NELSON ADVANCED STUDIES IN HISTORY

Nationmaking in Nineteenth Century Europe

The National Unification of Italy and Germany 1815–1914

W G SHREEVES

Nelson

Thomas Nelson and Sons Ltd
Nelson House, Mayfield Road
Walton-on-Thames, Surrey KT12 5PL

51 York Place,
Edinburgh EH1 3JD

P.O. Box 18123
Nairobi Kenya

Yi Xiu Factory Building
Unit 05–06 5th Floor
65 Sims Avenue, Singapore 1438

Thomas Nelson (Hong Kong) Ltd
Toppan Building 10/F
22A Westlands Road
Quarry Bay Hong Kong

© W. G. Shreeves 1984

First published by Thomas Nelson and Sons Ltd 1984

ISBN 0-17-445156-3

NCN 240-3254-0

Printed in Hong Kong

Contents

Acknowledgements

The author and publishers are grateful for permission to draw extensively on material from the following books and to reproduce pictures from the collections listed below:

S. J. Woolf	*The Italian Risorgimento* (Longman 1969)
G. Martin	*The Red Shirt and the Cross of Savoy* (Eyre and Spottiswoode 1970)
P. Ginsborg	*Daniele Manin and the Venetian Revolution 1848–9* (OUP 1979)
W. M. Simon	*Germany in the Age of Bismarck* (Allen and Unwin 1968)
H. Kohn	*The Mind of Germany* (Macmillan 1965)
H. Bohme (ed)	*The Foundation of the German Empire* (OUP 1971)
D. Mack Smith (ed)	*The Making of Italy 1796–1870* (Harper and Row 1968)
O. Pflanze	*Bismarck and the Development of Germany* (Holt, Rinehart and Winston 1963)
T. S. Hamerow	*The Social Foundations of German Unification 1858–71* (Princeton University Press 1969)
F. Stern	*Gold and Iron: Bismarck, Bleichroder and the building of the German Empire* (Knopf 1977)
L. Steefel	*Bismarck, the Hohenzollern Candidature and the Origins of the Franco-German War of 1870* (Harvard University Press 1962)
G. Bonnin (ed)	*Bismarck and the Hohenzollern Candidature for the Spanish throne* (Chatto and Windus 1957)
E. Minogue	*Nationalism* (Methuen 1969)

Illustrated London News Picture Library pp 22, 41; Mansell-Bulloz Collection p 41; Mansell Collection pp 42, 44, 86, 137; Radio Times Hulton Picture Library pp 45, 86, 137.

Cover illustration: detail from Garibaldi's attack on St. Fermo by Carlo Bissoli. Reproduced by kind permission of The Mansell Collection.

Series Preface

This is a new venture designed, first, to take account of some of the fresh ideas which have been canvassed over the past decade among teachers of history in schools, colleges and universities, and, secondly, to meet the needs of students preparing for advanced examinations, which in future will contain a greater emphasis on primary sources than hitherto. Each book will have a theme. Lord Acton's century-old advice, 'Study problems not periods' remains sound. Within a rough fifty-hundred year compass a particular argument will be explored, and sharp focus brought to bear on particular issues. In this way the series is intended to complement rather than supplement existing methods of work, and to provide teachers with evidence and lines of argument for seminar work or class discussion.

The series has two special features. History is about change and continuity, and the student will be required to set a premium on understanding, to think about what has happened and why, and to see connections. One of the GCE Boards offers succinct advice to its Advanced Level candidates: 'Analyse, argue, judge.' It is the series' intention to promote these qualities, and exorcise that bane of a student's life – dictated notes, one text and minimum discussion, a feeling that history is 'just one damn'd thing after another'. Textbooks have their reference uses, but for the student they suffer from one serious defect: a problem is solved at the outset. They are *too* complete, with insufficient consideration being given to the process of arriving at a conclusion; the student becomes the passive recipient of someone else's work. This series will offer a blend of narrative, analysis and, at a variety of points, studies to be undertaken. Some of these will be open-ended, some will require sifting of information or problem-solving; each author will make a few observations – not model answers, rather comments to the student on how a question might be approached.

The second feature is the extensive use made of source material woven into the main narrative. Students coming fresh to a period have often found original documentation difficult to obtain or handle – tucked away as it so often is in appendices or in separate, extensive volumes, with little guidance on a mass of detail. This series hopes that by constantly seeing edited portions of documents as integral parts of their work, students will treat primary evidence as a normal component of their study furniture, something though to be handled with care, showing proper concern for the pitfalls of bias, motivation and accuracy. Quotations have also been included from historians past and present, to give some flavour of rival authorities in interpretation of evidence, and to show how new research has modified traditional received opinion. The trust is that by including both primary and secondary sources students will be encouraged to seek out the full document or historical authority. A bibliographical note will feature in each book, with major text references identified, brief comments made by the author on reading matter, and some clearly directed further reading given, which a student should regard as obligatory.

B. W.   January 1983

Series Editor:

Barry Williams. Head of the History side and University Adviser, Sherborne School for Girls, Dorset. Sometime Schoolmaster Fellow, Pembroke College, Oxford.

Titles in the series:

Elusive Settlement by Barry Williams.
Nationmaking in Nineteenth-century Europe by W. G. Shreeves, Gillingham Comprehensive School, Dorset.

Forthcoming titles:

Parliaments, Puritans and Papists: England 1558–1630 by Brigid Davies.
Left and Right in France 1815–1914 by Dr David Pearse.

Author's Preface

This book has been deliberately divided into three parts each of which explores the theme of national unification at a different level. Part I of the two sections on Italy and Germany narrates and describes the momentous events surrounding the unification of the two countries. These sections attempt to provide more than the usual one dimensional account of bloodless battles and impersonal decisions and treaties. Hopefully they give some flavour of the ideas that drove men into action, the weapons they used, the dilemmas of the politicians and generals who attempted to control the events, and the feelings of those who were caught up in them at ground level. In the study sections in chapters 2, 3, 8 and 9, students are required to integrate maps, documents and pictures with the text, use the glossary to check the meaning of terms, and exercise skills in historical simulation and decision-making.

The second part of each of the sections on Italy and Germany is designed to stimulate analysis of the problems raised by nation building. Source materials and references to more detailed books are provided as the necessary data for solving the problems. Chapters 3 and 7 ask what caused the nationalist movements and how powerful they were. Chapters 4, 5, 8 and 9 invite discussion of why unification eventually succeeded in Italy and Germany. Finally, the problem of whether the unification of Italy and Germany was actually beneficial is explored in chapters 6 and 12. The study sections, especially in chapters 5 and 11, are intended to develop the higher historical skills demanded by new trends in the A level history examinations. Evidence has to be classified, and assessed for bias and propaganda; theories have to be tested, compared and revised; decisions have to be reached and converted into reports or essays.

The third part of the book is the conclusion which is intended to encourage reflection on the relevance of the nineteenth century nationalist movements to the twentieth century and to encourage further study of the problems of nation building in other parts of Europe and the world. Comparisons between the different nationalist movements are required, connections between the nineteenth century nationalists and their twentieth century successors are sought and decisions are invited about the whole desirability of nationalism in general.

The structure of the book should be sufficiently flexible for it to be used by both teacher and students in different ways. It is possible for teacher and students to work their way through each of the sections on Italy and Germany, one at a time, pausing for seminar type discussions along the way, which can be based on the ideas and material provided in the studies. Alternatively, having covered the narrative parts on both countries first, teacher and students can compare the situations in Italy and Germany by, for example, taking the chapters on nationalism (3 and 9) together. For those who prefer their students to follow a more individual work scheme, students or groups of students can be assigned different chapters from each of the second parts and brought together to compare their results. It is also possible for individual students to be encouraged to work their way through the book at their own pace.

Further work can be based on the books listed in the bibliography. Many of these are referred to in the text and it is intended that they be used selectively to follow up specific topics as well as for more general background reading. References to major questions in the text consist of the author or editor, the number of the book in the bibliography and the relevant page numbers. There are three bibliographies at the end of the relevant sections: on Italy, Germany and nationalism in general. The glossary can be found at the end of the book and words listed in it appear in bold in the text.

Finally, this book would not have been possible without the assistance of several friends and colleagues, especially: Mrs V. Collis and Miss O. Green who turned my illegible first drafts into the finished typescripts; Dr J. Whittam, Robert Fyson and my history teaching colleagues at Gillingham School who all read parts of the book, made helpful suggestions and tracked down errors; and the history sixth at Gillingham School who acted as guinea-pigs in the testing of the study sections and identified yet more errors.

Dedication

With Gratitude to Judy,
Rosamund and Gavin, who
suffered severe summer
holiday deprivation to enable
this book to be put together

The Vienna Settlement

1815

Between October 1814 and June 1815, Vienna, the capital city of the Austrian Empire, was the centre of a perpetual whirl of entertainment. The Emperor Francis of Austria accommodated the Tsar of Russia, four Kings, two Crown Princes, three Grand Duchesses, 32 minor German royalties, not to mention their vast train of chamberlains, aides-de-camp, masters of the horse, mistresses of the robes, equerries and adjutants, in his own Palace. Each evening 40 tables had to be laid for dinner. The Imperial stables had to accommodate 1,400 horses. The cost of this hospitality was estimated at 30,000,000 florins (£7 million). Lodged outside the Palace in Vienna itself were 215 princely families and the diplomatic representatives of every state in Europe. Every day the Emperor's Festivals Committee provided an assortment of entertainments ranging from balls, banquets, tournaments, theatrical performances and ballets to sleighing expeditions, hunting parties and the sight of the deaf, short and stout figure of the great Beethoven conducting his 'Battle' symphony.

However, behind this world of endless recreation lay the serious world of politics and decision making. Most mornings the representatives of the 'Big Five', Russia, Prussia, Britain, France and Austria, met in the office of Metternich, Chancellor of the Austrian Empire. Since 1792 Europe had been torn apart by almost continual warfare, when French armies had time and time again invaded Germany and Italy. With Napoleon Bonaparte defeated and confined to the Island of Elba in 1814 (map 1) it was their unenviable task to restore peace to Europe. They persisted in their work even when Napoleon succeeded in breaking out of Elba and returning to France as her Emperor for the famous '100 Days'. With Napoleon defeated again and, this time, to be finally imprisoned on St. Helena, they brought their work to its conclusion. Their decisions can be examined by studying map 1 on page 2. It can immediately be seen that the two countries which are the theme of this book did not exist. Italy, to use one of Metternich's favourite sayings, was only a 'geographical expression'. It consisted of nine separate states. One of these was ruled directly by the Austrian Empire. Three others were controlled indirectly by the Austrian Emperor through rulers related to the Austrian Hapsburg family. Germany was made up from 39 separate states and free cities each with their own form of government. It was less of a 'geographical expression' than Italy because the 39 states were united into a **confederation**. But the federal

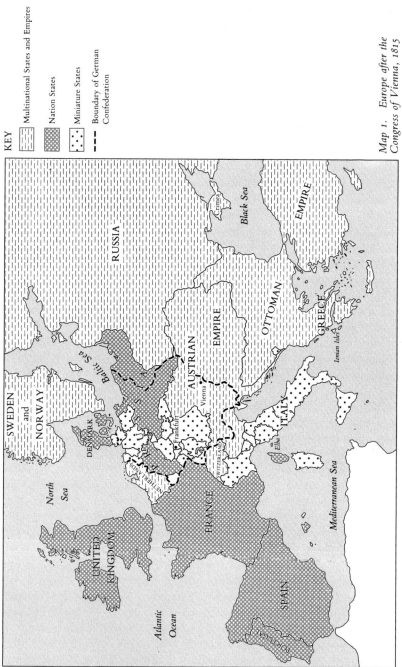

KEY

Multinational States and Empires

Nation States

Miniature States

Boundary of German
Confederation

Map 1. *Europe after the*
Congress of Vienna, 1815

assembly at Frankfurt, to which the states sent their ambassadors, was powerless and could make no real decisions.

It is not unreasonable to ask why the 'Big Five' failed to set up a united Germany or a united Italy. The short answer is that such countries had not existed for hundreds of years, that few people wanted them in 1815 and that there were very good reasons why they should not be called into existence. Italy had never really been a united country since the fall of the Roman Empire in the sixth century. The nearest she had come to unity since then was when Napoleon had reduced the eleven states of the 1780s to three. Germany had last been united under the great medieval kings of the thirteenth century. When Napoleon invaded Germany he had found 360 separate states loosely united into a fossilized institution called the 'Holy Roman Empire'. With his usual drastic efficiency he closed down that 'miserable monkey house', the assembly of the Holy Roman Empire, and reduced the number of separate states to around sixteen. Of course there were a few visionaries and intellectuals in 1815 who wanted Italy and Germany to become independent and united. Many Italians respected the poet Ugo Foscolo who had tried and failed to persuade the soldiers of Napoleon's army of Italy to set up an Italian **republic** in 1815. A few Germans like the reformer Baron Stein hoped for a powerful German confederation which might evolve into a united Germany. But these groups were in a minority and, more important, Metternich, Castlereagh and the other makers of the Vienna settlement had powerful reasons for refusing to accept their schemes. To Metternich and the British foreign secretary, Castlereagh, Europe could only enjoy peace if it could be based on a **Balance of Power**. In their view there were two countries which might threaten Europe's future tranquility: France, which had just done so and might try again, and Russia, whose army had recently marched across Europe to Paris and whose Tsar, Alexander I, had grand plans and visions. The best hope of deterring either of these countries from dangerous adventures was to make sure that the Austrian Empire remained powerful enough to counterbalance them. Now any attempt to set up independent national states would have exactly the opposite result. If Italians or Germans were given their independence then the other numerous national groups who lived within the two Empires would soon be clamouring for similar treatment. Czechs, Slovaks, Rumanians, Bulgars, Hungarians, Serbs and Croats would be in rebellion, the Empires would collapse and the numerous small states which emerged would make a tempting vacuum for an ambitious France or Russia to expand into. So the politicians at Vienna resolutely refused to sanction any changes which might weaken the Empires. Indeed, Metternich had at his disposal the 'Holy Alliance' between Austria, Prussia and Russia which he planned to use to crush any attempts at national revolution.

In spite of this, a quick glance ahead to map 7 on page 197 will show that by 1926 the very changes which the Vienna Settlement had tried to avoid had in fact taken place. Germany and Italy had both become independent and united countries. Chapters 1, 2, 7 and 8 in this book will attempt to tell the dramatic story of *how* this happened. The remaining chapters are concerned with trying to explain *why* this happened and whether the German and Italian people really derived much benefit from this change. Now these matters are contraversial so no attempt has been made to provide complete solutions. Rather the evidence has been presented in such a way that you will have to make up your own mind. Central to the whole problem is the idea known as **nationalism** A typical dictionary definition reads, 'a political movement to encourage the right of a people to assert their independence when this is thought to be suppressed by the power of another nation'. It sounds pretty dull and political until you realise that thousands of Germans and Italians and many from other national groups, died in the nineteenth century to make their beliefs come true. Nor, as you will see if you complete this book by looking at the conclusion, did nationalism end in 1914. When an I.R.A. terrorist blows up a building in Northern Ireland, a Basque nationalist bombs a Spanish seaside resort, an African guerrilla fighter murders white settlers, or a Palestinian Liberation Group hi-jacks innocent tourists on an aeroplane, they are perhaps guided by a similar belief in nationalism as that held by their Italian and German predecessors. Hopefully this book may help you to understand today's problems as well as what happened between 1815 and 1914.

----- CHAPTER 1 -----

The Years of Failure
1815 - 49

Restoration Italy 1815–31

When the Congress of Vienna had completed its work and Napoleon was safely locked up on St. Helena the restored rulers of Italy's states began to return to their capitals. The new political map of the Peninsula was to be superimposed on a land which was already deeply divided by geography. The Apennine mountains divided the West from the East. The fertile plains of the Po Valley in the North with their regular rainfall, contrasted sharply with the dry, hot, malarial and flood prone South.

Thanks to British sea power two of the returning kings had continued to rule the island parts of their kingdom throughout the Napoleonic period. King Victor Emmanuel I, of the House of Savoy, returned from the Island of Sardinia (I, v) to a Kingdom confusingly known as either Piedmont or Sardinia (I, i) which had now increased considerably in size. Restored to his capital city, Turin (a, population 78,000) he was now not only confirmed in his possession of the two provinces of Savoy (I, iv) and Nice (I, iii), but was also awarded the former republic of Genoa (I, ii). At the other end of Italy King Ferdinand I, of the House of Bourbon, had spent the war in Sicily (8, ii), using Palermo (g, pop. 140,000) as his capital city and protected by Nelson's fleet. In 1815 he was able to return to the mainland part of his 'Kingdom of Two Sicilies' (8, i) and take up residence in his royal palace at Naples (f, pop. 350,000). Pope Pius VII, long held prisoner by Napoleon, returned to the Vatican Palace in Rome (e, pop. 153,000). He had regained the province of Rome (7, iii) and also of the two Papal legations of Romagna (7, i) and Umbria (7, ii).

Officials of the Austrian Empire were meanwhile arriving in Milan (b, pop. 170,000) and Venice (c, pop. 137,000) to take control of the province of Lombardy-Venetia (2, i and ii) for their Emperor, Francis I of the House of Hapsburg. Relatives of the Hapsburg rulers of the Austrian Empire arrived to take over the smaller central states. Duke Francis IV reigned in Modena (3); Ferdinand III returned as Duke of Tuscany (6) taking up residence in his beautiful city of Florence (d). Napoleon's wife, Marie Louise, daughter of the Austrian Emperor, became Duchess of Parma (4). She obtained consolation for the separation from her husband by a series of lovers, some of them thoughtfully provided by her father. The tiny state of Lucca (5) originally like

KEY

The Quadrilateral

1 – 9 The Independent States of Italy

a – g Their capital cities

i – v Important regions

Map 2. Italy 1815–49

Genoa and Venetia a republic, now became a Duchy under the rule of Maria Louisa of the house of Bourbon. Out of the four **republics** which had existed in the peninsula before the Napoleonic wars only the minute city of San Marino (9) remained.

Study 1

The numbers and letters in brackets refer to map 2 on page 000. The figures show the rough population of the leading cities. When studying a foreign country it is very necessary for a historian to get to know it. For this reason you should now carry out the following tasks:

1. Draw or trace the map
2. Use the information from page 000 to draw up a key for it as shown below:

Number on map	Name of state & its regions	Name of ruler	Letter of main town(s)	Name and pop. of main town(s)

3. Devise a code of colours to indicate the following:

Ruled directly by Austria

Ruled indirectly by Austria through Hapsburg relatives

Other states independent of Austrian Empire

The inhabitants of the Italian Peninsula, now liberated from Napoleonic rule, had been waiting anxiously to see what changes the restored rulers would make. By far the greatest number of them could be classified roughly as **peasants**. In Italy the rapid growth of population, from about 13 million in 1700 to 18 million in 1800, meant that most of the peasant class were desperately short of land. The great landowners were noblemen or rich townsmen who rented their estates to the peasants. Not only were the parcels of land usually too small to support a peasant's family but they were also often leased on very short contracts which the landowner could cancel at any time. Most peasants needed **cottage industry** work, put out to them by merchants in the towns, to survive. The typical peasant home was shared with his animals and its windows were sealed with the dried dung which they provided. Peasant diet was hopelessly deficient in vitamins which often resulted in a terrible disease called pellagra. The classic symptoms were a swollen and inflamed tongue, diarrhoea and mental derangement. In February 1817, 95,000 cases were reported in Venetia alone. Although Napoleon had eased the peasants' burden by abolishing feudal taxes (see **feudalism**) and selling off the extensive church lands, their general position had not improved. This was because the church lands usually fell into the hands of rich city dwellers and the heavy costs of Napoleon's wars continually led to increases in general taxation. Predictably the restored rulers did nothing to improve the peasants' position. Indeed King Victor Emmanuel I of Sardinia actually revived the feudal taxes which they had to pay to the landowners.

Italian towns in 1815 were inhabited by four main layers of society. First there were the so called professional classes: the lawyers, the civil servants employed by the government departments, the writers, the artists and the students studying in Italy's 24 universities. Under Napoleon's rule the administration had used Italian and the introduction of France's Code of Laws had meant that there was a big demand for advocates to plead cases in the law courts. In Lombardy-Venetia the arrival of direct Austrian rule led to widespread loss of jobs for, since the language of administration was now to be German, the new government only employed Austrian judges, civil servants, police and army officers. Furthermore there was no provision for advocates in Austrian law so many lawyers lost work. Both Pope Pius VII and King Victor Emmanuel I abolished the French Legal Code. In the Roman States only ecclesiastics were allowed into government employment. In Sardinia all clerks who wrote the letter 'R' in the French manner were dismissed! Intellectuals who had criticized Napoleon's repression of freedom of speech found little cause for celebration under the new governments. An English lady wrote with horror in 1829 that:

> When an Italian in the Austrian states wishes to travel, he applies to the Minister at Vienna for permission. The usual form is for the Minister to write to the head of the Police of the town where the applicant lives, and to enquire what are his opinions and habits and what is his real object for wishing to leave the country. If all these questions are answered satisfactorily by the police then he may in the course of a year obtain leave, but it is more frequently refused. (Trevelyan, 16, p.23)

The secret orders issued to the Austrian police in Venice in about 1820 gave very precise instructions. Orders number three and four told them to watch the effect on public opinion of theatres, newspapers and pictures; number ten recommended surveillance over private correspondence. Sardinians now needed a permit from the King to read foreign newspapers. Students in Lombardy-Venetia were forbidden to read that dangerous subject 'modern history', while in Sardinia they were obliged to attend mass and confess once a month, and, since beards and long hair were considered revolutionary, they were frequently marched off to the barbers by the police for forced shaving!

The second layer of society in Italy's cities consisted of the bankers, the merchants, the industrialists and engineers. In Milan in 1838 for example there were 42 bankers, 25 money changers, 76 silk merchants, 196 textile manufacturers, 106 traders in clothes, 155 wholesale merchants in cereals, food and drink and 500 engineers. This group had been delighted when Napoleon's rule had swept away tariff barriers between the different states, standardized weights and measures, introduced street lighting and attempted to improve transport. They were less pleased with the high level of taxation and the discrimination in favour of French goods which brought ruin to the Italian silk industry. What would the resored rulers do to help them? In the Papal States Pius VII cancelled the laws which had introduced uniform weights and measures, street lighting and vaccination against smallpox. Produce travelling 120 miles from Bologna in the Romagna to Lucca, now had to cross seven customs posts each of which added to the cost of the article. The King of Sardinia closed the new road over Mont Cenis because the French had built it. As late as 1845 it was maintained that letters to Milan came more quickly from New York or even India than from Naples. In 1826 the French novelist Stendhal reported that the Duke of Modena 'had refused to allow the stage coach to cut across his estates on the grounds that all travellers are dangerous revolutionaries.' Discrimination was now in favour of Austrian instead of French industry. Count Cotti di Brusaco pointed out in a memorandum sent to the Tsar of Russia in 1818 that, 'trade communications with other Italian states are artificially hampered while the entry of Austrian products and manufacturers is highly promoted so that Italian products and trade are sacrificed.' (Mack Smith, 8, p.19)

Dependent on the two top layers of the town communities, were the third and fourth groups. The vast majority of the town workers were not yet employed in factories but in the workshops and shops of the skilled craftsmen. In 1838 Genoa had 21,000 masters and apprentices and 6,400 shopkeepers while Milan boasted over 100 watchmakers, 150 jewellers, over 300 tailors, 188 shoemakers, and over 1,200 house renovators and carriage makers. There was no class segregation in Italian cities and these traders and artisans often lived close to the groups above them and even to the fourth group of miscellaneous hawkers, rag pickers, road sweepers, beggars, acrobats, organ grinders, pimps, prostitutes, pickpockets and many others who made up 'the mob'. Life was crowded and unhealthy: in one suburb of Turin there was an average of nearly 80 people to a house; cholera and typhus epidemics were frequent. To some extent the return of the lavish spending courts of the new rulers brought prosperity to these groups, but in Sicily the departure of the court from Palermo caused serious unemployment. Nor did the richer classes treat the poor any better for living closer to them. In his memoirs D'Azeglio recalled that when, during the 1835 outbreak of cholera in Turin, a rich lady's washerwoman told her the rumour that the nobles were giving the doctors 20 francs for each poor person that had died, she was told that the story must be a lie – because poor people just were not worth that much!

Besides the aristocracy the one group that gained from the arrival of the restored rulers was the Roman Catholic Church. It had been persecuted and deprived of its power by Napoleon, but now came bouncing back to its former powerful position in Sardinia and the Papal States. In his memoirs the great novelist, painter and politician, Massimo D'Azeglio, described how he went one day to repaint the murals of a church in the Papal States. Inside were three brigands who had been living in the church for months because the pope had restored the laws of church asylum which gave criminals full protection from the police. In Sardinia the Roman Catholic Church was given immunity from taxation, full control over education, and its own law courts in which it dealt with problems of alleged heresy, blasphemy and family life and marriage.

Soon general dissatisfaction with the restored rulers began to take the form of the growth of secret societies. The most famous of these was the Carbonari, or Charcoal-burners. The name came from the 'shops', supposedly for the sale of charcoal, into which the society was divided. 'The aim of the order is the Independence of Italy our country. To give her a single constitutional Government, or at least to unite the various Italian governments in a confederation; all governments shall however be based on a constitution, freedom of the press and worship, the same laws, currency and measures' so ran the aims of the society (Woolf, 10, doc.18). The organisation of the Carbonari owed a lot to Freemasonry, it had seven grades of initiation at each of which members had to swear an oath. Those who reached the seventh grade had learnt that Christ was 'The Good Cousin' who had come to earth to preach liberty, equality and philosophy. The society was strongest in Naples. It also spread north to the Papal states and Sardinia. In opposition to the Carbonari other societies grew up, the most notorious being the Sanfedisti. A loyal member of this organisation had to 'swear not to spare anyone belonging to the infamous gang of liberals, regardless of his birth, lineage or fortune; to show no pity for the wailing of children or the old, and to spill the blood of the infamous liberals to the last drop, regardless of sex or rank.' (Woolf, 10, doc.21).

In 1820–1 and again in 1831, the rising dissatisfaction with the restored governments was guided by the Carbonari into attempts at revolution. The Neapolitan army, which had been infiltrated by the Carbonari, forced Ferdinand I to grant a constitution. A rebellion in Palermo demanded a separate parliament for Sicily. In Sardinia a group of army officers demanded a constitution and forced Victor Emmanuel to abdicate. But by the end of 1821, with the full support of his Holy Alliance allies Russia and Prussia, (p.3) Metternich had sent the Austrian army to restore order. In 1831 revolutions in Parma and Modena drove the Duchess and Duke into exile and infected most of the main cities in the Papal legations of Romagna and Umbria. Once again however an Austrian army moved in and the revolutionaries, armed only with sporting guns, pikes and scythes, could do nothing against them. With Prussia and Russia giving Metternich full backing and France and England unable or unwilling to interfere, the 1815 settlement still held.

Plans for Italy's Future 1831–47

The first attempts to alter the face of the Italian Peninsula had ended in disaster. Now new men with new ideas appeared on the scene. Basically there were two problems for them to solve. How could the rulers of the different states be forced to make reforms when the Austrian army stood behind them opposing every alteration to the 1815 settlement? If the Austrian army could somehow be defeated or neutralized, what sort of changes ought to be made?

The first new scheme to appear on the scene was launched by 26 year old Giuseppe Mazzini. The son of a doctor and professor at Genoa university, Mazzini had joined the Carbonari but had been arrested in November 1830 before the revolutions of 1831 had time to get off the ground. Forbidden to live in Genoa by the Sardinian government he had gone into exile in France. His new society was called Young Italy and its solution to the first problem was different from that of the Carbonari. French help, he argued, was totally unnecessary. Austria and the rulers who sheltered behind her armies could be defeated by the Italian people themselves. All that was needed was for the new society to recruit the younger generation and to educate them in the belief of a united Italy. Newspaper propaganda, plots and even possibly assassinations were to keep their imagination at fever pitch. At last when the time was ripe the masses would rise against their rulers and, using a type of guerrilla warfare, would drive the Austrians out of the peninsula. To realise these aims Young Italy became a typical secret society. They had a secret greeting ('What is the time'? 'Time for the struggle') and a secret sign (hands crossed and folded across the chest). Mazzini wrote endless letters – one estimate is that he wrote fifty thousand, ten thousand of which have been found. Since he was always on the run from the police many were written in invisible ink and he stretched hairs across the seals to see whether they were being tampered with. To confuse the censors his letters to his mother were usually signed 'Emily'. The society's newspaper was smuggled into Italy in a whole variety of ways – in trunks with false bottoms, in boxes of fish and with false addresses to baffle the police and customs. Mazzini believed that, when Austria had been driven out, the separate states should all be abolished and one united Italy should be created. This new Italy would be a republic with a centralized government elected democratically (see **democracy**).

The next man to produce an influential scheme for the reform of the Italian peninsula was another exile, Vincenzo Gioberti. When his book was published in 1843, Gioberti was 42 and a priest, philosopher and aspiring politician. Born in Turin, Sardinia, he had been much influenced by Mazzini and had been sent into exile in Belgium by King Charles Albert. His book, *On the Moral and Civil Primacy of the Italians*, argued that reforms in the states could be encouraged by the Papacy setting a good example. It implied that if the Austrians (not actually mentioned by name) should oppose the reforms, the Sardinian King and his army could defend Italy. The Italy which he envisaged in his book was not at all like Mazzini's. The existing rulers and their governments were to remain but as part of a **federation** under the Presidency of the Pope.

A year later another Sardinian entered the field of planning Italy's future. Cesare Balbo, like Gioberti had been exiled; in his case for associating with the army rebels of 1821 (p.10). Unlike Gioberti he had been allowed to return in 1823 but only on condition that he lived the quiet life of an ordinary country aristocrat on his villa. His book *On the Hopes of Italy*, argued very forcefully that it was the Sardinian Monarchy who must drive out the Austrians from the peninsula. Only Sardinia, with its extra territory gained from the Vienna settlement, had the power to stand against Austria. He agreed with Gioberti that the future of Italy must be in a federation but, he argued, this must be led, not by the Pope, but by the Sardinian Monarchy. He argued that Lombardy and Venetia should become part of Sardinia but accepted that the other states should retain their rulers. Both Count Balbo and Gioberti were agreed on one important issue – popular revolution by the people to be followed by democracy was quite unthinkable.

Another writer in the field was Carlo Cattaneo, a professor at Milan University. Like Mazzini he was a convinced republican. But like Gioberti and Balbo he had no faith in a unified and centralized Italy. In his view there were too many differences in laws, customs and languages for this to work. In his opinion the best hope for a future Italy was a federal **republic** based on the existing pattern of states.

Study 2

Check that you now understand the disagreements between Mazzini, Cattaneo, Gioberti and Balbo by doing the two following questions:

NARRATIVE

1. Complete the following statements:

a) The writer who believed that the Austrians could be driven out by the Italian people was...

b) The writers who believed that the Sardinian army would be needed to deal with the Austrians were...

c) The writer who believed that the reformed Italy must be a centralized and democratic republic was...

d) The writer who believed that the new Italy should be a federal republic was...

e) The writer who believed that Italy should be a federation of independent states under the presidency of the Pope was...

f) The writer who believed that Italy should be a federation of states under the King of Sardinia was...

2. Below are four extracts all by the writers we have been discussing. Read them carefully and say who you think wrote each one, giving your reasons.

(a) I intend to prove that mainly because of religion Italy possesses within herself all the necessary conditions for her national and political rebirth and that to achieve this in practice she has no need of internal revolutions nor of foreign invasions... That the Pope is naturally, and should be effectively, the civil head of Italy is a truth forecast in the nature of things, confirmed by many centuries of history... The benefits Italy would gain from a political confederation under the moderating authority of the Pope are beyond enumeration... for such an association would increase the strength of the various Princes without damaging their independence... it would remove the causes of disruptive wars and revolutions at home... it would eliminate or at least reduce the differences in weights, measures, currencies, customs duties, speech and systems of commercial and civil administration which so wretchedly and meanly divide the various provinces... (Woolf, 10, doc.24)

(b) We are a brotherhood of Italians... who believe that Italy is destined to become one nation... we are republican and unitarian... republican because theoretically every nation is destined, by the law of God and humanity, to form a free and equal community of brothers... unitarian because federation by reducing Italy to the political impotence of Switzerland would necessarily place her under the influence of one of the neighbouring nations... The means by which we propose to reach our aims are education and insurrection by means of guerrilla bands which is the true method of warfare for all nations desirous of emancipating themselves from a foreign yoke... we are convinced that Italy is strong enough to free herself without external help. (Woolf, 10, doc.26)

(c) Confederations are the type of constitution most suited to Italy's nature and history... the only obstacle to an Italian confederation is foreign rule which penetrates deep into the peninsula... The Peace of Utrecht in 1714 founded a new Kingdom in Italy for that worthy house of Savoy which has upheld the sacred fire of Italian virtue for the last century and a half... one should note that in the course of the century it increased by a third in population and almost doubled in territory. Equally notable is the method by which these additions were acquired – all at the expense of Austria... (Woolf, 10, doc.23)

(d) The dream of many people is that a single law for all Italy can be improvised by the wave of a magic wand. No! For many generations in Turin, Parma, Rome, Naples, Sicily, signed contracts and customary rights based on ancient and modern laws will continue... our cities form the ancient centres of the communication networks of large

13

and populous provinces... whoever ignores this love of the independent patria in Italy will always build on sand... two states alone, the American and the Swiss Federations have shown how to rule without continual use of a standing army... (Woolf, 10, doc.27)

Very soon people began trying to put their ideas into practice. Mazzini's Young Italy started to make plots for spreading his republican ideas. In 1833 the society's attempts to penetrate the Sardinian army were uncovered and King Charles Albert had twelve of the soldiers shot. The following year an attempt to invade Savoy from Switzerland and at the same time provoke a revolution in Genoa ended in disaster. After this Young Italy ceased to be an effective organisation but Mazzini's writings from his exile first in Switzerland and then in England continued to have an influence. So much so that Emilio and Attilio Bandiera, whose father was an Admiral in the Austrian navy, succeeded in forming a branch among the sailors at Venice. Soon afterwards, in 1844, with 19 comrades they landed on the Calabrian coast of Naples. Two days later they were attacked by local peasants and townspeople. They were captured, and nine of them, including the Bandiera brothers, were executed. Their last words were 'Viva l'Italia'.

In the late 1830s the ideas of Balbo and Gioberti seemed about to be put into practice. After becoming King of Sardinia in 1831, Charles Albert had appeared to be very much under Austria's control. However, from 1837 he began to introduce laws abolishing feudal practices. Plans for building railways and reducing tariffs were laid down and, most interesting of all, the army was reformed. Even more promising, the death of Pope Gregory XVI in 1846 was followed by the election of the liberal Giovanni Mastai-Ferretti as Pius IX. It is said that one of the books he had brought with him to Rome before his election was Gioberti's *Primacy*. On the evening of 17 July Romans were amazed to find that more than a thousand political prisoners were to be released and hundreds more were to be allowed to return from exile. Before the end of 1846 plans were in progress for gas lighting in the streets, railways and an agricultural institute. In the following year, 1847, schemes for an elected consultative assembly, the admission of laymen into government and freedom of the press were launched. Rome went wild with enthusiasm. A Professor at the Sorbonne, who was in Rome, described a torch light procession held to thank the Pope on 22 April 1847:

Torches were being distributed, and those who took them ranged ten abreast, with a leader of the file... men with lighted torches... a band of military music... more men with torches to the number, it is estimated of six thousand... nothing was more touching than to see walking side by side, in the same ranks, men of the highest classes, workmen in blouses, priests... all united in the same feeling expressed in the same cry, Viva Pio Nono! (Hayles, 18, p50)

The news that Italy had a liberal Pope spread through the country like a forest fire. In Venice at the ninth Congress of Italian Scientists a speaker who constantly mentioned Pius IX received rapturous applause. In Milan the arrival of a new Archbishop was used as an excuse for young men to surge through the city singing hymns to Pio Nono. In Tuscany Grand Duke Leopold emulated the Pope by freeing the press. Alarmed by this popular hysteria Metternich made it treason to shout 'Viva Pio Nono' in Lombardy-Venetia, and was reluctantly forced to move Austrian troops from the Papal city of Ferrara. In Naples King Ferdinand II cursed 'the wretched little priest' and forbade cheers for him. The year 1848 in Italy promised to be an interesting one.

The Revolutions that Failed: 1848–9

1848 turned out to be the year of revolutions throughout Europe. In Germany, the Austrian Empire and Italy alone there were over 50. Even today Italians still use the expression 'a regular forty-eight' which means, roughly, 'Good Lord, what a confusing mess!' By 22 March 1848 Charles Albert, King of Sardinia, was in the position where he had to make a vital decision. The citizens of Venice and Milan had risen in revolution against their Austrian rulers. Public opinion was boiling over with excitement in Sardinia and putting pressure on Charles Albert to declare war on Austria and go to their aid. Perhaps the time had come for the Sardinian Monarchy to carry out Balbo's schemes (p.12) and take over the north of Italy? But could the Sardinian army tackle the Austrian army on their own? Maybe Charles Albert ought to try to obtain help from France? Or might Charles Albert's best plan be to wait and do nothing until it became clear whether the Venetians and Milanese would succeed? However, in this case would Sardinian public opinion be satisfied or would there be a risk of revolutionary demonstrations against the King by the growing republican party? And, if Charles Albert did go to the rescue of the Venetians and Milanese, would they welcome him? After all, many of them were likely to be republicans who might resent the intervention of a **monarchist** or even use his army to help along their own plans to set up a **republic**.

—————————————— *Study 3* ——————————————

Suppose you were called upon to advise the King, which of the following courses of action would you recommend and why? After reading the evidence set out below, draw up a table like the one overleaf.

Possible courses of action	Advantages	Disadvantages	Order of preference
1. Wait patiently and do nothing			
2. Approach the French Government for help against the Austrians			
3. Offer to help the Lombards and Venetians on condition that they agree to become part of the Kingdom of Sardinia			
4. Declare war on Austria immediately and help the Lombards and Venetians unconditionally			

Evidence to be considered:

1 *The Strengths of the Armies*

	The Sardinian army	The Austrian army
Size	25,000 regulars 20,000 reserves	70,000 regulars, including 20,000 Italians. Also reserves available.
Commander-in-Chief	King Charles Albert. 51 years old. Had fought briefly in Spain.	General Radetzky. 82 years old. Had fathered a bastard child three years before. 17 campaigns. Wounded seven times.
Officers	Mostly amateur aristocrats.	Professionals who had entered army for life.
Men	Chosen for training by lot. 14 months service. Reserves might not have been on active duty for six years.	At least eight years training.
Other factors	No maps of Lombardy ready.	The quadrilateral of forts (Map 2, p.6) apparently easy to hold against the Sardinians.

2. *The Diplomatic Situation*

(a) France. A revolution on 24 February had replaced King Louis Philippe with a republic. The new foreign secretary, Lamartine, had declared on 4 March: 'France will only interfere if Italy asks her to'.

(b) Austria. There had been a revolution in Vienna itself on 13 March. Metternich had fled from the city. The Emperor of Austria's subjects in Hungary and Bohemia seemed about to break away from his control.

(c) The rest of Italy. Not only were the Venetians and Milanese fighting the Austrians but other regions also had risen against their traditional rulers. The people of Sicily had defeated the King of Two Sicilies' army and proclaimed their independence by the end of January. In February the King had given his mainland territory a constitution. Later in February the Duke of Tuscany had been forced to do the same and, in March, Pope Pius IX had imitated them. There was a possibility that Charles Albert might be able to draw on support from these reformed states.

3. *The popularity of Charles Albert's Monarchy*

However Charles Albert was not too popular with nationalists (see **nationalism**) in Italy. The leader of the Venetians, Daniel Manin, was a republican. The revolutionaries in Milan were split between a conservative group who were known to favour union with Sardinia and a more radical group led by Cattaneo (see p.12). Massimo D'Azeglio had made a report on a visit to Tuscany and the Papal states in 1845. He spoke to the nationalists and pointed out that Sardinia had 'money in reserve, an army and a navy. At the word Sardinia my debater grimaced (as everyone did right up to the end of my journey) and replied ironically, "Charles Albert... you want us to put some hope in him? What about 1821 and 1833?".' In 1821 Charles Albert had been unable to make up his mind whether to join the army revolutionaries (see p.10). For this lack of decision he earned the nicknames 'King Wobble' and the 'Hamlet of Savoy'. In 1833 he added a further nickname ('King Executioner') to his collection, when he had 12 men killed (see p.14). Only on 4 March 1848 had Charles Albert finally granted a **constitution** to Sardinia.

In fact on 24 March, Charles Albert did declare war on Austria unconditionally. 'Italy will make herself' he announced. By that time, against all odds the Milanese had actually succeeded in driving Radetzky out of Milan. The trouble in Milan dated back to January when the Milanese had given up smoking and refused to take part in lotteries. The Austrians stood to lose 4 million lire a year from the cigar tax and $1\frac{1}{2}$ million from the boycott on gambling. Austrian soldiers contemptuously went around puffing smoke into Milanese faces. Predictably there was soon an incident in which five Milanese were killed and 59 wounded. When news of the revolutions in Vienna reached Milan on 17 March, a demonstration of 15 to 20 thousand Milanese marched on the Town Hall, smashed windows, mirrors and furniture and forced the Austrian Governor to agree to reforms. That is where the revolution might have been expected to end. After all what could the city's untrained population of 156,000, with only 650 firearms, be expected to achieve against the Austrian garrison of 12,000 fully trained and armed soldiers with their 30 field guns under the leadership of the ruthless General Radetzky, whose motto was 'Three days of bloodshed secure 30 years of peace'? In fact, Radetzky was defeated by the citizens of Milan in the 'Five Glorious Days' as they came to be known. His own dispatches show how it happened. On 21 March, the first note of desperation crept in:

> The streets have been pulled up to an extent you can hardly imagine. Barricades close them by the hundred, even by the thousand. The character of this people has been altered as if by magic and fanaticism has taken hold of every age group, every class and both sexes. I have still a few days of bread left... I cannot obtain anything more... because the streets to the citadel are closed; and though I repeatedly demolished the barricades they were always re-erected! (Mack Smith, 8, p.143).

The 1,700 barricades which had helped to defeat Radetzky were described by an eye witness: 'In the rich quarters they used carriages, expensive furniture, elegant sofas, beds, mirrors; in the business quarters, barrels, bales of cloth, pumps, packing cases; in the poor quarters, the lowly broom, hen coops, small tables, anvils, benches; near the schools, desks and benches... then the whole was completed with faggots, shutters, doors, paving stones, beer bottles and dirt.' (Martin, 23, p.303) Meanwhile, behind the scenes numerous Milanese chemists slaved away making gunpowder and the revolutionaries pulled up the manhole covers to incapacitate the Austrian cavalry. On 22 March Radetzky wrote: 'It is the most frightful decision of my life but I can no longer hold Milan'. He retreated with all his men into the quadrilateral (see map 2).

At first it seemed that Charles Albert's decision had been the right one. By the end of March the Austrians had been driven out of Venice and most of their Italian regiments had been disbanded and sent home. In April, Charles Albert had defeated the Austrian army in two battles on the edge of the quadrilateral (map 2). Armies from Tuscany, Naples and even the Papal States had indeed come to help him. In May the duchies of Parma and Modena had voted to join Sardinia, in June Lombardy joined them and in early July the Venetians also agreed to do so. But already the signposts of eventual defeat had begun to appear. Charles Albert's reign as King of all North Italy was to last only three weeks. The first ominous sign appeared on 29 April when the Pope made it quite clear that he had no intention of declaring a holy war against Austria. 'We seek after and embrace all races, peoples and nations with an equal devotion of paternal love', he declared. In the second half of May came the next drawback when King Ferdinand II of Naples cancelled his constitution and ordered his army to withdraw from the war. All this time Radetzky had been patiently collecting reserves in the quadrilateral. According to Cattaneo, 'while Charles Albert was collecting votes, (to persuade Lombardy to unite with Sardinia) Radetzky was collecting men.' The crafty Austrian General, who in his time had had nine horses shot from under him, turned against Charles Albert and in a three day battle from 22 to 25 July defeated him at Custozza. The Sardinian army now began a long and dismal retreat in the course of which they abandoned Milan to the Austrians. Too late Charles Albert asked for French aid only to be informed mockingly by the French Foreign Minister that he regretted 'that a noble nationalist sensitivity did not permit you to call upon us sooner.' On 9 August Charles Albert signed an armistice with the Austrians in which Sardinia was forced to withdraw from Parma and Modena as well as from Venice and Lombardy.

However, Charles Albert still maintained in his last proclamation to the now dismantled North Italian Kingdom that 'the cause of Italian Independence is not lost' and he did not disband the Sardinian Army. On 12 March 1849, Charles Albert declared the armistice to be at an end and once again prepared to try the fortunes of war. But the cunning old Austrian General with the white hair and handle-bar moustache once again outmanoeuvred his Sardinian enemies. Too late they discovered that he had marched his whitecoats between them and Turin. On 23 March in the battle of Novara (map 2) they were completely defeated. Charles Albert told his officers:

> I have not been able to find death on the field of battle, as I would have wished it. Perhaps my person now is the only obstacle to winning from the enemy a fair treaty. And as there is no way of continuing to fight, I now abdicate the throne in favour of my son Victor Emmanuel, in the hope that a new King may be able to obtain more honourable terms... (Martin, 23, pp.342–3)

Four months later, an exile in Portugal, he was dead.

However, the 1848 revolutions in Italy did not come to an end with the defeat of Charles Albert. In June 1849, just two months after Novara, another very different sort of man was confronted with an agonising decision:

'On 3 June about 3 o'clock I was awakened by the sound of cannon... I sprang out of bed... jumped on my horse and galloped off to the St. Pancrazio Gate'; so wrote Garibaldi in his autobiography (Dumas, 12, p.290) The year was 1849, the St. Pancrazio Gate was part of the fortified wall which protected the Republic of Rome, the cannon were being fired by the soldiers of the Republic of France whose President was Louis Napoleon; the red bearded

Garibaldi, wearing an American style poncho thrown over his red shirt, was in charge of the defence of the Roman Republic at that point. Like Charles Albert, he now had decisions to make. But who was he? Why and how had the popular liberal Pope Pius IX's capital become a republic? Why on earth were the soldiers of a French republic under a President, Louis Napoleon, attacking a fellow republican state? This situation was typical of the confusions of the great revolutionary upheavals of 1848–9 so, before joining Garibaldi in his decision making, it must be briefly explained.

Pope Pius IX had soon discovered, like so many reformers before him, that the more concessions he made, the more his people wanted. His declaration of 29 April 1848 (p.19) turned them against him and all his earlier reforms (p.14) now began to backfire. His amnesty meant that Rome was full of republicans ready to campaign against him. The freedom of the press meant that they broadcast their views in the hundred or so newspapers which had appeared. To make matters worse, the limited consultative body which the Pope had allowed was neither popular nor worked well. In desperation he called into office Count Pellegrino Rossi. The Count was a liberal but determined to restore law and order. The Pope's enemies had other ideas. On 15 November, the Count collapsed on the second step of the stone staircase leading up to the council chamber with a great fountain of blood streaming from the carotid artery on the left side of his throat; he had been stabbed with a long hunting knife. Other conspirators raised their cloaks to conceal the murderer and the whole gang hurried off unidentified. The next day a crowd of six thousand advanced on the Pope's palace demanding a government which would declare war on behalf of Italian unity. When the Pope's Swiss guards tried to resist, shots were exchanged, a bishop was killed and the crowd brought up a field gun. The Pope was forced to give in and become a prisoner. On 24 November he succeeded in escaping disguised as a simple priest and reached safety in the Kingdom of Two Sicilies. On 5 February 1849, Rome was proclaimed a Republic and Mazzini (p.11) became the dominant personality in the government.

From Gaeta, Pope Pius IX had appealed for military aid to defeat the new Republican Government and restore him to Rome. Naples, Spain and Austria were soon offering their support but it was a French army which landed on 25 April 1849 near Rome. Louis Napoleon had been elected President of the French Republic in December 1848. His decision to allow the French army to advance on Rome was probably based on the need to limit Austrian power in Italy, to gain support from the Roman Catholic voters of France and possibly on friendship for Pius IX who had helped Napoleon to wriggle out of some tight spots in his youth. A final reason was added to these three when the French General Oudinot was unexpectedly defeated under the walls of Rome by the soldiers of the Republic; a Bonaparte could not tolerate a defeat. The 42 year old general who had inflicted this defeat on the French professional army was Giuseppe Garibaldi. His career up until then reads like a fictitious adventure story. At the age of 15 he had run away to sea. At 26 he had been condemned to death for taking part in Mazzini's Sardinian invasion plan (p.14). He had escaped to South America where he formed an Italian legion and learned the art of guerrilla warfare. Returning home in 1848 he had hurried to help the Milanese against the Austrians. Finally he had appeared in Rome to help the Republic. Almost immediately he had helped to defeat a Neapolitan army which had advanced on Rome and driven it back across the borders. Suffering from a painful wound, he had re-entered Rome on 31 May. There was to be no rest however. Armistice talks with the French had broken down. General Oudinot informed the Roman republican army that he was 'deferring the attack upon the place until Monday morning' (4 June) in order to give civilians a chance to leave the city. So the news that the French were attacking on Sunday morning, 3 June, came as a bitter shock to Rome's defenders.

Study 4

To understand the gravity of Garibaldi's problems at 3 a.m. on that fatal day, it is necessary to study both map 3 and picture 1 from the *Illustrated London News* (p.22), in conjunction with the extract from Garibaldi's memoirs given below. Using the three together fill in a chart like the one below. (Note that two of the places are not visible on picture 1.)

Name of place	Number on picture	Letter on map and in memoirs
e.g. St. Pancrazio Gate	1	a

When I arrived at the St. Pancrazio Gate [a], the villas Corsini [b], Valentini [c], and the Convent of St. Pancrazio [d], were all taken. The Vascello [e] alone remained in our hands. Allow me to give an idea of the field of battle where the destiny of the day was to be played out. From the St. Pancrazio Gate [a] there is a road [f] leading directly to Vascello; this road is about 250 paces along. At the end of that the road divides. The principle branch descends to the right [g] along the gardens of the Villa Corsini [b]... the second branch becomes a garden path [h] leading directly to the Villa Corsini, distant about 300 metres. This path is flanked on each side by high and thick hedges of myrtle. The third [i] turns to the left and keeps close along the opposite side of the high wall of the Villa Corsini garden. At 100 paces from its separation from the main road there are two other small houses, the one behind the garden of the Villa Corsini [j] and the other [Casa Giacometti k] 20 paces forwarder. The Villa Corsini [b], placed upon an eminence, dominates the whole neighbourhood. The position of the villa is very strong as if attacked

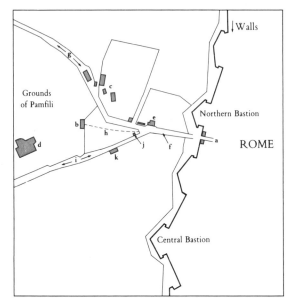

KEY **a – k** buildings and roads in battle

Map 3.   The Battle of the Villa Corsini, June 1849

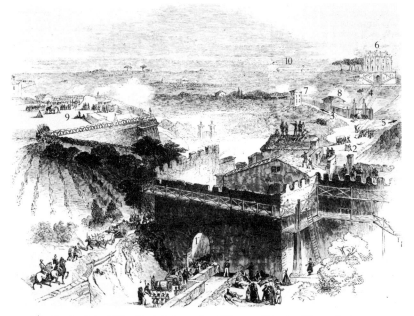

1.   The Battle of the Villa Corsini, June 1849 (Illustrated London News 1849)

simply and without making any works of approach it would be necessary to pass through the gate which is at the extremity of the garden and undergo, before reaching the Villa, the concentrated fire which the enemy, sheltered by the hedges, vases, parapets, statues and by the house itself, could make upon the point where the walls of the garden meet at the sharp angle. Now the Villa Corsini being taken was a tremendous loss to us; for as long as we were masters of that the French could not draw their artillery parallels. At any price it had to be retaken, it was for Rome a question of life or death! (Dumas, 12, p.290)

Next consider the table below which shows the military resources of the two sides.

	French	Romans
Number of soldiers	20,000 and another 10,000 reinforcements on way.	7,400 but only 6,000 under Garibaldi's orders.
Position of forces	15,000 in Pamfili grounds (map 3) 5,000 in action 5 miles north	Scattered all over Rome and officers not even in barracks with men.
Artillery	6 batteries of artillery	Batteries to north and south of San Pancrazio gate in range of Villa Corsini (see picture 1, point 9).

Now decide what you think Garibaldi should have done by completing a table like the one below. Remember: a) to use the information you have already been given; b) that to Garibaldi the campaign was not fought with much hope of finally winning but to create a romantic legend that Italians could in fact fight and die for an ideal.

Course of action	Arguments in favour	Arguments against	Order of preference
1. As soon as the first men arrive from Rome storm the Villa Corsini [b] via the garden path [h].			
2. Wait until most of his men have arrived, then storm the villa as in 1.			
3. Wait until the gunners on the bastions have had a good chance to bombard the French in the villa, and the outposts like Casa Giacometti [k] and Villa Valentini [c] have been taken, before attacking as in 1.			

table continued.

Course of action	Arguments in favour	Arguments against	Order of preference
4. Wait for all his men to arrive and then try to out-flank the French in Villa Corsini by moving up roads [g] and [i].			
5. Concede defeat immediately and avoid useless bloodshed.			

STOP HERE UNTIL YOU HAVE COMPLETED STUDY 4!

What in reality did Garibaldi do? In effect he chose the first alternative. By 5.30 a.m. his own legion had been assembled and he flung them up the path against the villa. In his own words, 'the Villa was retaken... but before arriving at it so many men were left along the garden path they could not resist the numerous columns that assailed them. They were obliged to fall back.' By 8 a.m. the villa was still in French hands. Garibaldi was now joined by Manara and his Lombard Bersaglieri. These men were not republicans but, driven out of Lombardy by the defeat of Charles Albert (p.19), they had opted to continue the struggle in Rome. Soon their broad brimmed hats decorated with the familiar plume of dark green cock's feathers could be seen charging up the deadly path to the villa. 'But from the terrace of the grand salon of the first storey, from the circular staircase which led to it and from all the windows, a murderous fire was poured on them... they had the French at once in front and on their flanks... I saw them fight and fall uselessly and therefore sounded the retreat. (Dumas, 12, p.290) In the afternoon Garibaldi was joined by more troops. This time his gunners preceded the attack by a bombardment and the Casa Giacometti was in his hands:

> Masina, on horseback... arrived at the foot of the villa staircase. There, clapping spurs to his horse he forced him up the stairs at the gallop so completely that for an instant he appeared upon the landing place which led into the grand salon like a fine equestrian statue. But a fusillade of guns close upon him brought down the brave horseman and his horse fell upon him... For a moment the villa was ours. That moment was short. The French brought up all their reserves and fell upon us before I could repair the disorder. I have seen very terrible fights but I never saw anything comparable to the butchery of the Villa Corsini. I came out the last, my poncho drilled with shot holes but without a single wound. (Dumas, 12, p.290).

One last attempt to regain the villa was made at dusk 'They went and returned leaving half their number behind them'. The Italian killed and wounded numbered between 500 and 1,000; all fell in the space of 600 paces by 300 between the Porta Pancrazio and the Villa Corsini. French losses were estimated at 264. Contrary to all expectations the Republicans went on fighting – it was not until 30 June that Rome was finally forced to capitulate. Mazzini escaped on board a ship, disguised as a steward. Garibaldi decided to fight on in the mountains. 'I offer neither pay nor quarters nor provisions. I offer hunger, thirst, forced marches, battle and death. Let him who loves his country in his heart and not with his lips only, follow me.' Remarkably, 4,000 men took up this challenge and joined Garibaldi. Of these, 1,500 escaped from the clutches of 65,000 French, Austrian, Neapolitan, Spanish and Tuscan troops to reach the neutral territory of San Marino (see map 2, p.6). A further 250 tried but failed to reach Venice with Garibaldi. So it was as a lonely fugitive (his pregnant wife died on the way) that Garibaldi escaped to safety on 2 September.

While Garibaldi had been defending Rome and carrying out his epic march the rest of the 1848 revolutions in Italy had been gradually terminated. By 15 May 1849 the King of the Two Sicilies had reconquered the rebellious island of Sicily. Deprived of Sardinian help by the defeat of Charles Albert at Novara (p.19) Manin had refused to give up the city of Venice to the Austrians. In late July the Austrians had dismounted their cannons so that they could attain an elevation of 45 degrees and thereby fire into two thirds of the city. Every 24 hours about 1,000 projectiles rained down upon the unfortunate citizens of Venice. Among these were the notorious 'Viennese oranges', red hot cannon balls, one of which dropped through the roof and into the bed of the British consul! In the third week of July about twenty small cloudlets drifted over Venice. These turned out to be the first recorded example of aerial bombardment; they were balloons loaded with bombs. But Venice was not broken by the bombardment (most of the balloons in any case had drifted right over the city and exploded in the Austrian lines on the other side!)

In early July, many citizens began to suffer from diarrhoea. Soon they began to vomit great quantities of watery fluid and lay moaning helplessly convulsed with muscular cramps. Between 11 July and 21 August 1849 a daily minimum of 306 dead, shrunken, desicated corpses were awaiting burial. The stink of the decomposing bodies was made all the worse by the hot summer weather (Ginsborg, 15). This deadly epidemic of cholera so reduced their ranks that the brave citizens of Venice finally surrendered to the Austrians on 22 August 1849. Manin joined the already long list of Italian leaders in exile and the attempts to alter the Vienna settlement of 1815 had ended in total failure. Austrian troops once again controlled North and Central Italy; French soldiers protected the Pope in Rome.

Study 5

No attempt has been made in this section on 'the Revolutions that Failed', to tell the story in chronological order – that is the order in which events actually happened. Rather the chapter has tried to get you involved with the complex decision making problems of two of the leading personalities and to convey something of the suffering of those years. To make sure you have grasped the main events use the dates given in the chapter to make yourself a timechart set out as below. Begin with January 1848 and end with August 1849.

Month & year	Events in:		
	North Italy (Sardinia, Lom-bardy, Venetia)	Central Italy (Rome, Tuscany)	South Italy (Sicily, Naples)
January 1848			

---- CHAPTER 2 ----

The Years of Success
1850 - 1919

Cavour and King Victor Emmanuel II lay the foundations 1850–59

After the abdication of Charles Albert, his son, Victor Emmanuel II, succeeded him as King of Sardinia. He was to be aided by a comparative newcomer on the Sardinian political scene, Count Camillo Cavour, the younger son of a Sardinian aristocrat. In 1850 Cavour was Minister of Agriculture; he soon progressed to Minister of Finance and in 1852 to Prime Minister. Between them they now began to lay the foundations for the ultimate unification of Italy under Sardinia's leadership. Success depended on three developments. First, Sardinia must be given a modern form of government which might attract the support of liberal reformers in other states. Second, her economy must be reformed and strengthened. Third, she must win allies abroad who could neutralise the Austrian power in the peninsula.

The King's decision to retain his father's **constitution**, with its elected chamber, meant that Sardinia was the only province in Italy with constitutional government. In addition, a series of laws pushed through the Chamber and Senate between 1850 and 1855 brought the Roman Catholic Church firmly under the control of the government. It was estimated in 1854 that Sardinia, with a population of 5 million had 41 archbishops and bishops overall, and one priest, monk or nun to every 214 inhabitants. In comparison Belgium, with a roughly similar population of $4\frac{1}{2}$ million, had 6 archbishops and bishops overall and one priest, monk or nun to every 500 inhabitants. A Sardinian bishop earned 30,000 lire a year compared to a cabinet minister's 15,000. The new laws attempted to remedy this state of affairs by forcing the church to pay taxes to the state, closing down many of the monastic houses, abolishing the separate church courts and the archaic laws of sanctuary. The increases in taxes, together with loans raised through great merchant bankers like Hambros, were used to promote the country's economic growth. Roads, bridges and railways improved the communications between the main cities. A series of free trade treaties with most of the leading European countries removed tariff barriers and forced Sardinian industries to be more efficient. The programme of reform was carried through by an alliance known as the *connubio* (marriage) between Cavour and a group of **liberals**. Faced with this

27

evidence of Sardinia's progress many former republicans began to agree that the only way to unify Italy and drive out the Austrians was to accept Sardinian leadership. Manin, the exiled leader of the Venetian rebellion (p.25) issued his famous press statement in September 1855: 'If regenerated Italy must have a king there must only be one, and that one the King of Sardinia. Convinced that before everything else we must make Italy the Republican says to the House of Savoy: "Make Italy and I am with you. If not, not".' (Mack-Walker, 30, p.18) Two years later the National Society was born (p.50). Its purpose 'to unify Italy, so that all the powerful elements which she embraces may co-operate in her liberation... we want... harmony between the House of Savoy and Italy.'

While the work of making Sardinia a modern state capable of leading a movement to free Italy was proceeding, Cavour was looking for foreign allies. The outbreak of the Crimean war between Russia on the one hand, and Britain, France and Turkey on the other, seemed to give him his chance. As a result of an alliance between Sardinia and Britain and France, signed in January 1855, 18,000 Sardinian troops went to help fight against the Russians in the Crimea (map 1). At the Congress of Paris, which met to settle the peace terms in 1856, Cavour was able to represent Sardinia and to attempt to get aid in his plans for removing Austrian power from northern Italy. Meanwhile he was also prepared to stoop to less dignified methods of winning support. He provided his golden haired 18 year old cousin with a secret code for corresponding with him and sent her to Paris with ominous instructions; 'Succeed cousin of mine, succeed by any means you like, only succeed'. He explained his aims clearly in a letter to Cibrario: 'I inform you that I have enrolled the very beautiful countess of Castiglione in the ranks of diplomacy, and have invited her to flirt with and seduce, if necessary, the Emperor of France.' (Holt, 1, p.194) At a house party at Compiègne her mission was accomplished (Many years later, when she died in 1899 in her sixties, her will requested that she should be buried in the lace and cambric nightdress of Compiègne!) Despite the Countess' undoubted charms little progress was being made when on 14 January 1858 Napoleon III and the Empress were on their way to the Opera in Paris. The Imperial carriage arrived under the crest of the main entrance to the opera and slowed down... 'at that moment three successive explosions like cannon shots took place at intervals of several seconds... the Imperial carriage was literally riddled; it had been struck in various places by 76 projectiles. Of the two horses drawing it, one, wounded in 25 places, died instantly, the other, seriously wounded had to be killed... On a ground strewn with debris and flooded with blood there lay many wounded... 156 persons were struck and the number of wounds reported by medical experts is no less than 511. On the long list of victims one notes 21 women, 11 children, 13 lancers, 11 guards, and 31 policemen.' (Mack Walker, 30, p.165) The plot to blow up the Emperor had been prepared in England by a group of Italian nationalists led by the 39 year old Felice Orsini. Cavour was afraid that his long struggle to gain Napoleon III's help against Austria had now been ruined. In fact the reverse happened. Napoleon III used the trial to arouse popular feeling against Austrian rule in north Italy. Orsini's lawyer was allowed to read a letter from his client to the court; 'this is the prayer I dare address your majesty from your dungeon cell... I entreat your majesty to render to Italy the independence which her children lost in 1849 through the fault of the French themselves'. The angry Austrian ambassador noted in his diary that at the trial Orsini, dressed in black even to the extent of his gloves, was a hero. 'Even the Empress is in raptures over this murderer in kid gloves', he commented bitterly. The newspapers reported how, at his execution, Orsini cried, 'Long live Italy, long live France', before giving himself over to the executioner. (Mack Walker, 30, p.181)

By May 1858, secret arrangements for a meeting between Cavour and the Emperor were being made with the latter's physician, Dr. Conneau. The telegraphic communications between Cavour and his ambassador in Paris, Nigra, still survive. At 5.55 p.m. on May 9 Cavour received a message from Nigra which read, 'Would your excellency let my wife know that I am well. I expect to leave soon'. This innocent sounding message really meant, when decoded, that Napoleon III had agreed to meet Cavour and that Dr. Conneau was coming to Turin to arrange the details. Travelling into France under the name of Giuseppe Benso, Cavour met Napoleon III at the French spa town of Plombières on 20 July. In a letter written four days later to King Victor Emmanuel, Cavour explained what had been agreed at a long meeting in the hotel from 11 a.m. to 3 p.m. and on a three hour drive in an elegant phaeton... 'which the Emperor drives himself'. (Mack Walker, 30, p.212) So secret was the meeting that Napoleon III's own foreign minister did not know it had been arranged and sent a message warning his Emperor that Cavour had been seen in the area! The agreement was then tidied up with a marriage between the 15 year old Sardinian princess and Napoleon's 36 year old cousin. It finally became a formal treaty signed by both parties on 30 January 1859. If Cavour could tempt Austria into declaring war on Sardinia and put 100,000 Italian soldiers into the fight, Napoleon would come to his aid with 200,000 men. Assuming the war was won, the territorial changes shown below in study 6 would take place.

--- *Study 6* ---

How far was the agreement actually carried out? Copy the chart overpage. Then using map 2 (p.6) and map 4 (p.32) and the rest of the chapter up to p.34, fill in the gaps as you go along.

Agreement	Letter on map 4.	Notes on: What happened? Was agreement kept?
Sardinia to obtain: Lombardy		
Venetia		
Modena		
Parma		
Romagna		
France to gain Savoy and Nice		
A kingdom of Central Italy to include Tuscany and Umbria		
The Pope to become President of a **federation** including these states and Naples		

Sardinia gains Lombardy and Central Italy 1859–60

At 1 a.m. on 19 April 1859 a secretary delivered a telegram to Cavour. Sitting half dressed on his iron bed, Cavour read it. 'There is nothing for me to do now but blow out my brains', he told his secretary. (Mack Smith, 8, p.274) Later he locked the door of his bedroom, refused to allow anyone in and began to burn his confidential papers. It seems that he may have been prevented from committing suicide by his close friend Angelo Castelli. When Castelli gained entry to the bedroom Cavour was clearly in despair, for it seemed at that moment as if all the careful plans which had culminated in the agreement at Plombières had collapsed in ruins. Cavour had used every ounce of his diplomatic skill to tempt the Austrians into the declaration of war which would bring French aid as agreed in the Treaty. King Victor Emmanuel had provoked the Austrians with his famous speech to the Sardinian Parliament in which he had referred to 'the cry of suffering which is raised towards us from so many parts of Italy'. War loans had been raised, the army prepared and mobilised, volunteers from all over Italy had been recruited. Yet still the Austrians had remained cool. The telegram he had just received seemed to indicate that his ally Napoleon III had finally cracked. Faced with opposition to his plans for Italy, particularly from the Roman Catholic party in France, Napoleon III had finally agreed to English plans to hold a Congress. Provided that she agreed to demobilise her troops, Sardinia would be allowed to attend the Congress as an equal to Austria. The Congress would then attempt to find a peaceful solution to the Italian problem – most likely along the lines of a federation which would leave Austria still in control of north Italy. Cavour felt obliged to accept the plan. Seven hours later he wired back, 'Since France joins England in demanding that Sardinia disarm in advance, the King's government, although foreseeing that this measure may have grievous consequences for Italy, declares itself disposed to submit'. However, two days later the man who had been on the point of suicide scored a triumphant victory. News came in that the Austrians had actually rejected the British proposal for a congress and had sent their own ultimatum giving Sardinia three days to disarm and disband the volunteers. In his diary Massari described how Cavour 'leapt up rubbing his hands even more energetically than usual' when the news arrived. (Mack Smith, 8, p.274) The war which he had planned could now begin; thoughts of suicide were banished.

North Italy became the scene of frantic military activity. In Sardinia itself an army of 60,000, containing the grenadiers with their light blue trousers, dark blue coats and white belts and the famous Bersaglieri, decked out in their broad rimmed hats with cock's feather decorations, were moving to the defence of Turin. Across the alpine passes into Savoy 120,000 French troops in dark blue tunics and red trousers raced to their aid. Moving north into the foothills of the Alps, with instructions to cut the Austrian supply lines, were the 3,500 volunteers of the 'Hunters of the Alps'. Their leader, General Garibaldi (p.21), now 52, was described by a British tourist who visited him during the campaign, as 'barely five foot seven inches or eight inches, broad shouldered and deep chested, beard and hair of chestnut brown bordering on reddish blond, cut short and slightly grissled'. (Parris, 5, p.168) Across Lombardy came General Gyulai with over 100,000 Austrian troops wearing their traditional white linen tunics, pale blue trousers and conical helmets adorned with the double eagle of Austria. On paper the armies were evenly matched. Both were using the percussion cap **rifles** which now replaced the old flintlock **muskets** of the Napoleonic wars. The French artillery's muzzle loading rifled cannon were, it is true, far superior to the Austrians' inaccurate smooth bores. However, the main difference between the two sides was in speed of movement. If the Austrians were to succeed they needed to defeat the smaller Sardinian army and occupy Turin before French help could arrive. But French troops had set out for the Alpine passes on 24 April; Gyulai and his Austrians only managed to move out on the thirtieth. Even then they moved with such caution that by the time they were within fifteen miles of Turin the French had arrived in strength. Gyulai retreated and a month later paid the penalty for his slowness. Using the railways for the first time in military history Napoleon III switched his troops across the Austrian front and defeated them at the battle of Magenta (see map 4, letter a) The regiments of soldiers who looked so romantic in their colourful uniforms were transformed

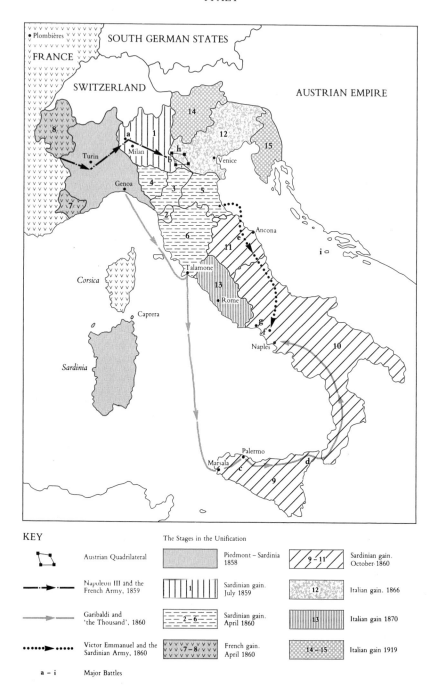

KEY

The Stages in the Unification

	Austrian Quadrilateral		Piedmont – Sardinia 1858		Sardinian gain. October·1860
	Napoleon III and the French Army, 1859		Sardinian gain. July 1859		Italian gain. 1866
	Garibaldi and 'the Thousand', 1860		Sardinian gain. April 1860		Italian gain 1870
	Victor Emmanuel and the Sardinian Army, 1860		French gain. April 1860		Italian gain 1919
a – i	Major Battles				

Map 4.   The Unification of Italy, 1859–1919

into the blood and chaos of the battlefield. 'Trees thrown down by the dreadful effect of artillery; heaps of dead bodies in all directions; human limbs scattered about, together with the carcasses of animals and military accoutrements:' such was the scene described by an eye-witness called Arrivabene in his book published in 1862. (Leeds, 2, p. 64) The Austrians retreated to the safety of their quadrilateral in Lombardy (map 4, no .1) and Napoleon III entered Milan on 8 June as 'the Liberator of Italy'.

This first Austrian defeat had even more wide ranging results. Austrian troops had to be withdrawn from the central Italian states of Modena, Parma and the Papal territories. Already on 27 April the Tuscans (map 4, no. 6) had rebelled against their Grand Duke and offered control of their country to Victor Emmanuel of Sardinia. Now the inhabitants of Modena, Parma (map 4, nos. 3 and 4) and the Papal States followed the same course. A papal army managed to subdue the western area of the Papal States (map 4, no. 13) but the Romagna (map 4, no. 5) was protected by 11,000 volunteers sent by Cavour to their aid. While all this was happening the combined French and Sardinian armies marched eastwards across Lombardy and met the Austrian army outside the quadrilateral on 24 June at Solferino (see Map 4, letter b) Three hundred thousand men were engaged in a massive battle ranging over almost 60 square miles. The carnage, 40,000 casualties, the looting of corpses by the Lombard peasants and the typhus which raged amongst the neglected wounded, combined to make a vision of hell. Henri Dunant, a young Swiss tourist caught up in this tragedy, published an account which later led to the formation of the Red Cross. The Austrians retreated once again but Napoleon III had now had enough. Mounting criticism of the war in France, the threat of the Prussian army mobilising on the Rhine, growing annoyance with the incompetence of the Sardinian army administration which had failed to order the necessary siege artillery, horror at the scale of the slaughter, and opposition to Cavour's attempts to take over central Italy, combined to persuade Napoleon III to sign a peace treaty at Villafranca. No Italian soldier or statesman of any rank was present when the agreement was signed. Sardinia's only territorial gain was to be Lombardy (map 4, no. 1) King Victor Emmanuel had the unpleasant task of communicating the news to Cavour. Losing his temper completely, Cavour handed in his resignation.

On 11 July 1859 the treaty of Villafranca seemed to have brought Cavour's schemes crashing down in ruins: Venetia (map 4, no. 12) remained under Austrian control, the central states were to be restored to their rulers. Yet on 2 April 1860 King Victor Emmanuel was welcoming delegates from Modena, the Romagna, Parma, Tuscany and Lucca (which had been part of Tuscany since 1848 – map 4, no. 2) to a new Italian Parliament, presided over by Cavour as Prime Minister. Once again Cavour had created a triumph out of apparent disaster. Two major developments had made this possible. First the central states of Italy absolutely refused to be handed back to their previous rulers. Under the influence of Baron Ricasoli, the aristocratic landowner whose estates produced some of the finest Chianti wines, the Tuscan assembly asserted on 20 August 1859, 'the firm intention of Tuscany (map 4, nos. 2 and 6) to make part of a strong Italian kingdom under the constitutional sceptre of Vittorio Emanuele.' On 31 October the three former regions of Modena, Parma and Romagna (map 4, nos. 3, 4 and 5) became united into one state to be called Emilia. They appointed Farini, a Romagnan who had been appointed Sardinian Commissioner, dictator and took immediate steps to be united to Sardinia. Since there was little the defeated Austrian army could do about this, everything depended on the attitude of Napoleon III. He was initially unfavourable. A citizen from the Romagna who urged Napoleon III to allow union with Sardinia was told: 'If annexation should cross the Apennines, unity would be accomplished and I will not have unity. It would stir up dangers in France itself on account of the Roman question (p.25) and France would not be pleased to see rise beside her a great nation that might diminish her preponderance. (Mack Walker, 30, p.236)

However, the second major development was that Napoleon III changed his mind. This came about partly through the new Liberal ministry under Palmerston in Britain who feared Napoleon's ambitions in Italy and hoped to check them by making Sardinia into a much more powerful state. Already by 22 August Palmerston was telling his ambassador in France that 'the annexation of the Duchies to Piedmont would be an unmixed good for Italy, and for France and for Europe.' The final conversion of Napoleon came when Cavour returned as Prime Minister and offered him the original bargain proposed at Plombières – the provinces of Nice and Savoy (map 4, nos. 7 & 8). In March and April everyone waited anxiously for the result of the **plebiscites** which it had been agreed to hold in the provinces. In Tuscany (map 4, no. 6) 534,000 voters were in favour of union with Sardinia and only 14,925 for a separate kingdom; in Emilia (map 4, nos. 3, 4 and 5) the figures were 426,006 in favour and only 756 against. In Savoy (map 4, no. 8) 30,533 favoured annexation by France and only 235 were against; in Nice (map 4, no. 7) Garibaldi's birthplace, 25,743 were for annexation and only 160 against. Despite protests from Garibaldi the transaction was complete. But had Sardinia's incredible growth now reached its climax or was there more to come?

--- *Study 7* ---

You should now have completed the chart from study 6. Next answer these questions:

1. Which parts of the Plombières agreement were actually carried out?
2. Which parts were not carried out?
3. Did Cavour and Napoleon III stick to their bargain honourably?

Sardinia gains the Kingdom of Two Sicilies and the Papal States 1860

It was the morning of 27 April 1860. A telegram was delivered to the Villa Spinola three miles outside the town of Genoa (see map 4). Waiting eagerly for it were Garibaldi and his lieutenants. They needed to know whether the plans initiated by Mazzini for a revolution in Sicily (map 4, no.9) were succeeding. Back in the first week of March Mazzini had written to his agents, 'For heaven's sake dare! You will be followed. But dare in the name of National Unity... Garibaldi is bound to aid.' The fourth of April was then marked down for the start of the revolution. It was planned that it would commence in Palermo (map 4) and would be maintained by the arrival in the city of bands of armed peasants from the surrounding countryside. Once it was under way the volunteers from all over Italy, who were already crowding into Genoa, would be led into Sicily by Garibaldi. The telegram read: 'offer barrels 160 rum America pence 45 Sold 66 English 47. Expect Lire 114 barrels 147 Brandy without offer. Reply immediately'. To the dismay of those waiting at the villa this was decoded as: 'Complete failure in the Provinces and in the city of Palermo. Many refugees received in British ships which have arrived at Malta.' After an angry discussion Garibaldi declared that, 'it would be folly to go'. But what was really happening in Sicily? It was quite true that the revolution had failed in Palermo but gangs of peasants, known as the *squadre*, had continued to resist in the mountains. Even they however, had been on the point of giving up when a Sicilian nobleman, Rosolino Pilo, arrived with the false news that Garibaldi was definitely coming to help. It was possibly reports of this renewed activity which changed Garibaldi's mind two days later and therefore changed the course of history. The news that the expedition to Sicily was definitely going ahead soon brought a steady stream of volunteers to Genoa. Among them was 21 year old Giuseppe Abba who kept a diary of the whole campaign. (Vincent, 4, entry for 4 May 1860) 'Last night we arrived late and it was impossible to get into any hotel; all were crowded with young men who had come into the city... the principal room was packed with people... chattering in all the dialects of Italy.' On the night of 56 May, Abba together with 1,088 other volunteers helped Garibaldi to seize two paddle steamers, the Piemonte and the Lombardo. The epic adventure of 'the Thousand' was ready to begin. These men were about to undertake a 600 mile journey with no coal, no food or water, no lubricating oil, charts or navigational instruments. With 1,000 antiquated muskets they were daring to tackle an island garrisoned with 25,000 Neapolitan troops. But they were going to win!

After two days at sea Garibaldi landed at the Tuscan village of Talamone (see map 4). Here he managed to remedy his shortage of provisions and, by putting on his Sardinian general's uniform, succeeded in bluffing the colonel in command of the Sardinian garrison into letting him have ammunition. Between 3 a.m. and 4 a.m. on the morning of 9 May the steamers put out to sea again. Early in the morning of 11 May Giuseppe Abba recalled that those on the Lombardo were rudely awakened: 'Get up, get up... a ship is making straight for us at full speed. Can it be a Bourbon ship? We could hear the angry threshing of its paddle wheels, then joy broke out... it was only the Piemonte!' When the expedition reached the harbour of Marsala later that afternoon (map 4) luck was on their side. Only the day before a battalion of Neapolitan infantry had marched away from the town. Two Neapolitan ships arrived on the scene just as the Thousand were landing but apparently, seeing the famous red shirts of some of the volunteers and a British warship in the harbour, jumped to the wrong conclusions and mistook them for British troops. By the time they had realised their mistake and opened fire with their ships' guns the Thousand had landed safely with the total loss of one man wounded in the shoulder and a stray dog hit in the leg!

On 12 May the 'army' set out for Palermo. Abba noted that 'Garibaldi rode a bay horse fit for a vizier... he wore a red shirt and grey trousers with a Hungarian style hat on his head and a silk handkerchief round his neck which he pulled up to shade his face when the sun was high...' The next day Abba came face to face with the first of the Sicilian squadre. They were 'armed with double barrelled sporting guns and strange pikes. Some wore sheep skins over their clothes. I have seen mountaineers armed to the teeth, some with rascally faces and eyes that menace one like the muzzles of pistols. They have cast in their lot with us.' Aided by these men Garibaldi's thousand now proceeded to win two remarkable victories; the first near Calatafimi (see map 4, c), the second the capture of Palermo itself. At the battle of Calatafimi on 15 May the Neapolitan riflemen in their colourful green uniforms and stovepipe hats decorated with yellow lace, commanded the terraced hillside. Garibaldi's men attacked them by charging up the hill taking each terrace in turn. Abba recorded what happened in his diary. 'When we came to the slopes of the opposite hill it was not pleasant to look upwards. I saw Garibaldi there on foot with his sheathed sword over his right shoulder walking slowly forward keeping the whole action in view. Our men were falling all around him and it seemed that those who wore the red shirts were the most numerous victims... The first, second and third terraces up the hillside were attacked at the point of the bayonet and passed but it was terrible to see the dead and the wounded. The dead Neapolitans were a piteous sight; many of them had been killed by the bayonet...' For a quarter of an hour Garibaldi and about 300 men sheltered beneath the overhang of the last terrace below the summit of the hill. Then he himself led the final bayonet charge which drove back the Neapolitans and brought victory. For such a small force the losses had been severe; 30 men had been killed and 150 seriously wounded – among the dead was a boy of thirteen. By 18 May the Garibaldini were on the march again. Abba was

horrified to see the devastation caused by the retreating Neapolitan troops.
'We ascended the slope on which the village of Partinico stands and the slight
breeze that freshened the air bore with it waves of unbearable stink. Having
burnt the village the Bourbon troops massacred the women and helpless of all
ages... When we arrived all the bells were ringing... and young girls, holding
hands and singing as though they were out of their minds, were dancing in a
ring around seven or eight already swollen corpses of Bourbon soldiers.' On
19 May Garibaldi's force could see Palermo but did not dare attack it. Instead
Garibaldi carried out a brilliant tactical manoeuvre. He marched south and
away from the town apparently in retreat. He lured 4,000 of the best troops in
Palermo, led by two of their most skilful commanders, into following him.
At the last moment his main 'army' slipped away into the mountains leaving
the Neapolitans chasing a decoy force composed mainly of wounded men.
This reduced the odds but only slightly. 21,000 Neapolitans with artillery and
fortresses now faced 750 Garibaldini and 3,000 Sicilian peasants!

'The air was growing chill at the approach of dawn', Abba wrote in his
diary for 27 May. 'Groups of houses were now more frequent and we could
see scared looking people peering at us as we went by... from the head of the
column came a shot, then a desperate cry, "to arms", a terrible yell, a sudden
fusillade, a rush; charge and we were in the fight... I can still hear the Genoese
who cried out in his dialect, "how can we pass here?" He was answered by a
bullet square in the forehead that toppled him over with a split skull...
Shoving forward and being shoved from behind we came to the crossroads of
the Termini gate which was swept by bursts of fire from a warship as well as
from a barricade ahead of us. Some of the most daring had already got across
under the eyes of Garibaldi whom I saw on a horse wonderfully cool and
collected.' Once through the gate Abba and the rest headed for 'Fiera
Vecchia,' a tiny market square in the centre of the oldest part of the city. From
here they tried unsuccessfully to persuade the inhabitants to join them. The
situation was saved by the Neapolitans who, instead of using their numerical
superiority to hunt down the invaders, decided to remain in their fort and
bombard the city with their artillery. A British admiral who witnessed the
scene reported, 'A whole district... about a thousand yards in length by a
hundred yards in width, was a crushed mass of ruins, still smouldering in its
ashes. Families had been burnt alive within the buildings, and the atrocities
committed by some miscreants of the Royal troops were frightful.' (Trevelyan, 17, p.304) Abba commented on the effect this had on the citizens: 'The
first shell came roaring through the air and fell... From that moment all the
bells of the city began to peal. About three in the afternoon citizens began
pouring out into the streets and we became more cheerful... Barricades now
rose as men and women worked with a will!' Even so, after three days of
fighting, with his ammunition almost gone, Garibaldi was facing certain
defeat. Once again the Neapolitans came to his rescue! They agreed to a truce

which Garibaldi used to strengthen the barricades in his area of the city. Abba's diary described the situation: 'The General has made a tour of the city wherever a horse can go. People knelt in the streets, touched his stirrups, kissed his hands. I saw children held up towards him as before a saint. He has seen barricades as high as the first floors of houses; there are eight or ten of these every 100 metres.' After the truce was due to expire, and despite the fact that the missing four thousand Neapolitan troops had now returned from their wild goose chase, the Neapolitans gave in. On 19 June, 24 ships steamed out of the harbour carrying the Neapolitan army back to Naples. Strengthened by the arrival of more volunteers on 18 June, Garibaldi was now able to go on to drive the rest of the Neapolitan army out of Sicily (map 4, no.9). After another major battle at Milazzo (see map 4, d) the remaining garrisons gave in. By 1 August, Garibaldi's army was looking across the straits to the Neapolitan mainland (map 4, no.10).

Study 8

Why did Garibaldi succeed in capturing Sicily? Consider the evidence below and what you have already read. Which of the following theories would you reject, which would you accept?
1. Garibaldi's qualities as a General.
2. Superior numbers and equipment.
3. The active support of the Sicilians.
4. The incompetence of the Neapolitan army.
5. Good luck.

Table A   Numbers and leaders involved in battles

Battle	Garibaldi	Neapolitans	Neapolitan leader
Calatafimi	1,000 volunteers, 200 *squadre* who fought and 800 who waited to see who would win.	2,000 and 1,000 in reserve.	General Landi, 70 years old; followed his troops in a carriage and was not himself at the battle. Remained with reserve.
Palermo	750 volunteers and 3,000 *squadre*.	21,000	General Lanza, 72, deaf.
Milazzo	4,500 volunteers.	4,636 but 1,000 were in castle.	Major Bosco who had been second in command of the force lured by Garibaldi out of Palermo.

Table B   Weapons

	Infantry	Artillery and Cavalry
Garibaldi	Flintlock **muskets** converted to percussion cap. Sighted to 300 yards but ineffective beyond 100. After Palermo Enfield **rifles** arrived sighted to 900 yards.	Two 1802 cannon and three pre-Napoleonic war 'museum pieces'. Used at Calatafimi but not at Palermo where they were in diversion force. No cavalry.
Neapolitans	Muzzle loading rifles sighted to 900 yards.	Full complements of cavalry and guns.

Table C   Eye witness reports

Name	Position	Comment
Patterson	British volunteer rewarded with a commission at Milazzo	'Success was obtained by the constant determined advance always under heavy fire and against a brave enemy in a strong position, superior in numbers and in training. Only the heroic leading of Garibaldi and his lieutenants made the victory possible.' (Trevelyan, 17, appendix E and p.328)
Maniscalco	Sicilian Minister writing to King Francis on 19 May 1860	'Public spirit is getting worse all the time ... civil servants are leaving their jobs and the voice of duty is no longer heard. What we are watching is a process of social disintegration ... even men of good will are now turning in favour of the revolution because they fear otherwise they will be devoured.' (Mack Smith, 22, ch.10)
Commander Forbes	British observer of campaign in 1861	'Garibaldi may be said to exercise an individual power over his followers wholly without parallel amongst modern commanders. With this imaginative race faith in their chief amounts to a superstition. This feeling combined with an utter contempt and, with the Sicilians, an implacable hatred for Neapolitans, has been the key-stone of Garibaldi's success.' (Mack Smith, 9, p.103)

King Francis II, the 24 year old King of the Two Sicilies had all this while been attempting to find ways of preventing the destruction of his kingdom. He had only been King since the death of his father Ferdinand II on 22 May 1859. Gentle and pious (he had once telegraphed for the pope's blessing five times in one day) he was not really the right person to handle the emergency. With Austria unable to help him, he desperately gambled on making his rule more popular by granting a constitution. But the new constitution of 25 June 1860 did more harm than good. Loyal **monarchists** were replaced by liberals who had no faith in the monarchy and preferred Garibaldi. Hopes that Napoleon III would prevent Garibaldi from crossing the straits into Naples vanished when the British refused to support him. Between 18 and 21 August, Garibaldi organized two successful crossings and his armies were soon advancing rapidly up the peninsula towards Naples (see map 4). Deserted by his leading ministers, Francis II decided to abandon Naples and concentrate his forces to the north at Capua (see map 4, f). His main hope now was that he could hold out long enough for the powers of Austria, Prussia and Russia to agree to send an army to his aid. Cavour now took a bold action. On 11 September the Sardinian army invaded the two Papal provinces of the Marches and Umbria (see map 4, no. 11). Outnumbering the Pope's small volunteer army by nearly three to one they defeated them at the Battle of Castelfidardo on 18 September 1860. (see map 4, e). By the beginning of October therefore, Francis II had a hostile Sardinian army poised on his borders to the North and Garibaldi to the South. He decided on a final effort to regain his lost capital of Naples. In this battle from 1 to 2 October, Gairbaldi's 20,000 men were forced on to the defensive by the 30,000 Neapolitan troops. But Garibaldi proved perfectly capable of fighting a defensive battle, and Francis II was obliged to fall back on Capua again (map 4, f). On the 6 October the unfortunate Francis was informed by Cavour that the Sardinian army would now enter Naples and restore order. It was agreed that Sicily, Naples, Umbria and the Marches would be annexed to Sardinia provided their peoples proved agreeable. The plebiscites held on 21 October produced large majorities in favour of annexation. Garibaldi and Victor Emmanuel met on 26 October and the Sardinian army, with their superior equipment, took over the siege of Capua. Even when it fell on 2 November Francis II refused to give up the struggle. Assisted by Napoleon III's fleet, he held out in the coastal fortress of Gaeta (see map, 4, g) until February 1861. Long before then his last hope of help had faded when the British government on 27 October unreservedly supported the new enlarged Italy and the Austrian attempt to get support from Russia and Prussia failed completely at a meeting in Warsaw. Apart from the area surrounding Rome itself (map 4, no. 13) and Venetia (map 4, no. 12) the unification of Italy had been completed.

Study 9

Events in Italian Unification:

Look carefully at pictures 2, 3 and 4 and then:
  (a) Arrange them in chronological order, the order in which the events, took place.
  (b) Write a brief description of each picture and the event shown in it.

2. *Garibaldi cutting down a captain of Neapolitan cavalry after a charge made near the bridge of Milazzo (Illustrated London News)*

3. *(Mansell–Bulloz Collection)*

4. (Mansell Collection)

Venetia, Rome, the Tyrol and Istria become united to Italy 1860–1919

On 6 June 1861, Cavour aged 51, having been bled no less than 5 times in the previous few days, lay dying with mustard plasters applied to his limbs and bladders filled with ice to his burning head. His last intelligible words before he died were supposed to have been: 'Italy is made – all is safe'. But Italy had not yet been completely unified – the Pope's excommunication of the parish priest who gave Cavour communion illustrated just one of the many problems still unsolved.

Cavour was the only leading creator of Italian unification who died before Venetia and Rome were added to the new state. Had he survived it is possible that the unification of Italy might have proceeded to a more glorious climax. As it was he was spared the disaster of Garibaldi's attempt to invade Rome (map 4, 13) with an army of volunteers in 1862. Whether or not Garibaldi had the support of the King for this venture is still not clear for the attempt ended in a skirmish between the King's regular army and Garibaldi's volunteers. Garibaldi was himself wounded and imprisoned, five royalist soldiers and seven of Garibaldi's volunteers were killed in the battle, and others, deserters from the regular army, shot without trial. Garibaldi remained undaunted and a popular hero. When the bullet was finally extracted from his ankle the sheets and bandages, stained with the blood of the martyr, were torn up and treasured as sacred relics. In England, after a visit in 1864 there was a flourishing trade in bottles of soap suds which were supposed to have come from the hero's own wash basin. In 1866 the 59 year old was back in action against his enemy Austria. In alliance with Bismarck's Prussia Italy had gone to war against Austria; the prize was to be Venetia (map 4, no. 12). Garibaldi's irregular troops succeeded in penetrating into the Trentino (map 4, no. 14).

The professional Italian army had retreated rather hastily after a minor reverse at Custoza (map 4, h) and the navy, in spite of complete superiority in numbers and equipment were defeated at the battle of Lissa. (map 4, i). In the end the good offices of Napoleon III secured Venetia for Italy in spite of her military defeats; the Austrians had promised him Venetia if he remained neutral in the war. He handed it over to Italy according to a prior agreement but the Trentino had to be returned to Austria. However, Napoleon was still inextricably fastened to the Italian problem. The army which had restored Pope Pius IX to Rome back in 1849 (see p.25) was still there. In December 1866 he must have felt that his problems were coming to an end. He was now prepared to honour the terms of the September convention signed back in 1864. In this agreement the Italians had promised to defend Rome from attack and to move their capital to Florence. In return Napoleon would honour his part of the bargain by withdrawing his troops from Rome. In under a year they were forced back again. Mazzini and Garibaldi had collaborated to invade Rome. A prisoner on his island home of Caprera (map 4), guarded by nine ships and now 60 years old, Garibaldi had evaded his guards by rowing solo across the straits and riding along the coast for 17 hours. But it was all in vain. The French army returned and Garibaldi's four thousand volunteers were defeated by a combined French and Papal army of nine thousand at a battle near Rome on 3 November 1867. Italy had to wait until 1870, when Napoleon's troops were withdrawn to help him defend France against the Prussians, before she was finally able to occupy Rome (see map 4, no. 13).

With this Italy became a reality. The leaders of the unification movement gradually vanished from the scene. Mazzini died in 1872; Napoleon III, no longer an Emperor but a lonely exile in England, in 1873. King Victor Emmanuel II, aged only 58, and Pius IX, Pope for 31 years, both died in 1878. Garibaldi, still living on his island home of Caprera, survived until 1882, aged 74. The Italian government refused to honour his request to be burned in the open dressed in his famous red shirt. As if in protest, when his body was lowered into the ground, the sky darkened and the block of granite which was supposed to cover his grave cracked and broke. In 1919 Italy was rewarded for aiding Britain and France in the First World War with the territory of Istria and the Trentino, which Garibaldi had so often fought in. (See map 4, nos. 15 and 14). Unification was now complete.

Study 10

Pictures 5 to 7 show the leaders of Italian unification, Cavour, Garibaldi, Mazzini. Use the clues given in the table overleaf to identify each of them.

5. *(Mansell Collection)*

6. *(Hulton Picture Library)*

7. *(Hulton Picture Library)*

Picture no.	Dates and father's occupation	Description	Name?
	1810–61 Landed aristocrat	'Scant thin hair, sharp grey eyes covered by goggle spectacles; black silk tie too tight for the swollen neck, waistcoat half unbuttoned.' (Dicey, 1861, quoted in Holt, 1, p.186)	?
	1807–82 Sailor from Nice	'Of middle height, well made, broad shouldered, light chestnut hair which fell loosely over his neck on to his shoulders, the nose with its exceedingly broad root.' (Koelman, 1849, quoted in Trevelyan, 17, p.117)	?
	1805–72 Genoese doctor	'Haggard and worn, with rather an agreeable face, dim black eyes, full forehead, straight black hair and grizzled beard.' (Wetmore 1849, quoted in Whitridge, 37, p.183)	?

Study 11

Just to make sure you have mastered the main events and the geography of this chapter make a tracing of map 4 and add a full key on the lines shown below.

Number	Name of State	How and when taken over by Sardinia
1, etc		
Letter	Name of Battle	Who fought it and the result
a, etc		

If you read the chapter correctly, by continually referring to the map as you went along, you should be able to do this without referring back!

CHAPTER 3

Italian Nationalism

1815 – 60

The story of Italian unification in Part A has shown how, again and again, armies marched, men fought and died, civilians laboured to build up barricades; one estimate is that from 1848 to 1866 nearly 28,000 Italians lost their lives, not to mention the Austrians and French who were killed in the wars of 1848–9 and 1859–60. But why did these men risk their lives? What sort of people were they? Why did success come in 1859–60 and not in 1848–9? Was the new Italian Kingdom really worth all the fighting and bloodshed? Chapters 3 to 6 are designed to help you think about these important problems and try to reach some conclusions of your own about them.

A very simple explanation of the wars and fighting which led up to the creation of the Kingdom of Italy in 1860 would be that they were caused by **nationalism**. It would be possible to draw up a theory which worked like this: the people living in the Italian peninsula had their own language and culture but were governed in many separate states, often by foreign rulers. As these governments grew steadily more oppressive the people grew more and more discontented. The French Revolution and Napoleonic Wars for a time swept away the old governments and showed them that change was possible. At the same time a whole new way of thinking was born known as **romanticism**. Romantics disagreed with the ideas of the eighteenth century which taught that government, music, poetry and painting needed to be based on universal rules and discipline. Influenced by these ideas, Italian writers, poets, and musicians began to teach that the people should be proud of being Italian and that sometime in the future the whole peninsula ought to be united in one great country, Italy. Secret societies were formed, revolutions were attempted, men died and became celebrated as martyrs. Gradually Italian nationalism became a vast popular movement which only needed great leaders like Cavour and Garibaldi to carry it to success. Like many theories this one sounds convincing. But in history no theory is acceptable unless it can be shown to be supported by evidence. If the evidence contradicts the theory then it must either be abandoned altogether or modified until it fits the facts. In the rest of this chapter you will be introduced to a selection of evidence and will be invited to make up your own mind as to whether the original theory outlined above holds good, needs to be modified, or to be abandoned altogether.

Study 12

(a)   Recently many historians have begun to doubt whether the whole Italian people became converted to the new religion of nationalism. They have argued that only a small minority from certain classes, regions and age groups ever participated in the movement. Study evidence 1 to 5, make up your own mind and write down your views —

      1. Does the evidence indicate a wide cross section supporting the wars and revolutions?

      2. If not, which regions, classes and age groups *are* most heavily represented?

(b)   In our original theory it was suggested that the various Italian nationalist societies may have played an important part in converting the people to nationalism. Some historians, however, have not been impressed with their achievements. Their membership, it has been claimed, was small and mainly on paper and in the minds of their leaders only. Study evidence 6–10 below and briefly report on what you think. It might help you to use the following estimates of Italy's population.

Date	1815	1833	1844	1852	1860/1
Population: (in millions)	19.7	21.2	22.9	24.4	25

(*Source:* Cipolla, 33, statistical appendix)

1. Of those listed by Garibaldi in his Memoirs as taking part in the attempt to force a constitution on the King of Sardinia in 1821, (see p.10) 'in all there were six superior officers, thirty secondary officers, five physicians, ten lawyers and one Prince.'

2. In the five days of revolution in Milan from 17 to 22 March 1848 (see ch. 1, p.18) 409 persons were listed as killed. These included 107 skilled workers, 41 workmen, 35 shopkeepers and clerks, 12 peasants, 26 servants, 4 students, 3 apprentices, 16 middle class merchants, 4 children, 9 'others' (e.g. riding master, singer) 152 unemployed or with no stated occupation. There were also 39 women killed. (Ginsborg, 15, p.128, note 3)

3. During the Venetian Revolution in 1848–9 (see ch. 1, p.25) many of the towns in the countryside asked for volunteers to become civic guards to resist the Austrians. In Lonigo, a small town south of Vicenza, 529 men volunteered, on 20 March, including 104 from the neighbouring villages. Their occupations were as follows: 48 peasants, 40 carpenters, 21 tailors, 21 masons, 10 innkeepers, 10 shoemakers, 6 students, 4 road workers, 1 shepherd, 49 unemployed. (Ginsborg, 15, p.106). (The information came from the state archive of Venetia in Venice; until recently rats had set up home amongst these valuable documents!)

4. In 1849 Garibaldi brought his legion of volunteers into Rome to defend the new Republic (ch. 1, p.21) 'There were few peasants in the legion. The

great majority belonged to the commercial classes and artisans from whom were chosen, by a process of voluntary natural selection, the most intelligent and enthusiastic partisans of reform together with the most adventurous spirits and lovers of a roving life. There were a large number of students in the ranks. One element in the legion consisted of a few convicts whom Garibaldi had admitted. Garibaldi called his legionaries "The cultivated classes of the towns".' (Trevelyan, 17, pp.88–9)

5. In 1860 the famour 'Thousand' set out with Garibaldi to invade Sicily (see ch.2, p.35) of which it is known that 349 came from the cities of Bergamo, Milan, Brescia and Pavia (originally Austrian Lombardy) 113 from Genoa and Turin (Sardinia), 50 from Sicily, 46 from Naples, 11 from the Papal States, 17 from outside Italy. Five hundred were urban working class, 150 lawyers, 100 doctors, 100 business men, 50 engineers, 30 sea captains, and there were also artists, authors, journalists, civil servants, barbers and cobblers. The oldest was over 60 and the youngest was 12. More than half were under 20 and indeed many of the professional men were still really students. Garibaldi himself said in his memoirs: 'They were splendid in the dress and cap of the student and in the more humble dress of the bricklayer, the carpenter and the smith. I wish from my heart that I could have added "and of the peasant": but I will not distort the truth. That sturdy and hard-working class belongs to the priests, who keep them in ignorance. There was not one case of them joining the volunteers.' (Ridley, 14, pp.443–4)

6. 'Coletta affirms in his history that the members of the Carbonari (ch.1, p.10) in the Kingdom of Naples amounted to 642,000; and, according to a document in the Aulic Chancery, even that number is below the mark. The number of Carbonari, says this paper, amounts to more than 800,000 in the Kingdom of Two Sicilies...' (Dumas, 12, p.12)

7. Young Italy's membership is unknown (ch.1, p.11). One estimate put it at 60,000 members in 1833. The trials of 1833–5 in Pavia showed that over 3,000 skilled and other workers had been enrolled in the society. (Holt, 1, p.88; Ginsborg, 15, p.130, note 11).

8. 'We must tell you privately but clearly that your sources of information about public opinion are wrong... They have deceived you into thinking the whole of Italy a volcano ready to erupt... The ordinary people are neither educated enough nor have they the strength to move or to support a revolution once it has begun.' (letter to Mazzini from Bertani 1858 – Mack Smith, 8, ch.6).

9. Young Italy was very different in reality from what it seemed to be on paper: 'The leaders were chosen from amongst those held in highest esteem for their position in civil life; counts, marquises, rich landowners, doctors and lawyers most of them complete strangers to the art of war. I myself have seen

a frightened dwarf taking the oath to this militant society. Meanwhile Mazzini was telling Europe of thousands of armed apostles straining for battle; and many of the local leaders, when they contrasted such boasts with the wretchedness of the people they had at their disposal, consoled themselves with the thought that their own circumstances were exceptional and that things were better elsewhere. It is always like this in conspiratorial enterprises... exiles dream up an imaginary world, regard every city or province where they have two or three correspondents as a key position in their command. Nevertheless... Mazzini deserves praise as a writer who gave impetus to the movement of ideas...' (Giuseppe Montanelli, *History of Tuscany*, 1814–50, published 1853. Fuller text in Mack Smith, 8, pp.60–61)

10. The National Society, (ch.2, p.28) founded in 1857 by Manin and Gioberti (ch.1, p.12) is estimated to have attained a membership of four to eight thousand. By 1860 its official newspaper had attained a circulation of 10,000 and its official statement of policy had reached a distribution of 100,000 copies. From 15 January to 25 March 1859 it succeeded in recruiting 20,000 volunteers from all over Italy. Most of these joined the Piedmontese army or were drafted into Garibaldi's 'Hunters of the Alps' (ch.2, p.31).

Study 13

One very useful method of testing a theory in history is to apply it to the lives of people who lived at the time. Below (11 to 15) are brief biographical notes on five famous Italian writers, poets, painters and composers. In our original theory it was suggested that, apart from the influence of nationalist societies, the Italian people converted to nationalism in the following ways:

1. The influence of the French Revolution and Napoleon.
2. The influence of the new Romantic writers.
3. The influence of their own writers, painters, poets and composers who taught them to be proud of Italian history and culture.
4. The oppressive governments who attempted to prevent freedom of speech and set up police states.

Read the biographical extracts and make a report on the evidence you have found for or against the above parts of the theory. It is only fair to warn you that some historians don't believe that there was much real oppression or that the so called 'influences' went further than a narrow circle of rich friends and relatives from middle class backgrounds. What are your views?

11. The Marchese MASSIMO D'AZEGLIO (1798–1866) was the younger son of a Piedmontese aristocrat. Instead of making a career in the army, as was usual for younger sons of aristocratic families, he became a painter, novelist and political journalist. In 1848 he joined the papal army and was wounded when it was defeated by Radetzky. After the defeat of Charles Albert he

became Victor Emmanuel's first Prime Minister until he was replaced by Cavour. Typical of his popular paintings, produced between 1833 and 1843 was his 'Battle of Legnano' which showed the German Emperor Barbarossa defeated by the Italian Lombards in 1176. His two novels were full of Italian patriotism and critical of foreigners who intervened in the peninsula. He did not feel, however, that the Austrian rulers of Lombardy were particularly tyrannical. In his autobiography he said: 'If I wished to breathe freely I had to return from Turin to Milan. Why? Because of all the subtle skill with which the Austrian authorities knew how to allay and soften the commands and to allow widespread freedom to the Milanese to grumble, to fool the police, make pronouncements... even on politics: only it was essential not to shout too loud, with prudence one could say anything.' (D'Azlegio, *Recollections*, 1868, quoted in Marshall, 20) In fact instead of getting his works published in Sardinia he usually turned to Lombardy, or, in the case of *On the recent events in Romagna*, to Tuscany. It is true that the Tuscan government seized and confiscated the second edition in 1846 and that the censor of Lombardy-Venetia lost his job after allowing the first novel through. But he never had to publish abroad. 'To call the present rulers of Italy tyrants would be ridiculous', he maintained. Like his cousin, Cesare Balbo, (ch. 1, p.12) to whom he dedicated his political writings, D'Azeglio believed in Italy united around the Sardinian monarchy.

12. UGO FOSCOLO (1778–1827) was the son of a Venetian doctor. He became a republican and was twice wounded when fighting for Napoleon I against the Austrians. However, when he discovered that Napoleon did not intend to free Italy he began to write poems and plays and to use his position as lecturer at Pavia University to attack Napoleon. In 1814 he tried to organise the Italian divisions in the French army to set up a republic in Italy. When this scheme failed he refused to live under Austrian rule. 'To have hated the tyranny with which Bonaparte was oppressing Italy does not imply that I must love the domination of the House of Austria', he wrote. 'The difference for me was that I hoped that Bonaparte's frenzied ambition might bring about, if not the independence of Italy, at least such great deeds as might raise the Italians; whereas the regular government of Austria precludes all such hopes.' (Martin, 23, p.191) The rest of his life was spent in exile in England. In 1871 his bones were transferred to Florence. His poems, such as 'On Tombs', written in 1807, urged young Italians to keep struggling and dying for their beliefs even if there was no hope. His novel, *The Last Letters of Jacopo Ortis*, told the story of a Venetian who was persecuted for his patriotic views and committed suicide. Mazzini as a young man is said to have learnt the whole novel by heart. In his diary for 14 July 1860, Abba (see p.35) writes about his companion on that day's march, Telesforo Catoni: 'He used to study law at Pavia... he adores the poet Foscolo and knows 'On Tombs' by heart and seems

to draw spiritual nourishment from it... Catoni is very Foscolian and if his portrait was prefixed to *Ortis* everyone would think that Jacopo must have looked like that.' When Garibaldi died in 1882 a book of Foscolo's poems was found open by his bedside.

13. ALESSANDRO MANZONI (1785–1873), spent the early part of his life in Paris living with his mother who had settled there with her lover, a rich Milanese banker. Here he became fascinated by the French Revolution and came to admire Napoleon I. 'His death shook men', he wrote, 'as if something essential was now lacking from the world.' Returning to his home town Milan, now under Austrian rule, he was soon in trouble with the authorities for supporting anti-Austrian newspapers. In 1827 the first edition of his novel, *The Betrothed*, was published. Banned initially in the Papal States, 600 copies were sold in 20 days and new editions have been coming out regularly ever since. The book was influenced by the English Romantic writer Sir Walter Scott and described the triumph of simple Catholic peasants over their wicked oppressors. 'A dangerous book' said one critic, 'because the peasants cut such a better figure than the nobles.' Further than this the 1840 edition of the book gave the Italians a national language. Up until then the national language was based on sixteenth century Italian which only a few scholars could read and speak. French was the language of government in Sardinia and the Kingdom of the Two Sicilies, the Papal States used Latin, and the Austrian controlled areas operated in German. Ordinary people used their local dialects which meant that, for example, a Tuscan could only talk to a Neapolitan with great difficulty. Foscolo's main languages were the Ionian and Venetian dialects; the families of Mazzini and Garibaldi spoke a Ligurian dialect first and French second; Manzoni's family spoke either French or the Milanese dialect. According to a contemporary, Brofferio, 'Cavour spoke in a clipped, Frenchified way and made so many howlers that it would have seemed an impossible task to anyone to make him agree with the Italian dictionary.' The 1840 edition of *The Betrothed* helped put an end to this by combining the dialect of Tuscany with the older academic Italian. Although he took no active part in the fighting in Milan in 1848 (ch. 1, p.18) Manzoni's sons fought on the barricades and his daughter married D'Azeglio (ch. 3, p.50). He published a poem, 'Oh days of our country's ransom', which later was quoted by many of Garibaldi's Thousand. In 1859 he abandoned his republican ideas in favour of support for King Victor Emmanuel's leadership. After unification he became a member of the Senate in Italy's parliament.

14. SILVIO PELLICO (1789–1854) was born in Piedmont. At the end of the Napoleonic wars Foscolo (p.51) left Pellico in charge of all his papers. Now settled in Lombardy, Pellico already had an important play, *Francesca da Rimini*, to his credit. One of the leading characters in the play makes a patriotic speech threatening foreigners with massacre. In 1818 Pellico edited a

new paper, *Il Conciliatore*, which opposed the Austrian financed *Biblioteca Italiana*. The paper collapsed in 1819 after Pellico was threatened with expulsion by the Austrian police. In October 1820 the Austrian Emperor passed a new law condemning to death anyone joining a secret society or plotting revolution, and imposing hard labour for life on any person failing to report a revolutionary. Unfortunately for Pellico he had now been initiated into the Carbonari (see ch. 1, p.10). The police had already rounded up more than 30 men; thirteen had been condemned to death but later had their sentences commuted to hard labour. Information from these arrests led to a trail which resulted in the arrest of Pellico in Milan on 13 October 1820. He was condemned to death but had his sentence reduced to 15 years hard labour in the Austrian fortress of Spielberg. Shortly after his release in 1830 he published his famous book *My Prisons*, which described conditions at the Spielburg. 'Our prison garb consisted of a pair of trousers of rough cloth, the right leg grey, the left a brown colour: a smock of the same two colours... and a jacket similarly coloured. The stockings were made of coarse wool, the shirt of rough hemp full of prickles, a real hairshirt... Fetters on our feet consisted of a chain from one leg to the other.' (Pellico, 11, p.124) The prisoners were not allowed to write or have any contact with their families though they communicated illegally with each other by writing with pieces of finger nail on toilet paper in flower juice. For some of the time at least they were allowed to read books from the volumes which the prisoners had themselves brought – among the 72 works in this 'library' were Shakespeare, Milton, Byron and Scott. Each day they had to work at sawing wood, preparing lint for dressing wounds and making stockings from 'wool so impregnated with oil and grease that the stench brought on headaches.' Of seven other prisoners mentioned in Pellico's book, who like him, had been originally sentenced to death, two died in prison, and the other five served between five and sixteen years. Pellico was himself very ill with arthritis and scurvy. Of the fourteen prisoners whose occupation can be identified, five were members of the aristocracy, there were three lawyers and three doctors or professors, and one merchant, one priest and one army officer. Contrary to Pellico's intentions the book aroused national indignation. Since 1832 there have been an average of six editions per year in Italy. Pellico, in company with his friend Gioberti, (ch. 1, p.12) believed originally in a papal **federation** for Italy. He always maintained: 'When I published those memoirs my only intention was to give witness to the excellence of the Catholic religion'.

15. GIUSEPPE VERDI (1813–1901) was born in Parma, the son of an innkeeper and grocer. Mazzini had once prophesied that a musician would come who would devote his art to Italian unification. Some music historians have argued that Verdi, originally a convinced republican, identified himself with this claim. The opera houses at this time were not only centres of musical

entertainment but of eating, drinking, gambling, business and politics, all of which could be indulged in because the chandeliers carried candles which burned continually even during the singing. It was not necessary to be literate to appreciate the meaning of the great choruses which Verdi provided in his operas. It was no accident that most of his operas were based on scripts which could be given a double meaning. Was it really the Jews who lamented their captivity under Babylon in *Nabucco* (1842) when they sang 'Oh my country so beautiful and lost'? When the tenor in *Lombardi* (1843) sang, 'The Holy Land will be ours', most audiences knew he meant Italy and not Israel. Wherever Verdi's operas were performed in 1847–9 there seemed to be disturbances and crowds. When *Nabucco* was played in Milan and Parma more seats were sold than the towns had inhabitants. In Venice in 1847 the audience erupted during each performance of *Macbeth* when the lines, 'Our country betrayed invites us to weep; brothers let us hasten to save the oppressed' were reached. Red and green bouquets, the colours of Italy, cascaded on to the stage. When the police forbade this the audience tossed down yellow and black ones, Austria's colours, and cheered when the singers trampled on them. In Rome in 1848–9, under the Republican government (see ch. 1, p.20) Verdi's new opera, the *Battle of Legnano* was produced. The hero in the opera is locked in a tower to prevent him from joining the gallant Lombard army in their struggle against the *German* Emperor Barbarossa. In his patriotic determination to fight for his country he leaps out of the window into the moat. A soldier in the opera house, his enthusiasm fired by the banners, the streamers thrown on to the stage and the audience participation in the choruses, actually did tear off his coat and jump out of the gallery into the orchestra pit! In 1849 Verdi was one among many who petitioned France to help save the city of Milan from Austrian recapture (ch. 1, p.19). By 1859 his republicanism had moderated sufficiently for him to become a firm supporter of Cavour. His name was chalked up on walls all over Austrian Italy because the letters spelled out the slogan, '*V*ictor *E*mmanuel *R*e (King) *D*'*I*talia'. When the citizens of Parma rebelled against their ruler (ch. 2, p.33) Verdi was chosen as a delegate to report their wish to join the kingdom of Sardinia. The defeat of the revolutions had meant that Verdi had to go back to his struggles to get his works past the censors. In 1858 the Neapolitan censor got to work on Verdi's new opera *A Masked Ball* which contains an assassination plot (Orsini? ch. 2, p.28). In a letter Verdi summed up the results: 'The original consisted of 884 verses, 297 are altered. Moreover what remains of my work in the drama as revised? The title? No. The poet? No. The period? No. The Place? No. The characters? No. The situations? No....' (Hussey, 32, p.117) From 1860 to 1865 Verdi was a member of the new Italian Parliament. Until Cavour's death he always voted as Cavour did – 'That way I can be sure of not making a mistake.' When his great friend Manzoni (p.52) died in 1873, Verdi composed his famous *Requiem*, to be performed on the anniversary of Manzoni's death.

—————————————— *Study 14* ——————————————

(a) Our original theory stated that the people of Italy rebelled because they had been convinced that their peninsula must become united into one Italian nation, an idea which you have just explored in some detail in studies 12 and 13. Many historians argue that the rebellions of 1848–9 and 1860 were not caused by this at all but by a much older and more obvious cause – poverty. Look at the evidence 16 to 19. Report briefly on whether this supports the critics of our original theory.

(b) Poverty is often linked to poor economic progress. Our original theory would suggest that in Italy this was due to oppressive foreign governments. If this were true we should expect the evidence to show three things:

1. Very poor economic progress in Italy compared to other countries.
2. The worst progress in areas governed by foreigners, e.g. Austrian Lombardy-Venetia.
3. Better progress in areas governed by Italian rulers, e.g. Piedmont-Sardinia, Naples-Sicily.

Examine the evidence 19 to 23 below and write a brief report saying to what extent these three statements are true.

16. *Price, tax and employment figures from Venice.*

Year	Wheat prices Maize prices (Wholesale: per Venetian bushel) Austrian lire		Numbers of silk workers employed	Amount of personal tax collected (in florins)
1819	16			
1845	16.22	10.61	639	616,000
1846	18.56			619,000
1847	31.92	24.49	410	602,000
1848 (Feb)	21.50			

(*Source:* Ginsborg, 15, p.74)

17. Three sources from Venetia in 1848 state that:
'The poorer classes lack any means of paying the personal tax (applied to all men aged 14 to 60)... instead of which the tax collector takes their beds and cooking pots.'
(Police report from Belluno Province Feb. 1848)

As for manufacturing concerns during February we can do no more than repeat the totally dismal picture which we have had to paint in the previous months. In the absence of any movement of trade... the consequences fall on to the class of workers whose conditions can only continue to deteriorate every day'.
(Chamber of Commerce report 6 March 1848).

'What the peasant suffers the lack of most is ready money. By continual drudgery the poor man manages to collect together a few lire. From these meagre earnings, for which the peasant has sweated, the tax collector takes the greatest part, and sometimes leaves none at all. You ask a villager what his greatest burden is. He'll reply the Filippo. The Filippo, or personal tax, is for him a misfortune, a calamity.'
(*The Voice of the People* – a Mazzinian newspaper – 31 March 1848.)
(Ginsborg, 15, p.74)

18. There were peasant rebellions in Sicily both in 1848 and in 1860 (chs. 1 and 2, p.17 and p.35). In his *History of Modern Sicily*, Mack Smith argues that the peasants' chief reason for rebellion was the price of food, the high 'macinato' (a tax on all grain before it was milled), and their desire for more land. In 1848 there were bad harvests and the peasant bands marched into Palermo, destroyed customs barriers, burned title deeds and tax records and seized large portions of the land for themselves. In 1860 it was much the same story. In a letter written in July 1860 Ippolito Nievo, one of Garibaldi's thousand, commented; 'We have been helped by auxiliary squads of volunteers made up for the most part of bands of brigands who are ready to fight against the Bourbons just as an excuse to make war on the landowners.' A broadsheet issued at Corleone on 8 September 1860 announced: 'People of Corleone, you have been turned into fleshless skeletons just because a few landowners have sucked out even the marrow from your bones. Avenge the blood of your forebears... kill all the cattle... burn hayricks... if you present a united front you can dethrone the landowners...' Such peasants did not understand anything about an Italian nation. Indeed they thought that the 'La Talia' which the Thousand were always talking about was the King of Sardinia's wife!

19. *International Comparisons*

Country	Km.s of railways in:		% illiterate c. 1850
	1840	1850	
Austria-Hungary	144	1,579	40–45*
Belgium	334	903	45–50
France	497	2,915	40–45
Germany	469	5,856	20
Great Britain	2,390	9,797	30–33
Ireland	21	865	30–50
Italy	20	620	75–80
Netherlands	17	176	30
Russia	27	501	90–95

(*Source:* Cipolla, 33, statistical appendix)

* Excluding Lombardy-Venice.   Excluding Prussia.

20. 'Our land [in the Kingdom of Two Sicilies] is as fertile as almost anywhere in Italy but it is deserted or else is cultivated by a handful of wretched, weary peasants. In such a fertile kingdom which could feed double its present population there is often a bread shortage and people can be found dead of starvation... Two railways have been built... the second to link up the two royal palaces of Naples and Caserta. Nothing is done for the Provinces, nothing for luckless Sicily. When Sicilians go to market they have to clamber over precipices or risk plunging into crevasses or drowning themselves in swollen rivers. There is only one road in Calabria and that a bad one. Sicily has two, short and bad.'★

(Written anonymously in 1847 by Luigi Settembrini, a political prisoner who spent four years in Neapolitan prisons. Full document in Mack Smith, 8 pp.117–23).

★ It might cost more to send goods from a farm to Palermo than from Palermo to London. (Mack Smith *History of Sicily*).

21. *Economic progress in the regions of Italy*

Item	a	b	c	d	e	f	g	h
Population 1830 (000s)	3,800		4,930	1,275	819	2,590	7,420	
National Income 1830 (million francs)	60		122	17	4	30	84	
Kms of Railroads 1848	8	0	112	160	-	0	85	0
Kms of Railroads 1859[1]	938	0	522	257	-	101	99	0
Foreign Trade 1858, ducats per head	40		-	32	-	2	7	
Percentage Literate 1861★	45.8	10.3	46.3[3]	26	22.4	16.6	13.7	11.4
Km of roads per km of area 1862[2]	1	0.10	1 +		0.75		0.10	0.05
Key a) Piedmont *b)* Sardinia *c)* Lombardy-Venetia *d)* Tuscany *e)* Modena-Parma *f)* Papal-States *g)* Naples *h)* Sicily								

(*Sources:* Tilly, 34, p.103; Mack Smith, 8, p.93)

★ Literacy in these figures refers to a regional dialect or a foreign language. Only 2.5% of Italians could speak the national language in 1860. (Woolf, 24, p.476).

1. Naples led the way in railway building in 1839. It also pioneered the first steamboat and the first gas lighting in Italy.
2. Some idea of the state of the roads in Italy before unification can be gained from the following: in 1845 letters reached Milan more quickly from New York or India than from Naples. There were seven customs posts along the 120 mile stretch of road from Bologna in the Papal States to Lucca. Goods could take over seven weeks to travel 200 miles from Florence to Milan. (Mack Smith, 22, ch. v.).
3. In 1830 one out of every thirteen children in Lombardy were in school. In England and Scotland the proportion was one out of sixteen.

22. The economy of Lombardy – extract from a speech given to the sixth Congress of Italian Scientists at Milan in 1844 by Carlo Cattaneo (see ch. 1, p.12)
'In 1840 our infirmaries numbered 72... in the course of a year the Milan hospital alone takes in 24,000 sick, Paris, which has more than four times the population, takes in only three times as many patients. The number of doctors is equivalent to one for every 13 square kilometres of the country while in Belgium each doctor has to serve an area twice that size. The country is similarly provided with engineers who in the city of Milan alone amount to around 450, whereas in France, the whole body of hydraulic and road engineers is only 568... Hence, all things considered, Lombardy may well have a larger number of educated families in relation to the uneducated population than any other country in Europe.' (Mack Smith, 8, p.93)

23. Austrian tax records have been used to construct the following statements: 'Lombardy-Venetia had one-eighth of the population of the Austrian Empire but paid one third of the Empire's tax revenue.' 'In the average year the Austrians drew between a quarter and a third of the total income of the Empire from Northern Italy.' 'In 1837 revenue per head in Lombardy was 7.44 florins, in Venetia 7.15, but in other parts of the Empire was much lower; in Bohemia 4.0, in the Tyrol 3.58, in Galicia 2.49.' 'By 1845 income from Venetia exceeded what the Austrians spent in that province by over 45 million Austrian lire.' (Ginsborg, 15, pp.2–3)

Study 15

Writing an essay on the nature and causes of Italian nationalism.
The time has now come for you to make up your mind about the nature of Italian nationalism and state your views in the form of an essay. Before doing this you might want to carry out some further research by
(a) re-reading chapters 1 and 2.
(b) following up some of the book references given in the evidence.
(c) consulting some of the books from the list on pages 101–2.
Before you can write an essay you must have clear views or arguments. These are then usually used in the first sentence of each paragraph, known as the 'key' or 'signpost'

sentence. The purpose of this sentence is to tell the reader precisely what you are about to argue in the rest of the paragraph. This is a very important technique. It should be possible for somebody pressed for time to read just the 'key' sentences of an article and still have a very precise idea of what it is arguing. This is of course particularly important for managers in industry or ministers in government. They can read quickly through an article and only read in detail the bits which they are doubtful about. Below are some groups of key sentences for your essay. Choose the *one* from each group which seems to fit your views best. It is possible that you may by now have abandoned or modified the original very simple theory with which this chapter started. The original theory is marked with a *.

Key Sentences

Group A *1. Between 1815 and 1860 Italians from all regions and classes were inspired to join in the movement to unite Italy.

2. The movement to change Italy between 1815 and 1860 was pathetically small and confined to a tiny group of upper and middle class Italians drawn from the north.

3. Although the percentage of Italians who were involved in the movement to reform Italy was normally a small one, there were times when the movement spread to involve not only the upper and middle class Italians but also the peasants and workers.

Group B 1. Dissatisfaction with the Austrian government's economic policies could not have been a major cause of the movement for change because the areas under Austrian rule were, on the whole, the most prosperous in Italy.

*2. Austrian muddle and mismanagement of the economies of the areas under their control was a major factor in causing the movement for Italian independence.

3. Generally speaking the prosperity of the areas of Italy under Austrian rule compared favourably with the other Italian regions; what made their inhabitants liable to rebellion was their unjust taxation policy and their refusal to modify this policy in times of bad harvests and poor trade.

Group C *1. One of the major causes of the revolutionary movement in Italy were the **police state** methods used by the rulers between 1815 and 1860.

2. It would be ridiculous to argue that the reform movement in Italy was a rebellion against police state methods similar to those used in communist or fascist states in the twentieth century; the rulers of Italy were incredibly mild by comparison.

3. The rulers of Italy between 1815 and 1860 brought about the movement for change by following the worst possible policy; their regulations were not stern enough to crush rebellions but they were sufficiently annoying to provoke irritated opposition.

Group D *1. The ideas of the great writers, artists and composers of the '**Risorgimento**' helped to inspire men and women all over Italy with a burning desire for independence from foreign rule and national unification.

2. There is no evidence whatsoever that the small group of friends and relations who poured out books, poems, music and paintings in the first half of the nineteenth century had any influence on the great mass of the Italian people. When people *did* rebel it was because of their poverty not because they believed in a united Italy.

3. The writers, artists and composers of the Risorgimento helped to stimulate the movement for reform by giving the educated classes a national language and culture which broke down regional barriers and inspired many of them, especially the young, into direct action.

Group E *1. The societies formed in Italy between 1815 and 1860 helped to convert the masses to nationalism and to organise them for action.

    2. The societies were too small, weak and badly organised to contribute much towards the movement for unification.

    3. Although the societies were small, weak and badly organised, they did help the movement for unification by spreading ideas and providing 'martyrs' whose example could be followed.

Now you must write five paragraphs, one to follow each key sentence. Check first though, that the key sentences you have chosen do not contradict each other. Each paragraph must contain argument and evidence to support the statement. An important point to remember is that, to be convincing, you must do more than simply use the arguments and evidence which favour your case; you must also deal with evidence or arguments which might seem to go against you. You wouldn't think much of a defence lawyer at a trial who didn't deal with the prosecution's arguments! Suppose for example that you have chosen key sentence C1. Evidence in 11 certainly goes against you and must be dealt with. If you can't deal with evidence which goes against your case then perhaps it is worth considering whether you have chosen the right key sentence. Finally, it is vital that all your arguments are supported by *evidence*. Some people find it hard to tell the difference between the two. Just to make sure you can, consider the two columns below. Which column contains arguments and which evidence? Which pieces of evidence could support which arguments?

X	Y
1. The Austrian government annoyed most of the educated classes by foolishly attempting to censor literature.	4. When Italians listened to the Jews lamenting their captivity in Verdi's *Nabucco* they were really lamenting their own captivity under Austria.
2. Many Italians learned their national attitudes at the opera.	5. Pellico's newspaper, *Il Conciliatore*, was forced to close down in 1819 by the Austrian government.
3. The peasants who sometimes joined the rebellions did so only at times of economic depression.	6. Wheat prices in Venetia rose from 16.22 Austrian lire per Venetian bushel in 1845 to 31.92 in 1847.

CHAPTER 4

Cavour's Part in the Unification

1859 - 60

One of the most puzzling problems in the history of Italian unification is why the movement failed in 1848–9 but succeeded in 1859–60. In many ways the external obstacles to unification seemed less severe in 1848–9 than they did in 1859–60. The most serious barrier to unification was the opposition not only of Austria but also of her Holy Alliance allies, Prussia and Russia (see p.10). This was not so important in 1848–9 since both Austria and Prussia were crippled by their own internal revolutions, but in 1859–60 all three were free from revolution and capable of interfering in Italy. France presented another obstacle: there was always the danger that she would take advantage of any trouble in the Italian peninsula to annex some of the territory which she had once governed in the time of Napoleon I. Italians would then, so to speak, be out of the Austrian frying pan and into the French fire. Yet in 1848–9 France was under a republican regime (see **republic**) which looked with sympathy towards a united Italy—far less dangerous than in 1859–60 when she was under the control of Napoleon III, the nephew of the great Napoleon, who could be expected to attempt as many gains as possible in the Italian peninsula. A further threat to Italian unification was the attitude of the Pope at Rome. He was unlikely to be in favour of giving up his extensive Papal territories and, as the head of a church in which the vast majority of Italians believed devoutly, his opinions were influential. In 1848–9 however, Pope Pius IX was initially in favour of reforms; in 1859–60 the situation was much less promising. By then Pius IX was a disillusioned man, unwilling to yield any of his territory and defended by French troops. Perhaps the biggest obstacle to Italian unification was within the peninsula itself. Italians put their own states first and Italy a long way second; they were unable even to understand each other's regional dialects and had totally different plans for the sort of Italy they wanted (see p.52). Yet even here 1848–9 had definite advantages over 1859–60. The food famine and trade depression of those years meant that there were plenty of people discontented enough to throw themselves into a revolution even if they were not sure what it was about. The years 1859–60 had no such advantages. But... 1859–60 ended in success and 1848–9 in failure. Why was that?

Italian historians at the end of the nineteenth century had no difficulty in coming up with the answer. This was an age when it was generally believed that the course of history could be decisively altered by great men. The great man who master minded 1859–60, they argued, was Cavour. With the help of King Victor Emmanuel and Garibaldi, he succeeded in 1859–60 because his clever brain and careful planning had given him five important advantages over the muddled leaders of 1848–9:

1. He had one clear and definite aim – to unite Italy under the Sardinian monarchy.
2. He had worked out a master plan so that Sardinia would have French and English allies in her mission.
3. By the year 1859 he had built Sardinia into an efficient modern state which could take on Austria and which other Italians would not be ashamed to support.
4. His careful training had made Victor Emmanuel into a popular King who trusted Cavour and followed his advice.
5. He was able to unite all those who wanted Italian unity, from the Sardinian **monarchists** to the republicans, and was not afraid to use popular rebellions to help him in his mission.

But can even great men change the course of history? Twentieth century historians are generally much less sure of this. So we shall have to examine the five above propositions very carefully. In the sections which follow each proposition will be looked at separately; the arguments in favour of its acceptance will be put first and will then be followed by arguments and evidence which may cause you to doubt the original proposition. The study sections will give you a chance to pause and reconsider your position.

1. *Success came in 1859–60 because Cavour had a clear and consistent aim – the unification of Italy under the Sardinian monarchy.*

There can be little doubt that in 1848–9 Charles Albert had no long term plans for the unification of Italy. His main aim was to increase the power of the royal House of Savoy. Throughout much of his reign he hoped to achieve this with Austrian help and not necessarily in north Italy. The royal family of Savoy were French rather than Italian and Charles Albert had plans and ambitions for interfering in Switzerland. Only when the revolutions broke out in 1848 did he develop an alternative plan to try to expand his power in north Italy against Austria. So sudden was this decision that the army did not even have any maps of Lombardy ready for the campaign. In contrast Cavour's aim was clear from the start – the unification of Italy under the leadership of the House of Savoy. Petruccelli della Gattina, a backbencher in the new Italian Parliament, expressed this point of view in 1862: 'Count Cavour', he said, 'has had a clear and precise aim; that of creating a unified and independent Italy'.

But is this view consistent with the evidence? Pause and consider the following facts and arguments. On 25 November 1858, Cavour wrote to his ambassador in Paris: 'If anyone talks to you seriously or jokingly about the reconstitution of Italy you must be bold and maintain that this can be solidly established only if Piedmont rests her head on the Alps and her feet on Ancona... (Mack Smith, 8, p.255). In his diary for 29 December 1859, Massari recorded Cavour as saying; 'We must leave Naples out of it. United Italy will be our children's achievement. I'm satisfied with what we've got, so long as we can reach Ancona (Mack Smith, 8, p.288). Many Italians doubted whether Cavour was really interested in the unification of Italy. In 1856 Mazzini attacked Cavour's policies in his newspaper, *Italia del Popolo*: 'Between you and us, sir, an abyss yawns. We represent Italy – you the old, covetous, faint hearted ambition of the House of Savoy. We desire above all National Unity – you territorial aggrandizement for Piedmont. (Mack Walker, 30, p.18) In August 1856 Cavour had met Garibaldi and hinted that he had plans for Italian unification. But the republican Pallavicini wrote to Manin on 24 August: 'It was all an act. What Cavour wants, and I'm sure of it, is just for Piedmont to be enlarged by a few square yards of soil.' (Mack Smith, 8, p.21)

2. *Success came in 1859–60 because Cavour's clever master plan gave Sardinia allies.* Charles Albert had deliberately rejected offers of French help because he hated and feared republicanism. Although the French foreign minister, Bastide, declared on 28 July 1848 that 'Italy knows that we desire her independence and that we are ready to help her if, by chance, her successes turn to disaster', Charles Albert chose to act alone against the Austrians. When, after defeat in 1849, he did turn to France for aid, he was not prepared to cede anything in exchange. Bastide refused to help him. In contrast Cavour was able to learn from Charles Albert's mistakes and prepare a master plan. This scheme worked as follows: Cavour sent Piedmontese troops to the Crimean war, to help Britain and France against Russia. In gratitude for this invaluable aid Britain and France allowed Cavour to represent Sardinia at the Congress of Paris and put the case for Italian unification. Cavour then used his new position to persuade Napoleon III to sign the agreement at Plombières (p.29). Unlike Charles Albert he saw the need to make concessions and promised to reward France with Savoy and Nice. His final master-stroke was to use the English friends won for him by the Crimean War to help to persuade Napoleon III to allow him to go much further than Plombières and add the central and southern states to the new Italy. Cavour's brilliant diplomacy meant that the unpromising situation in 1859 led to Italian unification, whereas the much more promising situation of 1848 had only led to failure.

But does this explanation of the 1859–60 triumph really fit the facts? Consider the following points. The Comte de Salmour maintained that Cavour did nothing about sending troops to the Crimea until he heard that King Victor Emmanuel planned to replace him with a new Prime Minister who would.

Cavour sent the troops without extracting any conditions or concessions from the British or French. Although 2,000 Piedmontese died of cholera their only fighting casualties were sustained in one battle. They suffered 188 killed and wounded in that engagement compared to 1,500 French casualties and 8,000 Russian. Prince Albert commented, 'The Piedmontese force has not done a day's work in the trenches and but for the 16 August battle they would not have heard a shot fired.' In addition Cavour's friend Alessandre Bixio was very critical of the way in which Cavour handled the Congress of Paris. In a letter of 31 March 1858, he wrote: 'You succeeded in making Sardinia enter the Congress of great nations but you did not acquire the smallest village, not even Mentona and Monaco. France and England showed you great deference in the way of recognition but Sardinia was not given any guarantees for the event of a war with Austria; she was given no assurances for the case of a re-arrangement of the map of Europe.' (Mack Walker, 30, p.210)

Consider also the view that Cavour owed a great deal of his success to good luck. He was lucky that France was led at that time by Napoleon III, himself a former Carbonaro, who wanted to overthrow Austrian power in Italy. He was lucky that the Orsini bomb incident strengthened rather than weakened Napoleon's resolve to help. He was lucky that the Crimean war shattered the Holy Alliance between Austria, Prussia and Russia which between 1815–49 had so often backed Austria's armies against nationalist revolutions in Italy (p.11). Infuriated by Austria's threat to join Britain and France against Russia in the Crimea and by her lack of gratitude for the way in which Russian troops had helped Austria to defeat the Hungarian rebels in 1849, Alexander II was only too pleased in March 1859 to make a secret alliance with Napoleon III. In it he promised Russian neutrality in an Italian war. In March 1860 he went even further than this and put pressure on Prussia, Austria's other former Holy Alliance ally, to refuse help to Austria. Cavour was fortunate too that Palmerston, Gladstone and Russell were in power in England during 1859–60. All were in favour of Italian unification not because they had been converted by Cavour but because they believed that a strong Italy was needed to counter the ambitions of Napoleon III. On three occasions the British government played a useful part. They supported the union of the central provinces with Sardinia (p.34) and thus helped to persuade Napoleon III to agree to this extension of unification. They refused to use the British navy to stop Garibaldi crossing to Naples from Sicily (p.40) and thus helped to persuade Napoleon III to refrain from intervention. They were the first government to uphold Cavour's addition of part of the Papal States to the Kingdom of Italy (p.40). Far from inducing the British government to follow this policy there were times when Cavour was in danger of losing its support. His cession of Savoy and Nice to Napoleon III (for example) almost convinced the British that he was merely a puppet of Napoleon III who could not be trusted. Palmerston remarked angrily: 'Cavour not only concealed the undertaking he made over Savoy before the war of 1859 (i.e. at Plombières) but he recently told us once again that he had not the slightest intention of ceding, exchanging or selling Savoy. All his talk of plebiscites, votes and parliamentary decisions is a farce. The surrender of these provinces [Nice and Savoy] is iniquitous especially because it was unnecessary. The Emperor would never have dared face the condemnation of Europe...' (Mack Smith, 8, p.305)

Finally it is worth considering whether Cavour ever had a 'master plan'. Petruccelli della Gattina remarked in 1862 that 'Count Cavour's strength does not lie in his principles for he has none that are altogether inflexible... Count Cavour has the talent to assess a situation and the possibilities of exploiting it. And it is this wonderful faculty that has contributed to form the Italy of today. As Minister of a fourth rate power he could not create situations like Napoleon III nor has he possessed the resources of a great nation like Palmerston. Count Cavour had to seek out an opening in the complicated fabric of European politics; he had to wriggle his way in, conceal himself, lay a mine and cause an explosion. And it was by these means that he defeated Austria and won the help of France and England.' (Mack Smith, 8, p.181) Like so many of the world's cleverest diplomatists Cavour was not a planner but an opportunist who knew how to make use of any incidents which chance threw out. During those agonising months in 1859 when Cavour was waiting for Austria to give him the excuse for the war which he needed to bring the Treaty of Plombières into operation, he made a very revealing remark to Castelli: 'All plans, all projects are useless, everything depends on an accident...' (Woolf, 24, p.445)

Study 16

1. Having studied section one where do you now feel the truth lies? Choose one of the statements below and write a brief defence of your choice:

   (a) The evidence presented in section one does not disprove the theory that Cavour had a clear and definite aim to unite the whole of Italy.
   (b) The evidence suggests that Cavour's aim was only to unify north and part of central Italy down as far as Ancona.
   (c) The evidence shows that Cavour's aims were no different from Charles Albert's; to gain as much territory for the House of Savoy as possible.

2. Do you still think Cavour had a master plan after studying section two? Which of the following three arguments would you prefer and why?

   (a) Cavour all the time had a clever master plan which meant that when he had contrived the war with Austria he had useful allies.
   (b) Cavour succeeded because he inherited a favourable diplomatic position and had a great deal of luck.
   (c) Cavour succeeded because he was a very skilful opportunistic diplomat who knew how to make use of any chances which were given to him and how to correct his errors.

3. *Success came in 1859–60 because Cavour's reforms had made Sardinia an efficient, modern state.*

In 1848–9 Charles Albert's Sardinia was too backward, both politically and economically, to be acceptable as the leader of the crusade against Austria. Although in the late 1830s Charles Albert's government had attempted to encourage trade, stimulate railway building and reform the army, the statistics in the table on page 57 show that Sardinia still lagged behind the other Italian states. For example, even Naples had a greater network of railways. Politically, with rigid censorship which did not allow the words **liberal** or **Constitution** to appear, and a system of ecclesiastical courts, Sardinia was even more barbaric. It was only at the last moment and under considerable pressure that Charles Albert was persuaded to yield the constitution (p.17) All this was reversed by the period of reforms between 1852 and 1859 when Cavour was Prime Minister. (see p.27) As a result Sardinia emerged as the undisputed economic leader of Italy. (see statistics p.57). Moreover all this was achieved through a properly elected parliament with debates, votes, a Prime Minister and a cabinet. Cavour admired Britain's constitutional monarchy. In 1860 he wrote to the Comtesse de Circourt: 'I have no confidence in dictatorships, above all not military dictatorships and I think that Parliament enables one to do things which would be impossible for an absolutist ruler. Thirteen years of experience have convinced me that an honest and energetic ministry has everything to gain from parliamentary controversy. I have never felt so powerless as when Parliament was shut.' (Mack Smith, 8, p.338) Sardinia's new parliamentary regime meant that many Italians from other states were now prepared to accept her leadership of the movement for unification. Her improved economy and army reforms gave her the strength to tackle Austria and gain the support of other powers.

But were these reforms largely an illusion? Consider the following points. As a result of literacy tests and tax qualifications the actual proportion of the Sardinian population allowed to vote was only $2\frac{1}{4}\%$; that is, even less than the percentage allowed to vote in Britain before the 1832 Reform Act came into operation. Some deputies were elected by as few as five or six voters. Such a small electorate was a tempting target for bribery and corruption. The government organised a special department to ensure that officially sponsored candidates were elected. Prefects (local government administrators) who failed to back government candidates in their areas were liable to be removed after an election. When the 1857 elections brought a victory for the right wing Catholic group (Cavour's enemies who opposed his religious reforms), he unconstitutionally refused to allow 10% of the deputies to sit in the parliament because they were ecclesiastics. Nor was the parliament, once it had been convened, an entirely independent body. One third or more of the deputies were salaried employees of the government, such as civil servants, army officers and magistrates, and could therefore be relied upon to vote as they were told. Even this very subservient parliament was not always consulted. They were not asked to discuss the entry to the Crimean War or the policy to be followed at the Congress of Paris, and were certainly not informed about the Plombières agreement. For that matter even the cabinet were often not asked their views; only one cabinet minister was approached by Cavour about Plombières. Cavour himself held so many offices that he often almost *was* the cabinet! Several times he was Prime Minister, Foreign Minister, Minister of both the Interior and Economic Affairs, all at once. On another occasion in 1859 he was Minister of War and Marine as well. Nor was that basic ingredient of liberal democracy, freedom of speech, always guaranteed. The Sardinian law did not prevent the economist Francesco Ferrara from being dismissed from his university post when he criticised the government in a lecture. Nor did it stop the system of freely elected juries from being suspended when Cavour wanted to get some Mazzinian republicans convicted.

How efficient was the new Piedmontese army which the economic and military reforms had made possible? Although the French had been promised an army of 100,000 men, the maximum number which the government succeeded in putting in the field was 60,000. Fifteen per cent of Piedmont's citizens bought themselves out of the army; only half of the conscripts called up in March 1859 appeared. There was a shortage of maps of Lombardy and when the armies reached the famous quadrilateral of forts they were unable to attack because there were insufficient numbers of horses and the siege artillery had been left 150 miles to the rear. The French in fact supplied twice as many men as the Sardinians and suffered twice as many casualties.

4. *Success came in 1859–60 because Victor Emmanuel became a popular, liberal leader capable of working harmoniously with Cavour.*

The stern ascetic king Charles Albert, with his admiration for the Jesuits and hi tendency to wear hair shirts, was never a sincere liberal. A Venetian revolutionary is supposed to have commented that Charles Albert 'supported liberty as if it were a ball and chain attached to his feet.' Mazzini referred to him as 'a political Hamlet condemned to a permanent want of equilibrium between his conceptions and the faculties which should realise them.' King Victor Emmanuel however, despite a certain lack of motivation (one of his teacher's reports commented, 'always asleep, thoroughly bored and indolent, an hour's lesson is not enough to get across to him the simplest point') was a definite improvement. His refusal to give up the constitution granted by Charles Albert, despite being put under pressure by the Austrians, made him popular throughout the Italian peninsula. The legend of 'il re galantuomo' (the honest King) was spread by means of pictures depicting him turning away indignantly from the offers of Radetzky, the white haired enemy of freedom. His lack of education and coarse manners were often commented on: Greville, who met him when he came to England described him as 'frightful in person, but a great strong burly athletic man, brusque in his manners, unrefined in his conversation, very loose in his conduct, and very eccentric in his habits, the most debauched, dissolute fellow in the world.' (Mack Smith, 22, ch. 2) Yet these same peculiarities made him popular with the ordinary Italian people. Although lacking in political finesse he had the good sense to listen to Cavour's advice and as a reward became ruler of Italy. He had played a small but important part in the success of 1859–60 particularly with the loyalty he inspired among men like Garibaldi who distrusted politicans of Cavour's variety.

But how far does this legend of the hearty, earthy, honest King fit the facts? One problem is that much of the evidence is still not available. When Italy became a republic in 1946 the Royal Family's papers were removed to Cascais in Portugal. One historian is supposed to have been put in prison for revealing the contents of a Victor Emmanuel letter, another who was allowed to compile a catalogue of the Royal Family's papers, was never allowed to see the originals. Even Giolitti, Italy's great liberal Prime Minister declared in 1912: 'It would not be right to have beautiful legends discredited by historical criticism'. However, the letters which *have* been published seem to show a much more cunning and devious man than the Victor Emmanuel of the legend. While in 1855 his government was working to bring the Roman Catholic Church in Sardinia under control (p.27) Victor Emmanuel wrote this letter to the Pope, Pius IX: 'Your Holiness should know that it was I who did not allow the Senate to pass the marriage law, and that it is I who will now do all in my power not to allow the law regarding religious orders to go through. Perhaps in a short time this Cavour ministry will fall: I shall then nominate a right wing ministry and make it a condition that it carries out for me a total adjustment with Rome. Have the charity to help me... Please burn this piece of paper.' (Mack Smith, 8, p.186) It could be that Baron Butenval, the French Ambassador in Turin, had correctly assessed Victor Emmanuel when he made the following report to the French foreign minister in 1852. 'King Victor Emmanuel is in no sense a liberal. He tells everyone that "My father bestowed institutions on the country which are quite unfitted to its needs and the temper of its inhabitants." To some people he will add, "But my father and myself have both given our word and I will not break it." To others, however, he will say confidentially, "I am only waiting for the right moment to change everything." He does not, I repeat, like the existing constitution nor does he like parliamentary liberties or a free press.' (Mack Smith, 8, pp.170–1) The Austrian documents which have been released seem to show that the Austrian Government were only too anxious to sign a reasonable agreement with Victor Emmanuel in case he was driven to search for a closer understanding with France; there is no evidence to support the story of his brave refusal to give up the constitution under Austrian pressure.

Was the relationship between Victor Emmanuel and Cavour really a harmonious one? In July 1859 the British envoy George Cadogan reported a conversation he had with the King shortly after Cavour's resignation which followed on Villafranca (p.33). 'Cavour is a muddle head who is always pushing me into some wasp's nest or other. Cavour is mad. I have often told him he was off his head.' (Mack Smith, 8, p.288) After Cavour's early death the King talked freely to Hudson (see p.80) about his former Prime Minister. On 30 June 1861 Hudson reported the conversation to Russell. 'The King could not shut his eyes to the fact that Cavour's great statesmanship was at times most hazardous to the state: "in his passion he has sometimes kicked over every chair in this room. He has called me traitor and worse."' (Mack Smith, 8, p.353) For his part Cavour was equally clear about his feelings. In a letter to Farini on 9 November 1860 he complained: 'The King does not like me and is often jealous; he endures me as a minister but is glad when I am not near him... As a representative of the Monarchical principle I am ready to sacrifice my life and property for the King... but as a man I only want one favour from him, to keep as far away as possible.' (Mack Smith, 8, p.329)

Study 17

1. Having studied the arguments and evidence in section three are you still happy with the view that success came in 1859–60 because Cavour had turned Sardinia into an efficient democratic state? Hopefully you will have noticed that in Study 16, questions 1 and 2, the arguments you were asked to choose from consisted in each case of two extremes (a) and (c) in 1, and (a) and (b) in 2. The third argument was a compromise. Try your hand at writing a compromise argument for section three which lies between the two following extremes.
(a) Success came in 1859–60 because Cavour had transformed Charles Albert's kingdom into an efficient modern state with a strong army, economy and a liberal form of government.
(b) The Sardinian state of 1859–60 was little more modern or efficient than the kingdom which Charles Albert left behind when he abdicated in 1849.
(c) ?
2. Report briefly on what you now think about the part played by Victor Emmanuel in the unification. Did he work harmoniously and sensibly with Cavour or did he do more to hinder the unification than to help it?
3. Now read on into section five. You will find that the evidence in this section seems to give two entirely different views of the part played by Cavour in the unification. The first one shows him cleverly using and encouraging the republicans and popular movements to help with his plans. The second shows him trying to stop the popular movements but being dragged along in their wake rather like an owner whose huge dog takes him for a walk. He ends up unifying much more of Italy than he intended. After reading the evidence in section five, which view do you find most convincing?

5. *Success came in 1859–60 because Cavour was able to unite all those who wanted Italian unity and was not afraid to make use of popular movements to secure his aim.*

The most important single reason for the failure in 1848–9 was the total lack of unity amongst the revolutionaries. This occurred at all levels: republicans could not combine with monarchists; states could not unite with each other even against a common enemy; towns and regions even within a single state wasted valuable time arguing with each other; peasants did not trust townsmen. As early as October 1848 a journalist making a speech in Leghorn asked: 'What was lacking in all those forces which rose up to fight for our independence?... we fought as Piedmontese, as Tuscans, as Neapolitans, as Romans, and not as Italians.' When in January 1849 Manin was trying to raise money to keep the Venetian war effort going, he asked Tuscany to buy 20 million cigars from Venice. The Tuscan Minister of Finance refused because of the harm it might do to the Florentine tobacco factories. Charles Albert was not sufficiently tolerant or flexible to inject any sense of unity into this confused picture. In a letter to Pius IX in April 1848 he said: 'Our greatest enemies are not the Imperial Soldiers but the anti-religious republican party.' His critics have argued that if he had spent as much time and energy in pursuing the war against Austria as he did in spreading anti-republican and pro-monarchist propaganda, the Austrians could have been annihilated. In an article in 1853 Manin wrote: 'I believed and still believe that the propaganda for the annexation of the Lombardo-Venetian provinces to Piedmont was the principal cause of the failure of the war of independence' (Ginsborg, 15, p.337).Piedmontese agents were certainly hard at work everywhere. Dr. Malutta from the Treviso area in Venetia wrote: 'There is a party here which is in favour of Charles Albert and it is headed by Guglielmo Onigo. He has brought with him from Tuscany two Piedmontese... one of them spends every day in the cafés... he has been giving away money and on 14 April organized a demonstration' (Ginsborg, 15, p.199). The republicans resented this monarchist intervention. After Charles Albert's defeat, Cattaneo (p.12) declared: 'Good news! The Piedmontese have been beaten. Now we shall be our own masters. We will fight a people's war; we will chase the Austrians out of Italy and set up a federal Republic.'

Nor were the leaders able to arouse much popular enthusiasm for the movement. Their reluctance to employ Garibaldi illustrates this point well. Charles Albert wrote to his war office: 'I hasten to warn you that I have today received in audience the famous General Garibaldi... if there were a naval war he might be employed as a leader of privateers but to employ him otherwise would be to dishonour the army... to encourage him and his brave fellows they might be given a subsidy on condition they go away.' The republican Manin was no more enthusiastic than Charles Albert. In November 1848 he wrote to his colleague Tomasseo: 'if... Garibaldi came we would fear for the city's tranquillity, the conservation of which is not the least of our worries.' (Ginsborg, 15, p.272) Neither Garibaldi nor the Piedmontese army could find much popular support in the rural areas. The Sardinian general della Rocca's *Memoirs* show that the Lombard peasants were somewhat less than enthusiastic: 'resenting our camping in their fields the peasants prepared to open the sluices of their canals to flood the country.' Garibaldi complained in his *Memoirs*: 'I could not find a single guide in Italy while the Austrians had as many as they wanted.' D'Azeglio's letters (p.50) sum up what many Italians felt about 1848–9; 'Italy as a nation had done nothing. Twenty-five million inhabitants have not given 50,000 volunteers.' 'All classes from Princes down to the humblest of the population have failed to produce anyone equal to the chance that was given.'

Thanks to the more tolerant and far sighted policies of Cavour, 1859–60 was a different story. Under his guidance Piedmont had welcomed exiles from other Italian states. With men like these working at Turin University, as editors of important newspapers and even as deputies in the Piedmontese Parliament, state rivalry began to diminish. Moreover, although he himself was a devout monarchist, he was tolerant enough to see that men of republican ideals could still be useful in the cause of unification. This time for example, Garibaldi was not ignored but given his own command (p.31). Cavour also appreciated that popular enthusiasm could be used to promote the movement for unity and was not something to be afraid of. With this end in view he gave his support to the National Society (p.28) and encouraged it to raise volunteers. Between 15 January and 25 March 1859 the Society helped to recruit 20,000 volunteers to take part in the war against Austria. When his efforts to unify Italy seemed to have been killed stone dead at Villafranca he was prepared to go still further. The National Society was encouraged to promote rebellions in the central Italian provinces with the result that the unity movement continued (p.34). Finally when the Sicilian peasants rebelled he was not afraid to give his secret encouragement to Garibaldi and his thousand (p.35). The success of 1859–60 owed a great deal to the greater unity which Cavour's more tolerant policy gave to the conduct of operations.

Once again, however, the question of whether this version fits the evidence must be raised. Much of Cavour's correspondence seems to indicate a violent hatred of republicans rather than any belief that they should be tolerated and used to promote the unification of Italy. It seems more likely that his policy was to sacrifice them in order to secure Napoleon III's support or at least to use them to scare Sardinians into yielding moderate reforms. In July 1857 Cavour wrote to the Piedmontese envoy in Paris: 'You should engage the French government to send us without delay an agent who they think can catch Mazzini... make no mistake we ardently desire to free Piedmont and Italy and Europe from this infamous conspirator... if we catch Mazzini I hope he will be condemned to death and hanged...' On 20 January 1858 Cavour was writing to his prefect at Genoa: 'If we are not to lose French friendship we must do something about the Mazzinians. Best of all would be to silence Mazzini's newspaper and for this I am ready to use all available means; should there be refugees from other Italian states among its contributors they must be expelled from the country forthwith. We must wage war to the death against that assassin's gazette.' (Mack Smith, 8, p.231). In 1859 when the defeat of Austria had led to rebellions in the central provinces Massari recorded the following incident in his diary: 'The leader of the Bologna deputation was shocked yesterday because having told Cavour that the Romagna was falling into the hands of Mazzini, Cavour rejoined: "So much the better, we shall intervene and shoot him."' Massari's diary for 25 August 1858 also throws some doubt on Cavour's motives for backing the National Society, recording him as saying: 'I don't know the people behind the National Society but as I see things it is against the Mazzinians and hence that much advantageous. Moreover I am convinced that all this talk about 'unification' or 'union' will go up in smoke with the first cannon shot. All you need tell people is that Count Cavour prefers the National Society to Mazzini's.' (Mack Smith, 8, p.249) Garibaldi always maintained that his command in 1859 was merely a device to get him out of the way: 'In 1859 I was kept as a flag to attract recruits... to summon volunteers in large numbers, but to command only a small portion of them and those least fit to bear arms.' Bertani (p.77) wrote that 'the Government is frightened to death of Garibaldi... they are afraid that his volunteer corps will gain too much glory and diminish the importance of the Piedmont army.'

The available evidence also seems to indicate that far from promoting the popular disturbances which ended by bringing the central states into the new Italy, Cavour had opposed them. On 20 March 1859 Cavour wrote to the Piedmontese representative in Florence: 'I exhort you to use all your influence to prevent street demonstrations; in the great enterprise for which Italy is preparing it is desirable that we should shun the errors of 1848–9 among which and not least should be numbered the disorderly shouting of multitudes.' (Beales, 7, p.165) At the most Cavour merely hoped to persuade Duke Leopold, the ruler of Tuscany, to break with Austria and send Tuscan troops to help the Piedmontese army. When Giuseppe Dolfi, a baker, a friend of Mazzini and not a member of the National Society, organized a disciplined mob of tough working class men to demonstrate, and scared Leopold off his throne, Cavour was as amazed as anyone. Luckily for him Baron Ricasoli, having failed to persuade Leopold to stay, took control of the situation. Whether Cavour gave any assistance or even encouragement to Garibaldi's Sicilian expedition is a very controversial question which you must study in more detail in chapter five. In a letter to Ricasoli on 16 May 1860 he wrote: 'To support him openly is not possible but neither is restraint of the individual efforts in his favour!' (Woolf, 24, p.462)

Study 18

By now you will probably be feeling totally confused! And so you should be. History is not just a matter of mastering a series of events but of thinking carefully and making decisions. *Before* making a final effort to sort out your views and write an essay you should:

1. Re-read the narrative chapters 1 and 2.
2. Read and carry out the exercises in chapter 5 which takes a much more detailed look at the problem of whether Cavour supported Garibaldi in Sicily.
3. Follow up any of the references in the text which may have caught your attention.
4. Take a look at any of the books in your school library listed on pp.101–2. The best way to use them is to find the chapters on unification and see whether they agree with your views or provide new evidence. Particularly useful are numbers 1, 3, 5, 6, 7, 22, 23 and 24.
5. Discuss your ideas with others to try to discover their weaknesses.

Writing an essay on why Italy was successfully united in 1859–60 but not in 1848–9.

This chapter has been written with a particular type of essay in mind. It is nicknamed an 'Aunt Sally' essay after the old fairground figures which used to be set up for people to knock down. Try to write your essay in this style, following the instructions set out below –

1. Pick out the theories for the success in 1859–60 which you think are the most *useless* and explain them (my number one on this list would be the idea that success came in 1859–60 because Cavour had a diplomatic master plan!) These are your 'Aunt Sallies'.
2. Demolish these theories utterly taking care to use your evidence. You have knocked down your 'Aunt Sallies'.
3. Put forward what you regard as the really useful theories for explaining the success of 1859–60. These might be some of the original theories used in this chapter which seem to you to have stood up to all criticism (I can't think of any!) More likely they might be considerably modified versions of the original theories. For example you might argue that Cavour's contribution to success was not that he supported the popular movements for unification, but that he knew how to take them over for Piedmont, once they looked like succeeding. Take care as always to support your views with plenty of detailed evidence and to write key sentences at the start of each paragraph as explained in study 15 page 58.
4. Try to sum up your arguments in a conclusion paragraph at the end of your essay. Would Italian unification have taken place if there had been no Cavour? My guess for what it is worth, is that it would, but might have been a very different *sort* of unification. Perhaps great men or women cannot make history but they can slightly influence which direction the flow of events takes and the speed at which it travels.

CHAPTER 5

Cavour, Victor Emmanuel and Garibaldi

1860 – 61:

Co-operation or Conflict?

For many years historians argued that the defeat of the Bourbon Kingdom of the Two Sicilies in 1860 (see chapter 2 for the narration of events) was brought about by the harmonious co-operation of the three heroes of Italian unification: King Victor Emmanuel of Sardinia, Count Cavour, his clever Prime Minister, and Garibaldi his dynamic guerrilla leader. Their argument ran something like this:

1. From April 1860, when rebellion broke out in Sicily, until 11 May when Garibaldi and his 'Thousand' landed at Marsala, Cavour and King Victor Emmanuel played a clever double game. In public they pretended to be against Garibaldi's adventure and appeared to be doing all they could to stop him. This policy was essential because, if the French or Austrians thought that a respectable country like Sardinia was using a disreputable guerrilla leader to overthrow a legal monarchy, they might well interfere and put an end to all hope of a united Italy. In private, however, they did all they could to encourage and help Garibaldi's expedition.

2. After 15 May, when Garibaldi won his victory at Calatafimi, Cavour was able for the first time to give him open public support. However by August 1860 Garibaldi was ready to cross the straits and invade Naples itself. Supposing this proved too much for the French to accept? They had an army in Rome to protect the Pope and Garibaldi had made no secret of his desire to liberate Rome next. So Cavour and the King returned to their original policy: in public they ordered Garibaldi to remain in Sicily, in private they encouraged him to invade Naples.

But is this version of the events correct? Recent research has thrown considerable doubt on the above interpretation. Denis Mack Smith, in his book *Victor Emmanuel, Cavour and the Risorgimento* (22) claims that 'Cavour played a less important and less helpful part than generally thought in the movement which conquered half Italy from the Bourbons. The facts only fit together if we assume, firstly that there was a kind of hiatus [breakdown] in his policy, and secondly, that initially he did more to hinder than to help the conquest of Sicily.' According to Mack Smith not only did Cavour *really* try to stop Garibaldi's expedition to Sicily but also he later did everything he could to stop Garibaldi crossing the Straits and taking over Naples. While Cavour was working against Garibaldi, King Victor Emmanuel was often working against Cavour and using his own private diplomatic service. Why were these three men opposing, instead of co-operating with, each other? Because Cavour and Victor Emmanuel were not in favour of Italian unity but of Sardinian control of Italy whereas Garibaldi at this time would have accepted any form of unity. Furthermore Cavour thought that Garibaldi was not to be trusted because Garibaldi was a former republican and was angry that Cavour had handed over his birthplace, Nice, to Napoleon III. King Victor Emmanuel was inclined to agree with Cavour but had another important aim. Not for him the position of a tame constitutional King doing what he was told by a politician like Cavour. There were times when he wanted freedom of action. He thought that an alliance with Garibaldi against Cavour might give him it. This is rather a long way from the older theory. The table below shows the differences between the two:

	'Old' theory	'New' theory
Aims Cavour	A united Italy	Sardinian control of Italy under a constitutional monarch
Victor Emmanuel	A united Italy	Sardinian control of Italy under a powerful monarch

Methods Cavour	Condemns Garibaldi in public but helps him in private	Does everything he can to stop Garibaldi
Victor Emmanuel	ditto	Keeps friendly with Garibaldi and uses him against Cavour

So which version is correct? The purpose of the rest of this chapter is to provide some of the evidence and leave you to make the decisions. But first you will need some guidance on how to use historical documents. The following four guidelines should be helpful:

1. The more primary the evidence, generally speaking, the more valuable it is. Primary means close to the time in which the events being investigated took place. Official records like cabinet minutes, letters, diaries and telegrams are usually more useful primary sources than memoirs which are generally written down some time after the events took place. Biographies and history books are

secondary evidence though they may contain or use primary evidence. Of course this doesn't mean that secondary works are of no value. A good history book has already made use of primary evidence and made decisions about it. It might be helpful to think of the writer of a secondary history as rather like an expert witness at a trial not present at the crime but listened to with care by the jury because he has made a special study of his subject.

2. The most useful evidence is first-hand. In an English law court second-hand evidence or 'hearsay' is not allowed. Witnesses must have immediate contact with the events they are describing – what someone else told them is not evidence. Historians often have to use second-hand evidence for want of anything better but it must be treated with great caution.

3. Evidence must be as free from bias as possible. Bias means prejudice and it is almost impossible to find evidence which is totally free from it. Historical witnesses may be swayed by chances of personal gain, political persuasion, religious conviction, or racial prejudice, amongst many other things. The historian's unenviable task is to act as judge and jury and decide which pieces are the most trustworthy.

4. Evidence must fit together with rival evidence. If it conflicts then you have to decide which piece to reject.

Study 19

With these rules in mind read through the evidence which follows and record your decisions on a chart like the one opposite. Besides the documents themselves you have been given brief biographical notes on some of the 'witnesses' which should help you with the problem of assessing bias. Note that the observations on la Farina's speech are just examples – read it and make your own assessment! Before starting remember to check the basic facts on Garibaldi's expedition in chapter 3, p.35 if you are uncertain of them.

The Evidence, part 1: 4 April–5 May 1860

(This was the period when Garibaldi was preparing his expedition to Genoa). Did Cavour and Victor Emmanuel help or hinder Garibaldi's plans for the invasion of Sicily?

1. Statement made by Dr. Agostino Bertani in a debate in the Italian Chamber, 19 June 1863:

> 'Next I ask the Hon. General Sirtori to tell the Chamber what answer he got from Count Cavour when he went to see him two evenings before 5 May [he meant on 23 April, like many of us he got his dates confused!]... Count Cavour... said "I don't know what to say or to do", and, in the sly way he had, ended, rubbing his hands, "I think they [Garibaldi and the thousand] will be taken."'

(References: Trevelyan, 17, p.336, Mack Smith, 22, pp.182–3, Parris, 5, pp.206–7.)

Docu-ment no.	Marks out of 10 for qualities explained above				Reasons for marks	Total
	Pri-mary	First hand	Bias	Fit		(out of 40)
9	3	8	3	2	La Farina was directly involved with the organisation of the 'Thousand' so a high mark for first hand experience. BUT this speech was made three years after the events described so does not score high on the primary scale. He was a very strong supporter of Cavour and probably was not pleased at being arrested by Garibaldi so his speech could have been strongly biassed. His speech doesn't fit at all well with Cavour's letter to Nigra (7) so a low mark here.	16

Dr. Agostino Bertani (1812–86):

Career – Milanese doctor, who organised ambulance services for Garibaldi during the siege of Rome in 1849 and in the Alpine campaign in 1859. He was in charge of recruiting volunteers for Garibaldi's Thousand 1860, for which most of the planning meetings were held at his house, and remained behind in Genoa to organise further recruitment. After Garibaldi's victories in Naples, he organised his administration there.

Views – extreme republican who opposed Cavour's use of French help and his abandonment of Nice; and who urged Garibaldi not to hand over Sicily to Victor Emmanuel too quickly so that he would be free to press on to Naples and then head for Rome.

Later career – eventually came to accept the monarchy but refused to join any of the governing groups; was unofficial leader of about 20 left wing deputies who campaigned for agrarian reform.

2. Statement made by Giuseppe Sirtori in reply to Bertani, 19 June 1863:
    'As to the expedition to the [Papal] Marches, he [Cavour] said absolutely: "No, the government will oppose it by every means in its power." As to the expedition to Sicily, Cavour said exactly these words: "Well and good. Begin at the south, to come up again by the north. When it is a question of

undertakings of that kind, however bold they may be, Count Cavour will be second to none." Those were his precise words. He said this naturally referring to all those means by which the government without compromising itself could help the expedition. He promised to help it, provided the responsibility of the government was completely concealed.'
(References: Trevelyan, 17, p.337, Mack Smith, 22, pp.182–3, Parris , 5, pp.206–7)

Giuseppe Sirtori (1813–74):
Career – once a priest, later Garibaldi's Chief of Staff, fought with the revolutionaries in 1848, opposed expedition to Sicily: 'I don't believe it will succeed, but if Garibaldi goes to Sicily, with many or with few, I go too.' Wounded three times in Sicily and saved Garibaldi's life at Calatafimi.
Views – a moderate republican who helped Garibaldi to stop extremists from attacking Sicilian Catholic priests and opposed scheme to carry on to attack Rome. Came to accept the monarchy.

3. Diary of Francesco Crispi. 23 April 1860 and letter 25 April:
Sirtori had 'great doubts' of the success of the expedition, Cavour's friends 'are constantly coming and going and trying to persuade Garibaldi to give up the attempt.' Letter contains the remark 'Piedmont can give us no help... we are on the point of despair.'
(References: Mack Smith, 22, pp.183–4, Parris, 5, pp.206–7)

Francesco Crispi (1819–1901):
Career – Sicilian lawyer, became an exile in 1849 but returned in 1859 to help plan Sicilian rebellion against Bourbons. Afterwards went to Genoa where he worked hard to persuade Garibaldi to help the rebels; and was political secretary for Garibaldi in Sicily until forced to resign by La Farina (see doc.9).
Views – extreme republican follower of Mazzini; expelled from Piedmont as a dangerous Mazzinian agent early 1860; encouraged Garibaldi to refuse to hand over Sicily to Victor Emmanuel too soon and to press on to Naples and Rome. By 1864 ('The Monarchy unites us while republicans would divide us') had come to accept the monarchy.
Later career became Prime Minister of Italy between 1887 and 1896.

4. Letter from King Victor Emmanuel of Piedmont to Francis II, King of Naples. 15 April 1860:
'We have reached a time in which Italy can be divided into two powerful states of the north and of the south, which if they adopt the same national policy, may uphold the great idea of our times – National Independence. But in order to realise this conception it is, I think, necessary that your majesty abandon the course you have held hitherto... the principle of

dualism if it is well established and honestly pursued, can still be accepted by Italians. But if you allow some months to pass without attending to my friendly suggestion, your Majesty will perhaps experience the bitterness of the terrible words too late.'

(This letter was written at the suggestion of Cavour)

(References: Trevelyan, 17, pp.185–6, Hibbert, 13, p.194, Ridley, 14, p.436)

5. Cabinet Minutes signed for 24 April 1860 by Cavour:
'It was unanimously decided to refuse Garibaldi the guns★ he requires for the Sicilian insurrection, lest the European capitals should thereby be alarmed, in view of the imprudent publicity given by him and his friends in Genoa to the preparations he has in hand for Sicily.'

(References: Mack Smith, 22, p.184, Hibbert, 13, p.193, Martin, 23, p.539, Trevelyan, 17, pp.182–4, 197–8, Parris, 5, pp.204–5.)

★ In January 1860 Garibaldi had been given permission to collect contributions for 'A Million Rifles Fund' but only on condition that they were put under government control. By April, 12,000 modern Enfield **rifles** were stored in Milan but when Garibaldi applied for permission to collect 200 Enfields on 16 April the Governor of Milan, D'Azeglio, (p.50) refused to allow this. Neither Farini, the Minister of the Interior, nor Cavour himself, were prepared to countermand D'Azeglio's order. In the event Garibaldi had to be content with 1,500 **muskets** which, on 14 April, Cavour had authorised La Farina, the secretary of the National Society, to issue to a Sicilian, La Masa, who was also planning an attack on Bourbon Sicily. La Masa joined forces with Garibaldi so that the Thousand eventually received these muskets at Genoa, registered as cases of 'books'. When unpacked they were found to be smooth-bore muskets, rusty with age, which had been converted from flint-locks into percussion caps, and finally sold as obsolete by the military authorities.

6. Reports from Sir James Hudson, British Ambassador to the British Foreign Secretary Lord John Russell (a) 4 May (b) 28 June 1860:

(a) 'If Garibaldi means to go he is sufficiently strong and sufficiently supported by public opinion to be able to go whether the Government likes it or not.'

(b) 'At the outset nobody believed in the possibility of Garibaldi's success; and Cavour thought the country well rid of him and of the unquiet spirits who went with him. The argument was, if he fails we are rid of a troublesome fellow, and if he succeeds Italy will derive some profit from his success.'

(References: Mack Smith, 21, pp.181–2, 22, p.30, Ridley, 14, p.441.)

Sir James Hudson (1810–85):
British Ambassador at Turin and close friend of Cavour's. In Spring 1859, for example, he showed Cavour confidential documents belonging to the British Government. In January 1860 he played a direct part in persuading King Victor Emmanuel to take Cavour back as chief minister. After Garibaldi's capture of Palermo Hudson became convinced that a union of northern and southern Italy was desirable; so far did he go in this direction that Queen Victoria wanted him dismissed on grounds of disloyalty. Russell told him to 'be very careful to keep the interests of Great Britain always in sight and not be led too far by your Italian sympathies.' (25 July)

7. Letter from Cavour to Costantino Nigra, 12 May 1860:
   'I regret Garibaldi's expedition as much as anyone... I could not stop his going for force would have been necessary. And the Ministry is in no position to face the immense unpopularity which would have been drawn upon it had Garibaldi been prevented. With the elections taking place, and depending as I do on the votes of every shade of moderate liberal to counter the opposition and get the French Treaty★ through, I could not take strong measures to stop him. At the same time I omitted nothing to persuade Garibaldi to stop his mad scheme.
   I sent La Farina [see doc.9] to see him, who assured me that Garibaldi had given up all thought of his expedition. Since the news from Palermo showed that the state of siege there had been lifted and the revolt was on the point of being extinguished, I thought Garibaldi would be obliged to stay at home whether he liked it or not.'
(References: Mack Smith, 22, pp.183–4, Hibbert, 5, pp.206–7.)

Costantino Nigra (1828–1907):
Cavour's favourite assistant and his private secretary, who acted as a sort of 'troubleshooter'. Cavour's personal representative in Paris 1858–59. Sent to Tuscany in 1859 to help arrange for its annexation, returned to Paris 1859–60, then sent to Naples December 1860 to report on problems there.
★ The French Treaty was the agreement whereby France was to annex Nice and Savoy, which required assent of the parliament.

8. Eye witness account of meeting between Cavour and King Victor Emmanuel thought to be at Bologna on 1 May 1860. Printed in a French Newspaper article by D'Haussonville 1862:
   'Cavour tried to stop everything and halt Garibaldi. He became very excited as he spoke about his plans, and when someone objected that no one could be found who would dare to stop the expedition, Cavour exclaimed, 'If no one else will do it, I will go myself and seize Garibaldi by the scruff of his neck.'

(References: Mack Smith, 22, p.138, Trevelyan, 17, p.197, Parris, 5, pp.211–12, Ridley, 14, pp.437–8.)

9. Statement made in Italian Parliament by Giuseppe La Farina 18 June 1863: 'Cavour's friends helped the expedition with every possible means'.
(References: Mack Smith, 22, p.176 and 21, p.23, Parris, 5, p.219.)

Guiseppe La Farina (1815–63):
Career – an exile from his country of birth, Sicily, once Mazzini's agent in Paris but became a loyal supporter of Cavour and secretary of the National Society (p.28). Worked for Cavour in order to procure annexation of Tuscany in 1859, was involved in preparations for the Thousand's expedition to Sicily (see notes to doc.5 and reference in doc.7) and was sent by Cavour to arrange for rapid annexation of Sicily on 6 June. A month later Garibaldi had him arrested and expelled from the island.

The Evidence, part 2: 5–11 May 1860

This was when Garibaldi was at sea with the Thousand. Did Cavour send the Piedmontese navy to help Garibaldi or to stop him?

10. Telegraphs from Cavour (a) to Governor of Cagliari in Sardinia on 7 May 1860, (b) to Governor of Cagliari in Sardinia on 8 May 1860:
    (a) 'Garibaldi has embarked with 400 volunteers on two Rubatino steamers for Sicily. If he enters a port of Sardinia, arrest the expedition. I authorise you to employ, if required, the Squadron commanded by Count Persano.' (See note on no.11)
    (b) 'Do not arrest the expedition out at sea. Only if it enters a port.'
(References: Trevelyan, 17, p.225, Mack Smith, 8, pp.186–7, Hibbert, 13, pp.203–4, Parris, 5, pp.218–9, Ridley, 14, pp.441–2)

11. Memoirs of Count Carlo Pellion di Persano published in 1869:
    In his memoirs Persano recorded that he received 8 May orders on 9 May and immediately wrote to Turin to ask if these were seriously meant. He received the reply that 'the Minstry had decided.' In his memoirs he said he interpreted this to mean that Cavour did not agree with the Ministry. So he telegraphed back 'I understand' and did nothing.
(References: Trevelyan, 17, p.226, Mack Smith, 22, pp.186–7, Hibbert, 13, p.204.)

Count Carlo Pellion di Persano (1806–83):
Career – distinguished himself by (a) running aground the navy's largest ship outside Genoa, (b) wrecking a ship off the coast of Sardinia when carrying the Sardinian royal family. Despite this seems to have been a favourite of the King's and became Minister of Navy in 1862. Just before the government in

which he was serving was forced to resign, he appointed himself full Admiral of the Fleet – the most senior post in the navy. When war broke out with Austria in 1866, he was ordered to attack an Austrian fleet much inferior in numbers. He did so reluctantly and was totally defeated at the battle of Lissa (p.43). Condemned after trial before the Italian Senate, he was dismissed from the service with loss of pension and decorations.

12. Telegrams in cipher from Farini, Minister of the Interior to Ricasoli in Tuscany on (a) 11 May (b) 12 May:
(a) 'Piedmontese Warships have been ordered to stop Garibaldi if he is in Tuscan or Roman waters.'
(b) Garibaldi to be arrested anywhere outside Sicilian waters, all expeditions to re-inforce him to be prevented at all costs, the words 'at all costs' underlined.
(References: Mack Smith, 22, p.183, Hibbert, 13, p.204, Parris, 5, pp.218–19.)

13. Letter from Garibaldi to Barrili, 24 August 1869:
Garibaldi writes that when Persano met him in Sicily in late May 1860 'he assured me that he had had orders to follow and arrest me, and if he did not carry them out, it was because luckily our expedition, instead of coasting Sardinia as we had at first planned was switched via Tuscany by unforeseen circumstances, and so escaped the claws of the Piedmontese fleet.'
(References: Mack Smith, 8, p.188.)

The Evidence, part 3: 7 June–3 September 1860

The period during which Garibaldi prepared and carried out the invasion of Naples. Did Cavour and Victor Emmanuel do all they could to help Garibaldi cross the Straits to Naples?

14. Letter from Cavour to Nigra, envoy in Paris, 12 July 1860:
'Garibaldi has become intoxicated by success and by the praise showered on him from all over Europe. He is planning the wildest, not to say absurdest schemes. As he remains devoted to King Victor Emmanuel, he will not help Mazzini or republicanism. But he feels it his vocation to liberate all Italy, stage by stage, before turning her over to the king. He is thus putting off the day when Sicily will demand annexation to Piedmont, for he wants to keep the dictatorial powers which will enable him to raise an army to conquer first Naples, then Rome, and in the end Venice... The Government here has no influence on him. On the contrary he mistrusts everybody whom he imagines to be in touch with us... Garibaldi has a generous character and the instincts of a poet, but at the same time he has a wild nature, and certain impressions have stamped him in a way that cannot be

effaced. He was deeply hurt by the cession of Nice which he views almost as a personal and unforgiveable insult... The King still retains some influence over him, but if he tried using it on this occasion he would lose it to no purpose. That would be a grave misfortune, as circumstances could arise in which the King's influence could be our only hope... We must therefore prevent Garibaldi from conquering Naples, and we must try to annex Sicily as soon as possible. Were Garibaldi to become master of all the Neapolitan provinces we would not be able to stop him from compromising us with France and Europe... Hence it follows that it is of the very greatest interest to us and the Emperor that, if the Bourbons have to fall, it should not be by Garibaldi's agency...'
(References: Mack Smith ed., 8, pp.317–8, Martin, 23, pp.597–9, Lloyd, 3, p.55.)

15. Letter from Cavour to Persano, 14 July 1860:
'We must at all costs on the one hand prevent Garibaldi from crossing the straits, and on the other excite a revolution in Naples. If this were to succeed, the government of Victor Emmanuel would at once be proclaimed there. In that case you would immediately sail with your whole squadron for Naples.'
(References: Trevelyan, 17, p.100, Mack Smith, 21, p.123.)

16. Diary of Count Litta revealed for first time 1910:
On 22 July Count Litta was given two notes by King Victor Emmanuel to deliver to Garibaldi. The first (published by Cavour) instructed Garibaldi NOT to cross the straits from Sicily to Naples. The second, which was found among Count Litta's papers *with its seal unbroken*, read as follows:
'To the Dictator General Garibaldi,
Now, having written as King, Victor Emmanuel suggests to you to reply in this sense, which I know is what you feel. Reply that you are full of devotion and reverence for your King, that you would like to obey his counsels, but that your duty to Italy forbids you to promise not to help the Neapolitans, when they appeal to you to free them from a government which true men and good Italians cannot trust: that you cannot therefore obey the wishes of the King but must reserve full freedom of action'.

Garibaldi's reply (published immediately by Cavour) read as follows:
'Sire, Your Majesty knows the high esteem and love I bear you. But the present state of things in Italy does not allow me to obey you as I should have wished. Called by the people I refrained as long as I could. But if now in spite of all the calls that reach me, I were longer to delay, I should fail in my duty and imperil the sacred cause of Italy. Allow me then Sire, this time to disobey you. As soon as I shall have fulfilled what I have undertaken, by

freeing the peoples from a hated yoke, I will lay down my sword at your feet and obey you for the rest of my life.'

(References: Trevelyan, 17, pp.101–2, Hibbert, 13, pp.255–6, Martin, 23, pp.569–70, Mack Smith, 21, pp.125–8, Holt, 1, p.244, Lloyd, 3, p.56, Parris, 5, pp.239–40, Ridley, 14, pp.473–4.)

17. Message in handwriting of Count Trecchi. Victor Emmanuel's aide-de-camp. Dictated to him by the King on 5 August 1860, published 1 June 1910:
'Words dictated by Victor Emmanuel to be conveyed to Garibaldi. Garibaldi in Naples. Will regulate himself according to opportunity, either occupying Umbria and the Marches with his troops, or allowing bands of volunteers to go. As soon as Garibaldi is in Naples he will proclaim its union to the rest of Italy as in Sicily. Prevent disorders which will harm our cause. Keep the Neapolitan army in being, for Austria will soon declare war. Let the King of Naples escape, and if he is taken by the people, save him and let him escape.'

(References: Trevelyan, 17, p.116 and note, Mack Smith ed., 8, pp.315–6, Martin, 23, p.570, Parris, 5, p.243.)

Study 20

1. You have picked out the most reliable sources. Now it is time to come off the fence and decide whether they support the old view, the new view or perhaps a different view altogether. Read through the documents again and record your observations in a chart like the one below; make up your own mind about doc.9.

Document	Which view does it fit?	Your reasons
9	The old view that Cavour did all he could to help Garibaldi	Very clearly put — Cavour's friends helped with 'every possible means'

2. Now using your two charts choose the statement you prefer out of each of the following groups and briefly list your reasons:
(i) Between 4 April 1860 when the Sicilians rebelled and 5 May when Garibaldi's Thousand set off to assist them, Cavour —
  (a) Did all he possibly could to help them in secret, while in public claiming that he was opposed to their escapade.
  (b) Did all he possibly could to stop them from going, short of risking the unpopularity of using force.
  (c) Played a clever opportunistic waiting game and skilfully refused to commit himself or his country to either helping or hindering them.
  (d) Could not make up his mind what to do and just hoped for the best.

(ii) Between 5 May when the Thousand set off in their paddle steamers and 11 May when they landed at Marsala in Sicily, Cavour –
- (a) Pretended to be using Persano and the Piedmontese navy to stop them.
- (b) Genuinely intended Persano and the Piedmontese navy to stop them.
- (c) Deliberately kept his policy vague while he waited to see how events would turn out.
- (d) Could not make up his mind what policy to follow.

(iii) Between 7 June, when the Thousand had completed the capture of Palermo in Sicily and 7 September when Garibaldi entered Naples, Cavour had –
- (a) Done all he possibly could to help Garibaldi to cross the straits from Sicily to conquer Naples.
- (b) Done his best to prevent, hamper and control Garibaldi's efforts to cross the straits and conquer Naples.
- (c) Been frequently deceived by King Victor Emmanuel who was following his own private policy of helping Garibaldi.
- (d) Cleverly encouraged the King to work with Garibaldi so that if his own policy failed there was an alternative to fall back on.

(iv) At the moment I think that –
- (a) Cavour, Garibaldi and King Victor Emmanuel worked together to liberate the Kingdom of the Two Sicilies.
- (b) Cavour did all he could to prevent, frustrate and control Garibaldi's efforts.
- (c) Cavour played a clever opportunistic waiting game until he was sure that Garibaldi would succeed and that there could be no foreign intervention.
- (d) There is not enough evidence to make even a provisional conclusion.

3. If there is one thing that the study of history should teach us, it is that decisions must never be inflexible and final. It is always possible that new evidence or a new way of looking at a problem may suggest a change in view. You have reached your first conclusions and should now be ready to put them to the test:
- (a) **By further reading and research** This is essential. This author may not have given you enough evidence. Worse still his own bias or ignorance may have accidentally given you an unfair selection of the available evidence. You can use the book list on pp.101–2 in two ways. If you look back at the documents you will find that each one is followed by its references. After these comes a number which refers to the full name of the book printed in the list. Using these references you can find out whether the authors interpreted the document in the same way as you do and whether they persuade you to change your mind. Alternatively, or in addition, you can find one of the books on pp.101–2 and see whether it contains additional evidence which is new. Of course you won't have time to use all the books even if they are available. A useful idea is to divide the available books between the rest of the class and report back any new evidence to the whole group.
- (b) **By discussion**. This is the final test. Does the teacher in charge agree with you? Can you persuade the rest of the class that your view is correct? Do their criticisms force you to reconsider your decision? After completing the further reading and the discussion modify or alter your decisions if necessary and record your reasons in writing.

4. It is not much use making decisions unless you can use them. Apply them to answering the two problems below:

(i) Study the two pictorial sources (8 and 9 overleaf) carefully. Which gives the more accurate impression of the way in which the Kingdom of the Two Sicilies became a part of united Italy?

(a) 'The Man in Possession'. *Punch*, 6 October 1860 (picture 8)

Advice: Start by working out who the two characters in the cartoon are and what they

8. *'The man in possession' (Mansell Collection)*

9. *Victor Emmanuel II, Cavour and Garibaldi (Hulton Picture Library)*

think of each other. At the time of publication all the world was waiting to see whether and how Garibaldi would hand over his conquests to Victor Emmanuel.

(b)   Victor Emmanuel, King of Sardinia, with Cavour and Garibaldi. Undated engraving. (picture 9)

Advice: Ask yourself what the purpose of this picture might have been and when it might have been made.

(ii) Read the passage below carefully. EITHER explain why you think it gives an accurate picture of the way in which Italy became united, OR rewrite it so that, in your opinion, it gives a more acceptable version of what happened, in not more than 100 words:

'Cavour could not risk an open war between Sardinia and Naples... Garibaldi agreed to be diverted to Sicily; and sailed with his thousand early in May. In August, he crossed to the mainland... Cavour did nothing to interfere with Garibaldi... By launching Garibaldi he had given the revolution a chance to organise itself...'

A.J.P. Taylor: *The Struggle for Mastery in Europe, 1848–1914.* Oxford 1954, p.119.

The decisions you have reached in this chapter and the evidence you have collected should finally be used as part of the essay set in study 18, p.73.

CHAPTER 6

Italian Unification
1860 – 1914
Triumph or Disaster?

One of the most fascinating things about history is the way in which its view of the past is continually being adjusted by events in the present. Take, for example, the problem of whether the unification was worthwhile. Down to the 1930s most historians were agreed that the unification had brought great benefit to Italy. In 1879 Luigi Settembrini had no doubts: 'Hear what posterity will say to us. It will say that this was a generation of giants because it carried out a task which had been impossible for many generations and many centuries.' (Woolf, 10, p.79) The great English historian G. M. Trevelyan, writing before the First World War, held the view that, during unification, firm foundations were laid for a stable Italy. He wrote 'that in the years 1859 and 1860 the Italians acquired their national independence, their civic freedom, and their political union under the guns of France and Austria. Nothing is more remarkable... than the stability of the Italian Kingdom... and the building is as safe as any in Europe. The foundations of human liberty and the foundations of social order exist there on a firm basis.' (Braun, 35, p.691) Three years later World War I broke out, four years later Italy entered the war on the side of Britain and France, eleven years later the fascist dictator Mussolini seized control (see **fascism**). The 'civic freedom' and 'human liberty' which Trevelyan had referred to had been swept away.

At first these events did not lead to any major changes in historical interpretation. Writing in 1932 the Italian historian Benedetto Croce remarked: 'If it were possible in political history to speak of masterpieces as we do in dealing with works of art, the process of Italy's independence, liberty and unity would deserve to be called the masterpiece of the liberal national movements of the nineteenth century.' (Martin, 23, p.722) Yet even as he wrote, the communist Antonio Gramsci, a Sardinian hunch-back with a head so large that it did not seem to belong to him, was in a fascist prison. From his confinement emerged his prison notebooks which contained a major criticism of the achievements of Italian unification. 'The leaders of the Risorgimento said they were aiming at the creation of a modern state in Italy, and they in fact produced a bastard. They aimed at stimulating the formation of an extensive and energetic ruling class and they did not succeed; at integrating the people into the framework of the new state, and they did not succeed. The paltry political life from 1870 to 1900, the fundamental rebelliousness of the Italian popular classes, the narrow existence of a cowardly ruling stratum, they are all consequences of that failure.' (Ginsborg, 15, p.377) Mussolini's fascist regime went down to defeat in the Second World War and Italy abolished her monarchy and became a republic. Gramsci's criticisms began to take root. Historians became much more critical of the unification. In particular a British historian, Denis Mack Smith, began to study the period. 'The Kingdom of Italy', he wrote, 'was one of the most notable achievements of the age... Nevertheless, in some important respects it was to prove highly unstable; and many Italians agreed that this was due to flaws in its original creation.' (Braun, 35, p.692) Of course not all Italians agree with this more critical view of their 'Risorgimento': one reviewer complained that Mack Smith had taken away 'it's Soul.' However the great Italian writer and novelist, Alberto Moravia joined the critics in 1963 when he wrote: 'The **Risorgimento** lacked men, made little impression on the masses, was full of humiliating contradictions, and was far behind the rest of Europe. A petty affair in all... it was a mean little enterprise... the men of the Risorgimento were provincial middle class and their mixture of nationalism and liberalism produced something very weak in alcoholic content.' (Martin, 23, p.723)

So who is right? Was the unification a great triumph or was it a disaster? The rest of this chapter will consist of two parts. In part one some of the main criticisms of the unification are explained. In part two a defence is put forward. At the end of the chapter you will be asked to make your own assessment. Please note that the two parts contain intentional distortions and over-statements. It will be your job to spot these and produce a superior historical assessment!

1. 'The Unification of Italy was a Disaster'

An examination of the reactions of the men who played a leading part in the unification movement provides clear evidence that it was not the great triumph it was claimed to be. D'Azeglio, a conservative, but originally in favour of the Risorgimento (see p.50), wrote to his nephew in 1863: 'I, who am a realist, cannot believe that any human association whatever can be founded on a series of tricks, perfidies and lies. The Government inspires neither esteem nor affection. And never was Italy as divided as she is now.' Garibaldi, the former republican but, like D'Azeglio, loyal to Victor Emmanuel, was equally disenchanted: 'It was a very different Italy which I spent my life dreaming of; not the impoverished and humiliated country which we now see ruled by the dregs of the nation,' he complained in 1880. (Mack Smith, 9, p.174) Verdi, like Garibaldi a former republican, but unlike him converted to the Risorgimento by his admiration for Cavour (see p.53) also soon lost all faith in the Government which had emerged from the unification. It was noticeable that when he composed his hymn of the nations for the London exhibition of 1862 Italy was not represented by the Royal March of Savoy but by Mameli's hymn which had been the signature tune of Mazzini's Roman Republic in 1849 (p.20). Mazzini, who had spent his life campaigning for Italian Unification (p.11) was bitterly disappointed with the result. He wrote to Ferretti in 1871: 'The Italy which we represent today is a living lie... Italians are now a vassal people; a narrow franchise means we are governed by a few rich men who are powerless for good. Our army is not popularly based and is used for internal repression. Rights of the press and free association are fettered and a corrupt political system is bringing a slow but growing financial collapse. Ordinary people say to themselves, "This is just the ghost of Italy."' (Mack Smith, 8, p.363) If four men, all with totally different political beliefs were all equally disillusioned, then it is reasonable to suspect that the Risorgimento had failed badly.

What had gone wrong with the unification was that its leaders had not made it popular. There were actually fewer popular revolts in 1859–60 than there had been in 1848–9. The glorious 'five days' of Milan (p.18) were not repeated in 1859. In the central provinces Napoleon complained that 'these particular regions seem to say, "Let French and Piedmont military power do everything while we sit and watch". I am sure that in Peking they are doing more for this war of independence than here.' (Mack Smith, 8, p.280) Where there were popular disturbances, as in Sicily, they were against local rulers and general poverty rather than in favour of unification. The massive **plebiscites** which apeared to give support to the unification (p.34) were either rigged or misinterpreted. One observer who watched the plebiscite in Naples noted that 'the method of voting left much to be desired. The ballot box was between two baskets one full of yes slips, the other full of no slips. An elector had to choose in full view of the Guards and the crowd. In the Monte Calvario district a man who voted 'no' with some bravado was punished with a stiletto blow – assassin and victim are now at the police station.' (Mack Smith, 8, p.322) The votes in Sicily were against a return to government from Naples not in favour of government from Turin. Indeed most Sicilians thought that they would be given a measure of regional autonomy. It was here that Cavour made his worst mistake. Although he himself had at one time favoured a **federation** for Italy he changed his mind and subjected all areas to rigid centralization. Committees which had been set up by Cavour to consider the problem in Lombardy and the central states, and others established by Garibaldi in Sicily and Naples, had asked for a certain amount of regional autonomy. Their advice was swept aside. Indeed the law of October 1859 which annexed Lombardy directly to Piedmont was passed by emergency powers when the Piedmont parliament was on holiday. In October 1860 Ferrari tried in vain to persuade the parliament not to adopt the same policy in dealing with the other states: 'The movement for liberating Italy was begun by people brought up in the Piedmontese system of government.... the general idea was to say to all the other areas of Italy: "Revolt for your grievances against your rulers is justified; but after the insurrection there must be no discussion: you must become Piedmontese"... a federal system would enable us to reach the very highest goals. In a federation every individual Italian state would continue to exist and have an assembly of its own to perpetuate its own particular traditions. Each of these assemblies would then nominate representatives to the national parliament.' (Mack Smith, 8, p.341) Amidst uproar Ferrari's arguments were rejected and the movement for Italian unification lost its chance of becoming popular and acceptable.

Cavour and the Piedmontese Government had three other chances of putting the unification on firm foundations; they missed all three. The one popular element in the Risorgimento had been the volunteers who had fought so successfully under Garibaldi. It was vital that this element in society should be integrated into the new Kingdom of Italy. It was not. Abba described how some 12,000 red shirted men waited near Naples for King Victor Emmanuel to pay tribute to their services. Incredibly he could not bring himself to do it. Only Garibaldi arrived. In his diary for 9 November Abba described the bitterness which this humiliating treatment caused. 'We longed to throw ourselves at General Garibaldi's feet crying out, "General, why do you not lead us on to death, that is the road to Rome..." but that meant civil war, ...here I feel a gale of discord blowing up...' (Abba, 4) In this he was correct. For their reward a quarter of the officers in Garibaldi's army who had wanted to join the new army of Italy were dismissed; those who were retained had first to survive a rigorous screening operation. In contrast officers from the defeated Neapolitan army had no difficulty in finding positions. In a painful scene in parliament in April 1861 Garibaldi accused Cavour of having almost caused a 'fratricidal war'; uproar followed as deputies struck each other across the face and the sitting had to be suspended for twenty minutes to allow tempers to cool. While alienating the men who had added half the peninsula to the new kingdom, the new Government failed to carry out the reforms which were needed to convince people that unification had been worthwhile. During his five month rule in Sicily Garibaldi had pointed the way with schemes for redistributing church lands, damming rivers, re-afforesting mountains, draining marshes, setting up nursery schools and doubling the number of university posts. But, when Garibaldi had handed over Naples and Sicily to the central government, reforms ceased and rebellion broke out in the South. Cavour made the government's policy quite clear in a letter to the King in December 1860: 'If riots break out the grenadiers are there to repress unrest with severity... the goal is clear and beyond discussion. We must impose national unification on the weakest and most corrupt part of Italy. As for the means there is little doubt; moral force, and if that is insufficient, then physical force.' (Mack Smith, 8, p.331) Soon a bitter civil war raged with 120,000 soldiers concentrated in Naples and Sicily. More people died in the war, which lasted from 1861 to 1865, than in all the wars of unification put together.

With a country angered by the treatment of the volunteers, the imposition of a Piedmontese bureaucracy and the failure to carry on Garibaldi's social reforms it was essential that the Government should get an agreement with the Pope. Although the leaders of the risorgimento were mostly **anticlerical** the majority of Italians were loyally Roman Catholic. Having had his volunteer army defeated at Castelfidardo (p.40) and most of his provinces annexed, Pope Pius IX was in a stubborn mood. Once again Cavour failed to understand the situation. As soon as the central states and Naples came under Piedmont's control he ordered an immediate enforcement of the Piedmontese religious laws (p.27) without waiting even to consult parliament. 'Put into force energetic measures against the friars', he wrote to the Royal Commissioner in Umbria, 'you have done well to occupy some of the convents.' (Martin, 23, p.640) In the southern provinces no fewer than 66 bishops were arrested. The Cardinal of Pisa was sent to prison for refusing to celebrate Independence Day in the cathedral. Not surprisingly the Pope could not reach agreement with Cavour under this sort of pressure. Good Catholics were instructed not to take part in Italy's politics. The Pope refused to recognise the new Kingdom.

The results of the failure to put the Risorgimento on a popular basis were catastrophic. The Piedmontese **constitution** was totally unsuited for extension to the whole of Italy. Consequently vital problems remained unsolved; the Southern provinces sank ever deeper into poverty, the Italian economy failed to develop and Italy remained a backward country. The strains of the First World War proved too much for the country to bear and so she fell the first victim to fascism. The electoral manipulation which Cavour had used in Sardinia (p.66) was now built into the new Italian parliament. In 1891, even after the percentage of Italians entitled to vote had been raised to seven by the reform of 1882, Pareto described how electoral corruption had its own technical language. 'It is called the 'blocco' when the whole contents of the voting urns are changed, or the 'pastetta' when one changes only a part of them. There is still no word for when absent people and even the dead are made to vote... such practices have always been endemic in southern Italy but for some little time now they have begun to infect the whole country.' (Mack Smith, 36, p.220) According to Mussolini's father 50 cows were once put on the register for the elections in Predappio. In 1886 Crispi described how, when an important vote was due, 'There is pandemonium in parliament... as government agents run through rooms and down corridors collecting votes and promising in exchange subsidies, canals, decorations, bridges...' Until 1911 deputies received no payment and so many were bribed. Over 100 deputies were implicated in the Banca Romana scandal when it was revealed that the Bank had exceeded the legal limits for issuing paper money; most of the additional notes had somehow found their way into the hands of the deputies. Cavour had used what came to be known as the system of 'transformism' for managing parliament. Instead of choosing his ministers from one party group he appointed men from many different outlooks. This system was continued in the Italian parliament. De Sanctis wrote in 1877: 'We have now reached the point where there are no solidly built parties in Italy except those based on either regional differences or the personal relation of client to patron.' (Mack Smith, 36, p.111) Cavour was clever and influential enough to use the system and still tackle major problems with success. In lesser hands it became an excuse to ignore a problem. If there were men with all manner of different views in your cabinet it was best to leave a problem alone. As a result politics became the art of keeping your government in power by continually changing your ministers. In the 74 years between 1850 when the Sardinian constitution was first granted and 1922 when Mussolini took over, there were 67 ministries. In the 38 years between 1887 and 1925 there were no less than 35 different ministers of education. To make this chaos worse the Sardinian constitution gave the King very wide and undefined powers. Many of the ministries after Cavour's fell because Victor Emmanuel had conspired against them and not because the chamber of deputies had voted them out. In the case of Ricasoli the King even subsidised an anti-government newspaper to campaign against his own prime minister. Worse still, clause five of the constitution stated that 'the King commands all forces on land and sea, he makes treaties of peace, alliance and commerce.' Victor Emmanuel took full advantage of these powers. According to Sir James Hudson in 1862 he employed his own 'ambassadors', 'backguards of the spy genus, male and female, who merely get money from him and tell him just what suits their purpose.' (Mack Smith, 22, ch. 13) General Cialdini tended to blame the King for the disasters in the 1866 war against Austria (p.43) 'The king is wholly ignorant and incompetent', he wrote. 'He should have stayed home like Franz Josef (the Austrian Emperor) instead of taking up a command whose duties he cannot seriously discharge.' (Mack Smith, 22, ch. 13) It is not altogether surprising that governments run on the Sardinian system failed to convert the unification into a lasting achievement.

But perhaps the worst result of the Risorgimento was the ever widening gulf which it opened between the North and South of Italy. In 1898 Alfredo Niceforo wrote, 'Within the single womb of political Italy two societies exist, north and south... to bundle together these two societies, ... by iron centralization and by covering both with the cloak of a single law damages the less advanced provinces.' (Woolf, 10, doc. 48) Cavour's spending in Sardinia was by 1860 exceeding revenue by about 50%. After unification the national debts of all the provinces were amalgamated. Sicily's national debt had been small so she now found herself facing a tax increase of about one third to pay the interest on a debt which she had not incurred. This would not have mattered so much if the new taxes had been fairly distributed or if government expenditure in Sicily had been increased. There is nothing wrong with a national debt if it has been created by spending on useful projects which will increase prosperity. Unfortunately although Italy had the lowest wages her indirect taxes on food were the highest in Europe. Taxes on food of course, as opposed to taxes on income, hit the poor much harder than the rich. There were senators like the Duke of Gualtieri who even opposed the scheme for trying to collect more government revenue through a progressive income tax on the grounds that 'the wealthy classes have a much greater number of needs than the lower classes.' When in 1869 the cost of paying the interest on the national debt climbed to over 60% of total state expenditure the finance minister did not tax the rich but put back the hated tax on grinding wheat and corn which had been removed after the unification. This was bad for the poorer classes all over Italy but it was particularly damaging in Sicily because here government expenditure was low. So, for example, with 10% of Italy's population Sicily received less than 3% of Government expenditure on irrigation projects. It was estimated that in 1910 Northern Italy with 48% of the country's wealth paid 40% of its taxes; the South with 27% of the wealth paid 32% of the taxes. (The remainder is accounted for by the Central states, not included here.) The sale of the church lands, estimated to cover about one tenth of the surface area of Sicily, might have been expected to ease the poverty of the peasants. In fact they were bought by the richer classes. A report in 1907–10 revealed that a few hundred great landowners owned half of Sicily but represented less than one tenth of 1% of the population. In 1900 four-fifths of Sicily's population were illiterate and nine-tenths of conscripts were medically unfit. Criminal organisations like the Mafia in Sicily and the Camorra in Naples gained a stranglehold in the South. When the desperate people rebelled in 1866 and 1893 thousands of troops were sent into Sicily to deal with them.

In fact the Risorgimento was a disaster. What could have become a popular revolution based on a federal constitution and social reforms was perverted by the wealthier sections of society into a Piedmontese political, military and economic conquest of the rest of Italy.

2. The unification of Italy defended

Criticism of the achievements of the Risorgimento arose in the first place when it became necessary to explain why the Italian state fell such an easy victim to Mussolini's fascist revolution. It was easy to argue that the state established by the unification had all along been defective. Unfortunately the critics who went on to say that the unification was therefore a disaster broke three vital historical rules. They failed to allow for the immense difficulty of the task which confronted the men who made the unification; they assumed that Cavour had the freedom to make different decisions to the ones which he made; they judged the achievements of the unification against impossibly severe modern standards of excellence, instead of against the achievements of the mid-nineteenth century.

Considered in the light of the problems which had to be surmounted the achievements of the Risorgimento were considerable. A 'geographical expression' became a nation of 27 million people despite the opposition of most of the rulers of the different separate states, the head of the Roman Catholic Church, the mighty Austrian Empire and her rival France, and the indifference of the majority of the Italian people. All this was achieved with remarkably little bloodshed – on one calculation 16,000 dead between 1848 and 1870. Compare this with Germany's unification which cost more men than that in one day's fighting in July 1870. Consider too that it was achieved without recourse to a dictator (no Oliver Cromwell or Napoleon Bonaparte stepped in to restore order); and with a minimum of civil war atrocities compared to the 40,000 Frenchmen executed in Paris after the commune in 1871. Perhaps Italy's economic growth after unification was not as spectactular as Germany's but then Italy had virtually no reserves of iron ore or coal, and she had inherited the desperate problem of the South. The leaders of the new Kingdom of Italy did not cause the deforestation, the voracious goats and the unpredictable rainfall of the South which robbed the hillsides of their vegetation and soil, and created floods, landslides and badly drained marshes where the mosquito bred and spread malaria. These were problems which had begun centuries before. In this light the removal of internal tariff barriers, the institution of a national system of weights and measures and currency, and the improvement in income per head and economic growth which had been initiated by the 1890s were no mean achievement!

The Kingdom of Italy's treatment of the South was, nevertheless, shameful. But can we in all honesty argue that the much more experienced British Parliament did any better with Ireland which had experienced a major famine in the 1840s? Indeed even in the twentieth century the problem of depressed and declining regions is still defeating governments. Since the decline of the textile industry, for example, the north west of England has become a depressed industrial area with unemployment well above the national average in Britain. In spite of all the efforts made to inject fresh life through industrial estates and regional policies such areas in Britain still lag behind the rest of the country.

Nobody would deny that the new Kingdom of Italy's political system also fell far short of excellence. But the historian should compare it with the achievements of other states *at that time* and not against some impossibly high abstract standard. The new Italy was not a perfect democracy in which all had the vote. But at that time the Russian people had no vote at all and negroes in America were steadily losing the vote which they so briefly gained after the Civil War. Even in Britain the 1884 Reform Act still excluded all women, domestic servants, service men, men living with their parents, and effectively anyone forced to change their lodgings frequently, from voting. True, the new state of Germany had gained universal manhood suffrage in 1870 but then the German Reichstag was merely a powerless shop window (p.177). For all its imperfections the Italian parliament did have some real power. It is to its credit that the Italian system which was set up in 1861 did not stagnate. In 1882 the vote was extended to 7% of the male population, and in 1911–12 to all men over 30 or who had served in the forces. Corruption there certainly was, but what country in Europe was free from it? France had her Panama scandal and even in Britain the secret ballot act did not reach the statute book until 1872. Of course, the Italians did not run a proper British style political system because they governed by coalitions instead of by the well tried two party system! But so for that matter did the French and, more to the point, who is to say that the two party system is more democratic? At present in Britain (1983) the new S.D.P. and Liberal alliance argue that the two party system in which one party follows one policy and the next party, when elected to power, then follows a completely different one, needs changing. If these critics win their case perhaps historians will begin to write in praise of the Italian system of government through coalitions of central groups?

Most critics of Cavour's unification settlement have failed to ask themselves whether he really had any alternatives open to him. It is easy for historians to sit at their desks and say that he should have conciliated the Pope, Garibaldi's army, taken more account of regional differences, made Italy more democratic and so on. But politics is the art of what is possible at the time. Politicians always have to operate within restraints; they have to make compromises and concessions in order to get anywhere at all. Cavour, it is true, failed to reach an agreement with the Pope. But his application of the Piedmontese anti-Catholic laws (p.27) was necessary if he was to keep the support of the anti-clericals who constituted the vast majority of the active group of men who had made the Risorgimento. In any case his chances of reaching an agreement with a Pope who argued 'This corner of the earth is mine; Christ has given it to me. I will give it up to him alone;' (Holt, I, ch.XIV) could never have been strong.

On the problem of the army Cavour did his best to reach a compromise. There were three main groups who needed to be reconciled. There were the King, the army and all the conservatives who feared Garibaldi and his volunteers in the same way as many people today fear communists; there were the Neapolitan soldiers and ruling class who had opposed unification and there were the Volunteers themselves. In October 1860 Cavour wrote to Farini, 'I don't mean that we must retain all the officers appointed by Garibaldi or by others on his behalf... but on the other hand we cannot send all the Garibaldians home with a gratuity.' (Holt, I, ch.XIV) His final solution was a reasonable compromise. No fewer than sixteen of the volunteers who were chosen to be drafted into the regular army became generals. Three of Garibaldi's own Generals served on the Commission which made the decisions as to which of the applicants were to be retained.

Cavour's critics have implied that he should have set up regional governments in Italy, elected by universal male suffrage, and that he should have left Garibaldi in charge in the south and free to carry through his social reform programme. But could he have done this? To carry out a programme you need convincing arguments, supporters, men who can carry out your schemes, and time. Cavour had none of these. The most convincing arguments were all against a federation. Before the Act of Union in 1800, Ireland, with her own Parliament, had been part of a British Federation but had almost sided with the French against Britain. The United States of America, the supreme example of a federation, was in the midst of a bitter civil war. Who would support democracy and social reform? The men who had carried through unification were not democrats but liberals who only believed in giving votes to people who were educated enough to know what they were voting for. With 78% of the new Italian Kingdom illiterate they were unlikely to support a policy of **democracy**. Even Garibaldi preferred a dictatorship to democracy. And could Cavour have left Garibaldi in charge of a reform programme in the South? The evidence suggests that Garibaldi would have spent his time trying to capture Rome. Such an action, as the politician and historian Nicomede Bianchi pointed out in 1863, might have led to the new Kingdom of Italy being 'abandoned by England, attacked sword in hand by France and Austria'. And where were the thousands of reliable politicians and administrators to be found for running the large number of regional governments which would be needed in a federation? The small number of Piedmontese administrators who filled the posts in the centralised system which Cavour finally chose may not have been popular but at least they were well trained, efficient and honest. And above all decisions had to be made rapidly. As Nigra pointed out when he became Governor of Naples in 1861, pressures were building up. 'There is a continual clamour. One side cries "Hurry up with unification, destroy every vestige of autonomy"; the other side replies "Respect the traditions and institutions already in existence."' (Mack Smith, 36, p.53) Slow decisions might well be rewarded with civil war. Because a regional system of government has, since the 1970s, been extended to most of Italy, it does not follow that Cavour could, or even should, have done the same over 100 years before.

Supposing Cavour had by some miracle defied all these pressures and set up a democratic federation with a programme of social reform? The critics of the unification imply that all would have been well. The Kingdom would have been firm and strong, fascism would never have taken root, Italy today would have been a prosperous constitutional monarchy. Clearly this sort of speculation about 'what might have been' is almost a science fiction approach which should not really be used by historians. Leaving this objection aside, however, have we really any grounds for supposing that a regional government system would have made any difference? In the USA it has been the state governments who have always frustrated reforms; despite pressure from the central federal government it was the state governments who deprived the Negro of education and the vote until the 1950s; it was the state governments who frustrated many of Roosevelt's New Deal reforms. There is every indication that a Sicilian or Neapolitan regional government would have delayed reform in their areas and been even more corrupt than the Italian central government. Naples had a magnificent municipal theatre but no proper system of drainage and water supply because the local Neapolitan town council preferred it that way. The attempt to preserve the common land in Calabria was frustrated by local Neapolitan politicians not by politicians in Rome. A survey in 1910 found 83 encroachments on the common land; two were by brothers of the mayor, 17 by his first cousins, two by his nephews.

Meanwhile the Mafia succeeded in spreading its tentacles even to Rome. The case of the Marquis Notbartolo in 1893 illustrates this point. He had collected information on the Mafia's penetration of the Palermo hospital board and even into the Bank of Sicily. A kidnapping in which he was forced to pay a ransom did not deter him. In a confidential letter to the Government he tried to reveal his information. Within a few hours he was brutally murdered. The chief suspect, Palizzolo, was not brought to trial until 1899; the conviction by a non Sicilian jury was set aside after the witnesses had all strangely changed their stories. 'The Mafia', Bolton King observed in 1900 'has its patrons in the Senate and the Chamber.' A regional government of Sicily could hardly have escaped becoming totally Mafia controlled.

But suppose that somehow a government had avoided all these pressures and passed laws giving the peasants a fair share of the land? In that case many economists doubt whether Italy's industrial revolution would ever have got off the ground. Industrial progress requires capital; even if this is borrowed from abroad the interest must still be paid back. So far no country has ever succeeded in industrialising without in some way sacrificing the interest of the lower classes in rural areas. By holding back their incomes and forcing them to farm for larger landowners in return for poor wages the surplus of capital needed for industrial investment is built up. This even holds true in Communist Russia where Stalin deliberately subjected the Russian peasantry to near starvation to achieve his five year plans.

Bearing in mind the policies of other countries at the time, the special problems which the Kingdom of Italy inherited and the restraints placed upon

Cavour's policies, there can be no doubt that the unification of Italy was a triumphant success. To judge it by any other standards would be naive and unhistorical.

Study 21

1. Having read the two passages try to sort out why they are in conflict
   (a) Are they disagreeing about the facts?
   (b) Has criticism of the Risorgimento arisen because new evidence has been uncovered?
   (c) Are they in disagreement because recent events have changed the way historians look at Italian history?
   (d) Are they quarrelling over how progress and achievement should be measured?
   (e) Are they disagreeing on whether history should concern itself over what might have been?

2. Now work out where you stand in the debate. Which approach do you find convincing? Can you reconcile the two approaches?

3. Write an essay giving your own view of whether Italian unification was a triumph or a disaster. Try to use the advice given in previous exercises about key sentences (pp.58–9) and 'Aunt Sally' style essays (p.73).

Sources

For the study of Italian Unification

Where does Italian history come from? Of course, like all other history it must originate from the state papers, documents, letters, diaries, etc which are generally referred to as primary sources. But where are these? As in most countries some are still in private hands. A good example is the Ricasoli Archive at Briola in Siena, Tuscany. Here it is possible to study the letters, diaries, estate ledgers, accounts, mortgages and sales of the Ricasoli family, which under Bettino Ricasoli (p.34) played a leading part in the Italian Risorgimento. The rest of the primary sources may either lie awaiting discovery in some forgotten attic or cellar or have been deposited in one of the state libraries or archives.

Apart from the obvious fact that all such documents require translation before non-Italian speakers can use them, what are the particular problems presented by Italian archives? One very important difficulty is that Italy was purely a 'geographical expression' until 1860. As a result documents can be found scattered in the state archives which exist wherever there was once the court of an independent state. The central state archive in Rome can only be relied upon to have administrative material from 1860 onwards. A further problem is that north Italy was at one time under Austrian control. As a result a sort of 'tug of war' has taken place. Originally the government documents were stored in the State Archive in Vienna. After the defeat of the Austrian Empire in World War I some, but not all, of this material had to be handed over to the Italian Government. A major problem for any historian of the Italian Risorgimento is the impossibility of using the Royal Archives of the Savoy Family (p.68). When Italy became a republic after the Second World War in 1946 these were taken off to Cascais in Portugal. Natural and man-made disasters have played a more than usually important part in the history of Italy's archives. Floods in the Florence State Archive, rats in the Venetian State Archive (p.48) and World War II bombing of the Naples Royal Archives, have between them destroyed much valuable primary historical material. It is important to understand that the bibliography which follows is composed of books and collections of documents which have all, directly or indirectly, had to overcome these problems.

Bibliography
On Italian Unification

I A Brief and Basic List

1. A readable basic textbook: E. Holt, *Risorgimento: The Making of Italy, 1815–70*, Macmillan, 1970.
2. A simple narrative account: C. A. Leeds, *The Unification of Italy*, Wayland, 1974.
3. Documents: R. L. H. Lloyd, *Cavour and Italian Unification 1854–60*, Arnold's Archive Series, 1975.
4. An exciting autobiography: *Giuseppe Cesare Abba – A Diary of one of Garibaldi's Thousand*, translated by E. Vincent, Oxford, 1962.
5. An enjoyable biography: John Parris, *The Lion of Caprera (Garibaldi)*, Barker, 1962.
6. An argumentative essay: L. Seaman, *From Vienna to Versailles*, Methuen, 1955 (first edition) chapter 10.

II A More Detailed List

a. Documents and Sources

7. D. Beales, *The Risorgimento and the Unification of Italy*, Allen & Unwin, 1971, (new edition by Longman, 1981).
8. D. Mack Smith (ed.), *The Making of Italy 1796–1870*, Harper, 1968.
9. D. Mack Smith (ed.), *Garibaldi*, Prentice Hall, 1969.
10. S. J. Woolf, *The Italian Risorgimento*, Problems and Perspectives, Longman, 1969.

b. Autobiographies

11. Silvio Pellico, *My Prisons*, translated by I. G. Capaldi, Oxford, 1963.
12. A. Dumas (ed.), *Garibaldi; an autobiography*, translated by W. Robson, Routledge, 1860.

c. Biographies

13. C. Hibbert, *Garibaldi and His Enemies*, Longman, 1965.
14. J. Ridley, *Garibaldi*, Constable, 1974.
15. P. Ginsborg, *Daniele Manin and The Venetian Revolution 1848–9*, Cambridge University Press, 1979.
16. G. M. Trevelyan, *Manin and The Venetian Revolution*, Longman, 1923.

17. G. M. Trevelyan, *Garibaldi*, Longman, 1933.
18. E. Hayles, *Pio Nono*, Eyre & Spottiswoode, 1954.
19. E. Hayles, *Mazzini and The Secret Societies*, Eyre & Spottiswoode, 1956.
20. R. Marshall, *Massimo D'Azeglio, an Artist in Politics, 1798–1866*, Oxford, 1966.

d. Histories

21. D. Mack Smith, *Cavour and Garibaldi, 1860 – A Study in Political Conflict*, Cambridge, 1954.
22. D. Mack Smith, *Victor Emmanuel, Cavour and the Risorgimento*, Oxford, 1971.
23. G. Martin, *The Red Shirt and the Cross of Savoy*, Eyre & Spottiswoode, 1970.
24. S. Woolf, *A History of Italy, 1700–1860*, Methuen, 1979.

e. Short Pamphlets

25. H. Hearder, *Cavour*, Historical Association Pamphlet, G.80, 1972.
26. A. Ramm, *The Risorgimento*, Historical Association Pamphlet, G.50, 1962.
27. Irene Collins, *Revolutionaries in Europe: 1815–48*, Historical Association, 1974.

f. Novels

28. G. di. Lampedusa, *The Leopard*, Collins, 1960.
29. Alessandro Manzoni, *The Betrothed*, translated by A. Colquhoun, Dent, 1951.

g. Other works referred to in text

30. Mack Walker (ed.) *Plombières: Secret Diplomacy and the Rebirth of Italy*, Oxford University Press, 1968.
31. D. Mack Smith, *A History of Sicily*, Chatto and Windus, 1968.
32. D. Hussey, *Verdi*, Dent (Master Musician Series), 1974.
33. C. Cipolla (ed.), *Fontana Economic History of Europe: The emergence of industrial societies, part 2*, Collins/Fontana, 1973.
34. C., L. and R. Tilly, *The Rebellious Century 1830–1930*, Harvard University, 1975.
35. M. Braun, 'Cavour and Garibaldi,' *History Today*, October, 1959.
36. D. Mack Smith, *Italy, A Modern History*, University of Michigan, 1959.
37. A. Whitridge, *Men in Crisis*, Archon, 1967.

III.   Audio Visual Aids

a. Films

Urban Insurrection, Open University, 1977, colour, 23 minutes (Milan in 1848).

b. Tape Recordings

The Italian Risorgimento, a discussion between D. Beales and D. Mack Smith, Sussex Tapes, one hour (also printed in *Europe in the Nineteenth Century*, ed. A. Hardman, Sussex Books, 1976.)
The Unification of Italy and the Italian Revolutions of 1848–9, H. Hearder & S. Woolf, Audio Learning, 56 minutes.

c. Overhead Projector Transparencies

The Unification of Italy, 6 OHP maps, Audio Visual Productions.

d. Gramophone Record

The World of Verdi, Philips, 6833223 (contains most of the music mentioned in chapter 4, page 54).

CHAPTER 7

'The Time when Nothing Happened'
1815 - 50

The Germany of 1815

On 1 April 1815 the peacemakers at Vienna were still putting the finishing touches to the German Act of **Confederation** which they hoped would restore peace to an area recently torn apart by the Napoleonic Wars. Yet in Paris their hard work appeared to be threatened with destruction before it had even been completed for Napoleon had escaped from Elba and returned as Emperor of France. Meanwhile, 60 miles from Berlin in the family mansion of Schönhausen in the Brandenburg province of Prussia, Otto von Bismarck had just been born. Surprisingly it was Bismarck and not Napoleon I who was to destroy the new German settlement. On 8 June the German Act of Confederation was completed and signed; on 18 June Napoleon's threat to the new German order was finally terminated by his defeat at Waterloo. But, 51 years later the diplomacy of Otto von Bismarck played a leading part in undermining the whole system and creating a united Germany. How did this happen?

The Vienna peacemakers had decided to restore 37 of the original 360 smaller German states. These ranged in size from the independent city states like Frankfurt and Hamburg to the larger kingdoms like Bavaria. But this decision had set them a problem. Small states like these would be a permanent invitation to some future French or Russian statesman to try to imitate Napoleon I. Metternich and Castlereagh (see p.3) therefore planned an ingenious system of balances to prevent another invasion of Germany. The first line of defence was Bismarck's country of birth, Prussia. Bismarck's ancestors had been among the supporters of the Elector of Brandenburg when, in 1701, he assumed the title of King of Prussia and founded the Hohenzollern dynasty. Since then, rather like the Sardinian House of Savoy (p.5), the Hohenzollerns had gradually added more and more territory to their kingdom. Under King Frederick William III, however, their successes had been abruptly halted when Napoleon I had smashed the illustrious Prussian Army at the battle of Jena in 1806. But Prussia had recovered sufficiently to play a leading part in Napoleon's final defeat and was now rewarded by being made the protector of the smaller German states. To the East she retained a portion of her former Polish territory, the Duchy of Posen. She was further strengthened by acquiring the northern part of Saxony and Swedish Pomerania. To the west she was put in the front line against France by being given a large block of territory lying on the Rhine. This brought the population of King Frederick William III's Prussia to $10\frac{1}{2}$ million which was small compared to Russia's 48 million or France's 30 million but large enough to deter either country from attempting to take advantage of the 37 small German states.

Behind Prussia the second line of defence was provided by Metternich's own country, the Austrian Empire. The 25 million people of the Empire covered an area of over 250,000 square miles and comprised about a seventh of Europe's total population. Twenty per cent of the Hapsburg Emperor's subjects were German, the remaining 80 per cent included Czechs, Slavs, Italians, Rumanians, Hungarians and Poles. Any attempt to interfere in Germany would be sure to involve the Austrian empire. There was the added advantage that if the Prussians should by any chance be tempted to try to gain further territory at the expense of the 37 small states they too would be deterred by the might of the Austrian Empire. Nor would France or Russia stand by idly if Prussia gave up her role of protecting the German sheep and attempted instead to herd them into an extended Prussian Kingdom.

This very clever system of checks and balances was given a third line of defence by the creation of the Germanic Confederation or Bund. The 39 members included all of Prussia, (except for her Polish province of Posen), the German and Bohemian provinces of Austria, and the 37 smaller German states. The members of the Bund promised to defend Germany and its member states against attack, to refrain from making alliances which threatened other members, and to bring their problems before the Confederation's Assembly or Diet. But supposing a popular nationalist movement tried to use the Diet to create a united Germany? This would completely upset the careful balances and threaten the unity of the Austrian Empire. To prevent such a disaster Metternich had carefully made sure that the machinery of the Diet could not possibly be used in this way. For a start the men who represented the 39 states at the meetings in Frankfurt were not elected but were ambassadors chosen by their royal rulers. Even supposing that popular **nationalism** managed to influence any of them the Diet's laws had to be passed both by an inner council and by a plenary session. There were 17 seats on the inner council, of which two belonged to each of the larger states. The remaining six were shared between the 28 smaller states. The votes at the plenary session were shared out on a population basis so that the seven largest states with a population of 26 million had 27 votes and the remaining states with a population of 4.2 million had 42. To get through these two a proposal had to have at least a two thirds majority and in many cases unanimity. Even if, against all odds and against the skilful manipulation of the Austrian ambassador who was always President of the Diet, any proposal was accepted, there was no civil service to execute it or German Federal Court to enforce it. Indeed the Diet did not even have its own stationery and conducted all its business on paper borrowed from the Austrian chancellery. In fact in 1815 the 37 small states, all determined to protect their own identity and not become submerged in a new German nation, were easily able to frustrate schemes to set up a German Federal Court, a German army united under one Commander-in-Chief, and a German area of free trade and commerce.

Even without the Congress of Vienna's clever system of checks and balances and the determined independence of the states, the Germany of 1815 seemed to be too divided by religion to contemplate unification. The older provinces of Prussia into which Bismarck had been born were Protestant as were most of the smaller north German states. But Posen and the new Prussian Rhineland were Catholic. At the age of 21 Bismarck narrowly escaped being beaten up in the Rhineland for refusing to kneel when a Catholic street procession went by. The south German states like Bavaria, Baden and Württemburg were also largely Catholic. So there was a religious divide between the north German states who tended to look towards Prussia as their protector and the southern areas which looked to Catholic Austria.

A final obstacle to any idea of unifying Germany was the power of the ruling class. This rested on the apparently invincible foundations of a loyal hereditary aristocracy of landowners, the army and the bureaucracy. Bismarck himself had been born into the Prussian landed aristocracy. Hereditary squires like Bismarck's father were known as **Junkers**. They were loyal to the King of Prussia. The liberation of their **serfs** between 1807 and 1811 had made little difference to their power. In theory **peasants** could now arrange their own marriages, move house if they wanted to, choose their own heirs, and farm their own land without being called to do compulsory labour for their lord. In practice the peasants had to compensate their Junker masters for their loss of feudal rights by handing over between a third and a half of their land. In many cases the land which remained in the peasants' possession was insufficient to support them so they were forced to sell even that to the Junkers. Unlike English landowners, who tended to lease out a large proportion of their land to tenants, the Prussian Junkers preferred to farm their land themselves. The result was that in Prussia the serfs became landless labourers. Since the Junkers still retained control of the local courts, police regulations, the appointment of mayors and the issue of certificates entitling a labourer to move to a new area, their control over local rural society remained as strong as when they were feudal owners of serfs. In other parts of Germany, notably in the Prussian Rhineland, a bigger percentage of the peasants retained their own farms or the landowners were more prepared to lease out farms in the English style. But as more than 90% of the German population lived in the countryside the landed aristocracy remained dominant.

Nor did there seem much hope in 1815 that the bureaucracy or army might be converted to the idea of German unification. Bismarck's mother, Wilhelmine, came not from the usual Junker background but from the other powerful element in Prussian society, the civil service. Wilhelmine's father had risen to be Minister of the Interior in Prussia. Although the younger sons of Junkers still often made a career in the Civil Service it had by 1815 become dominated by men like Wilhelmine's father with a legal or university training. This trend had been accentuated when an order of 1807 made government posts open to all regardless of birth. Generally these bureaucrats despised the ignorant hunting and shooting Junkers. It was probably only because her father died when she was twelve that Wilhelmine was obliged to marry into the Junker Bismarck family. However the civil servants, like the Junkers, were totally loyal to the King who employed them and every so often rewarded them with titles of nobility. Although defeat by Napoleon had forced King Frederick William III to make reforms in the Prussian army it too remained aristocratic and loyal to the crown. One of the leading reformers, Scharnhorst, had actually dared to write to the King: 'If aristocratic children with their crass lack of knowledge and their feeble childishness alone should have the privilege of becoming officers... the army will become bad.' In 1808 the reformers seemed to have won their case when promotion in future was to be on merit and not on birth. But the majority of army officers remained aristocrats because each regiment retained the right to propose their own candidates for commissions and the cadet schools only admitted the sons of officers.

The biggest challenge to German society seemed likely to come from the towns because liberal and nationalist elements were more likely to arise there than in the more tradition-bound countryside. The Municipal Act of 1808 in Prussia had set them free from the control of the Junkers and they now had their own elected councils. But only 10% of Germans lived in towns in 1815. The total town population of Germany was only half as much again as the population of Paris. The councils of the towns were mostly run by local merchants, lawyers or industrialists. But these industrialists were not large scale factory owners. They were masters who controlled small workshops of skilled journeymen and apprentices or who employed large numbers of part time domestic workers in the surrounding countryside. In Prussia the numbers of these workers and masters had begun to increase considerably because in 1810–11 the Guilds had been deprived of their privileges, so that it was now possible for anyone to set up as an employer without being a member of a Guild. Although the first mechanized cotton spinning mill had been set up in 1784 there were still very few factories to compete with the handicraft workers and those that did exist were small and ran on water power. On the whole the towns in 1815 remained quiet and contented, and the German settlement of 1815 looked secure.

GERMANY

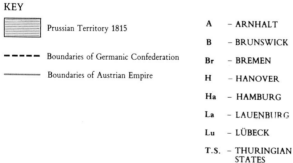

KEY

▨ Prussian Territory 1815

- - - - Boundaries of Germanic Confederation

——— Boundaries of Austrian Empire

A	– ARNHALT
B	– BRUNSWICK
Br	– BREMEN
H	– HANOVER
Ha	– HAMBURG
La	– LAUENBURG
Lu	– LÜBECK
T.S.	– THURINGIAN STATES

Map 5. Germany in 1815

Study 22

Look carefully at map 5 on page 108 and at pages 104–107 above. Answer the following questions:

1. **The Problems of Prussia.**
How many separate pieces of territory was the Prussian Kingdom divided into?
Name the states which shared their frontiers with Prussia.
How many different ambassadors and/or customs agreements would Prussia therefore have to make?
Answering these questions should give you some insight into the complexities of politics in a fragmented area like the Germany of 1815.

2. **The German Confederation.**
Which three Prussian provinces were excluded from the Confederation and why?
Which parts of the Austrian Empire were included?
Of the two states to the south of Denmark which was included and which was excluded?
Was Luxemburg in the Confederation?
Where did the Diet of the Confederation meet?

3. **Bismarck's early career.**
Find the following places on the map and, as you read on to pages 109–113, explain the part they played in Bismarck's early career: Brandenburg, Schönhausen, Berlin, Göttingen, Aachen.

4. **Further Developments 1815–50.**
Find the following places on the map and as you read on to pages 109–118 write down their importance: Dresden, Baden, Frankfurt, Erfurt, Olmutz, Eisenach, Carlsbad, Stuttgart.
What states are they in?

The Pressures for Change 1815–47

In 1836, when Bismarck was 21 and about to take up his first post in the Prussian Civil Service, it was clear that the 1815 settlement was under considerable pressure, for German writers had begun to attack it from three different directions. First were those who followed the great German philosophers like Goethe (1749–1832) and Schiller (1759–1805). These argued that the main purpose of a government was to protect an individual's freedom of speech, religion and property. Intelligent men, they argued, should be given a say in the running of the government. They admired the clear thought of the Greeks and of the French philosophers of the eighteenth century. Most of them welcomed the arrival of the French revolutionary armies in Germany and even at first had supported Napoleon when he introduced the logical laws of the Napoleonic code. Followers of this line of thinking worked hard to make the 39 states of the Bund grant constitutions to their peoples.

A second group of writers were less interested in the freedoms of the individual than they were in the creation of a German nation. Some of the leading writers in this group were Fichte (1762–1814), Arndt (1769–1860) and

Jahn (1778–1852). Basically they argued that the main purpose of a government was to preserve the pure language and culture of the people. German culture, they claimed, was superior to most others because it had never been tamed by Roman occupation and in the Middle Ages had reigned supreme. Government should not be based on alien French and British ideas but on the true 'Volksgeist' of the German people. No Germans could be truly free unless they lived under a totally German government in which all those speaking the German language were united together. Followers of this line of thought spent much time collecting folk tales and poetry like the *Nibelungen* which they claimed compared favourably to the famous Greek legends of the *Illiad*.

A third group compared the backward state of industry and trade in Germany with their flourishing growth in Britain. The reason for this, they argued, was that Germany consisted of 39 states all with their own tariff barriers; there were innumerable systems of weights and measures, seven different currencies, many different legal systems. Was it surprising that the German market was invaded by British manufactured goods with which German producers could not compete? The solution to the problem was to form a customs union in Germany which could then develop later into a German national state.

Two other vital problems which divided German writers were those of how Germany was to be converted into a nation and what territory should be included. Many argued that when the time was right education would persuade the separate states to voluntarily join together in a **federation**. Others like Jahn and the philosopher Hegel (1770–1831) suggested that the movement would have to be initiated and led by Prussia. The **'Kleindeutsch'** group held that the new Germany should include Prussia and the smaller German states. They were opposed by those in the **'Grossdeutsch'** movement who argued that the Germans in the Austrian Empire must also be included. This then raised the problem of the Empire's other nationalities. Should Czechs or Poles be part of the German State? List (1789–1846) and Jahn were even in favour of including Switzerland and the Low Countries.

Study 23

Ideas are always hard to follow and it would be fair to say that German political ideas are among the hardest. To check that you have understood the three lines of thought described above read the extracts below and say which they belong to and why.

(a) 'Thirty-eight customs boundaries cripple inland trade and produce much the same effect as ligatures which prevent the circulation of the blood. The merchant trading between Hamburg and Austria or Berlin and the other states must learn ten customs tarriffs and must pay ten successive traffic dues. Switzerland must traverse ten. Anyone who is so unfortunate as to live on the boundary line between three or four states spends his days among hostile tax gatherers and custom house officials; he is a man without a country.' List, 1819 (Snyder, 34, p.17)

(b) 'I do not desire national unity without political liberty and I prefer liberty without unity to unity without liberty. I reject unity under the wings of the Prussian or Austrian eagle.' Karl von Rotteck, 1832 (Kohn, 31, p.134)

(c) 'It is much more appropriate for the human race to be strictly separated into nations than for several nations to be united as has happened in recent times... each state is an independent individual existing for itself; it is unconditionally its own master governed by its own laws, habits and customs.' 'Every literature must and should be national. The growth of a nation depends on its store of national memories often lost in the darkness of time but preserved and enhanced by the poets. Such national memories are the most wonderful heritage that a people can have.' Lectures given in 1804–6 and 1812 by Friedrich Schlegel (1767–1845), (Kohn, 31, pp.60–2).

Bismarck's career in this period shows that some of these ideas were already being translated into action. In 1822 when he was seven years old his mother insisted on sending him to a fashionable school in Berlin. Here he was subjected to Jahn's educational system. Germans, Jahn believed, were as yet too soft and effeminate to fight for freedom and unity. Along with the other pupils Otto von Bismarck was subjected to a carefully planned series of gymnastic exercises designed to make him strong and self assertive. From the ages of twelve to sixteen Bismarck was educated at two different grammar schools in Berlin. Here his cultural needs were attended to and he studied Greek and Latin and the great German writers Goethe and Schiller. At seventeen in 1832 he entered Göttingen University in Hanover. On the staff of the university were some of the leading thinkers of the time. Dahlman was lecturing the students on the virtues of English constitutional government. The Grimm brothers were working on their famous collection of German fairy tales. 'I strove to penetrate into the wild forests of our ancestors listening to their whole language and watching their pure customs', wrote Jakob Grimm (1785–1863). 'The love for the fatherland is so Godlike and a feeling so deeply impressed in every human breast that it is not weakened but rather strengthened by the sorrows of misfortunes which happen to us in the land of our birth', he told the students in a lecture the year before Bismarck arrived at the university (Snyder, 34, p.40). For a while Bismarck took part in the *Burschenshaften* students' movement. This was another one of Jahn's ideas. Usually the students joined the traditional regional groups which attacked each other, drank and fought countless duels. Jahn encouraged the students to form political clubs instead which taught them to give up their womanising in favour of the more elevating pursuit of 'Honour, Liberty and Fatherland'. But at this point Bismarck threw overboard all his earlier training. He preferred the drinking and womanising of the traditional club he belonged to, the aristocratic Hanovera corps, and proceeded to fight 25 duels in nine months; by the following year he had left Göttingen and transferred to the University of Berlin.

Yet although the new ideas were definitely beginning to put pressure on the German settlement of 1815, they resulted in few definite changes. In 1818–20 six of the south German states adopted constitutions which gave their citizens representation and liberties. In the 1830s small scale revolutions persuaded some of the northern states like Hanover and Brunswick to do the same. Impressive nationalist demonstrations were put on at the Wartburg near Eisenach in 1817 and at Hambach in Bavaria in 1832. At the Wartburg Festival about 700 students and professors enjoyed a banquet, listened to speeches and sermons, watched gymnastic displays and burnt reactionary objects and books on a large bonfire. At Hambach invitations were sent to all 'German men and youths... whose breasts are aglow with the sacred spark of fatherland and liberty... and German women and girls whose political rights are so disgracefully neglected.' About 35,000 answered this call and, as bells rang and cannons boomed, they marched up the hill to an old ruined castle where they listened to stirring speeches.

These measures and protests were, however, scattered and ineffective. To begin with, closer study reveals that the constitutions were mostly very limited. Few of the state rulers gave up their powers of veto; most of them retained an upper aristocratic house which could be relied upon to throw out unwelcome ideas; the lower assemblies were controlled by restricting the vote to the wealthy, making it indirect (see **indirect voting**) or by the ingenious system of organising people to vote in separate estates so that the richer ones always elected more candidates than the poorer. Many of those elected were state officials who stood to lose their jobs if they voted against their rulers. Progress towards attaining individual freedoms was regularly halted by Metternich. For example, when in 1819 a student murdered Kotzebue, a German writer who made periodical reports to the Tsar of Russia, Metternich used the incident to frighten the Diet at Frankfurt with the prospect of a breakdown in law and order. As a result it passed the Carlsbad decrees which meant that the 39 states promised to put all books with more than 20 pages under censorship, dismiss outspoken professors and teachers, ban the Burschenshaften and bar ex-members of it from the civil service. Metternich used the panic created by the Hambach festival in the minds of the rulers to repeat the exercise in 1834.

The fate of some of Germany's leading writers indicates that little progress had been made in securing freedom of speech. At the time of the Kotzebue murder, List was sent to prison for ten months and forced into exile in the USA for trying to obtain the right to public trials in Württemburg. Arndt was forbidden to lecture for 20 years, and Jahn went to prison for two years and was banned for 20 years from living in any town which had a secondary school or university. The organisers of the Hambach festival were released by the jury in an ordinary court but were then tried by a special police court which sentenced them to prison. When in 1837 seven professors, including the

Grimm brothers and Dahlman, protested because the King of Hanover had overthrown the constitution granted only four years before, they were all dismissed from their University posts at Göttingen.

Meanwhile Bismarck had finished at Berlin university and managed to obtain the necessary qualifications for entry to the civil service. In 1836 he took up his first post in Aachen in the Rhineland where he was attached to the Rhenish governing Board. The board's job was to integrate the area into the new **Zollverein**. Bismarck was more interested in pursuing very pretty English girls and by 1838, having taken time off to pursue one of them, found himself suspended from the service without pay. The Zollverein, however, was the first break in the German Settlement of 1815. It had its origin in the Prussian customs law of 1818. Finding themselves with $10\frac{1}{2}$ million subjects scattered all over Germany and operating 67 different tariffs the efficient Prussian civil servants decided to remove all their internal customs barriers and set up one free market. They retained a very low external tariff not exceeding 10%. However, goods travelling through were charged a transit tax which the small states in and around Prussia found very annoying. Very soon they began to make treaties in which they agreed to adopt the Prussian system. The numbers joining Prussia grew steadily until in 1835 the Zollverein had been formed. Eighteen of Germany's states belonged, thus giving the area a trading population of $23\frac{1}{2}$ million. The agreement was to last for eight years and decisions about the customs were made in a yearly congress in which unanimous decisions were required. The income obtained from the tariffs was divided up among the members on a population basis. By 1841 the number of states belonging to the Zollverein had risen to 25 and it had signed a trade treaty with Belgium. This looked as if it might be the beginning of the fulfilment of List's idea for an economic union of Germany which could lead to the formation of a German national state.

The Failure of the Revolutions: 1847–51

On Tuesday, 21 March 1848, Otto von Bismarck, now 33, sat on a train from Potsdam approaching Berlin, the capital city of Prussia. He was determined to rescue his King, Frederick William IV, from the Berlin mob. In a way it was the new railways which had started all the trouble. Since 1835 they had begun to spread all over Germany except in east Prussia. The Prussian Junkers badly needed a railway to link their farmlands via Berlin to markets in the rest of Europe, but nobody would put up the capital. It was decided therefore that the Prussian government must build the railway but to do that it needed money. Frederick William IV had become King in 1840 and he believed firmly in the absolute power of Kings. But he also had the romantic notion that he must be popular with his people. Instead of just collecting the necessary taxes he decided to call a United Diet. This was an assembly representing the aristocratic local diets which were the nearest things that Prussia had to representative government. The United Diet had met against a background of mounting popular violence. The rye and potato crops had failed and food prices were rising. Skilled artisans and handicraft workers were beginning to suffer from the competition of factory products encouraged by the coming of the railways. Since 1815 five promises had been made to give Prussia a **constitution** like the other states in Germany but none of them had been fulfilled. To the dismay of the King and the Junkers the United Diet refused to grant the money for the new railway until these promises had been kept. The Diet was speedily dissolved but pressure for change mounted. Things reached their climax on 18 March 1848. Revolutions were breaking out all over Europe and the King had announced that he would recall the United Diet and ask it to draw up a constitution. A large mob appeared in front of the Royal Palace in Berlin, the army attempted to disperse them, shots were fired. Very soon huge barricades were built across the streets and the army found that they could only take them at the cost of very heavy casualties. It was decided to withdraw the army from Berlin but in the confusion the King was left behind in the Palace and surrounded by the mob. On the 19 March he was forced to pay his respects to the 216 citizens killed in the riots whose bodies had been brought into the Palace courtyard. As he descended from the train Bismarck was determined to change all this, and persuade the King to call back the army and smash the revolution.

Since his marriage the previous year the failed civil servant, who had spent the last eight years as a Junker farmer on his estates, had acquired a religious determination: 'I believe that I am obeying God when I serve the King', he claimed. As a member of the United Diet in 1847 the tall and powerful Junker squire's defence of the King delivered in his sarcastic squeaky voice, had infuriated the liberal members. When he was a boy he had played with the young Frederick William and on his honeymoon in Venice the previous year had been invited to dine with him. So he had high hopes of success in his mission. But by the end of the day he had totally failed. Refused admittance to the Palace he crept around Berlin, shaved off his beard to try to disguise his identity and was forced to escape from a group of citizens who had recognised him. The King meanwhile had ridden around Berlin in the revolutionary colours of black, red and gold and announced to the people, 'Prussia merges into Germany.' Prussia, the first line of defence of the carefully planned German settlement of 1815, had been swept away.

Meanwhile the other lines of defence had also crumbled. Five days before the rising in Berlin, on 13 March, a revolution in Vienna had caused Metternich to run for his life to England. With the Hungarians and the Czechoslovakians demanding local self government within the Empire, a constitution being drawn up in Vienna and a war in north Italy (p.18), there was little chance that the Hapsburgs could interfere in German affairs. The French too had been plunged into revolution as long ago as 22 February and were powerless to take advantage of the state of affairs. This left the third line of defence, the German Confederation at Frankfurt. But by March 1848 this too had collapsed. Nearly every state in Germany had by now experienced some sort of revolution, with the result that new delegates with more liberal views had been sent to Frankfurt. Under the influence of further **radical** groups of reformers, who had made their way independently to the city, the Diet agreed to set up a special preliminary parliament. Meeting from 31 March to 3 April, this parliament decided that elections should be held in each of the 39 states of Germany for a National Assembly. Each state held elections using its own electoral system and on 18 May the old Diet was replaced by the new National Assembly for Germany. With the careful balances which the Vienna peacemakers had constructed in total ruin, for the moment at least, the new Assembly had the opportunity to translate the dreams of a new united Germany into reality. But what sort of Germany would they make?

Study 24

You should pause now to consider the options open to the Frankfurt Assembly. The table below summarises them

1. Electorate	Limited by wealth or education	Universal male suffrage	Indirect univ-ersal male suffrage	Universal suffrage, direct or indirect
2. Type of Government	Centralized	Federation		
3. Extent of Germany	Klein-deutsch	Grossdeutsch	Grossdeutsch and to in-clude Czechs in Bohemia, Poles in Posen and Danes in Holstein★	
4. Ruler	King of Prussia	Emperor of Austria	Republic with President	

★ All of these areas had substantial German minorities.

Usually, but by no means always, people's choices of alternatives are governed by their own personal interests. A good historian has to be able to understand how these interests cause people to make different choices. Consider each of the following people and work out which alternative you think they would choose in the four categories.

(i) A Prussian Junker
(ii) A liberal (see **liberalism**) Catholic lawyer from Bavaria
(iii) A liberal university professor from Austria
(iv) A protestant civil servant from Hanover
(v) A radical journalist from Brunswick
(vi) A liberal merchant from Saxony

Please note that there are no right or definitely wrong answers here except that some decisions would be out of character. For example I should be rather amazed if, for 1 (electorate), a Prussian Junker chose direct universal male suffrage and for 4 (ruler) the Emperor of Austria!

It took the Frankfurt Assembly until 28 March 1849 to make up its mind. The People's house was to be chosen by direct universal male suffrage. There was to be centralized government but the 39 states were to be left with some powers and were to elect members of the State House which was to share government with the People's House. Germany was to consist of the Grossdeutsch area including if possible the duchy of Schleswig. Unfortunately for the Frankfurt Assembly, by the time it had reached its conclusions the favourable political situation which had made its creation possible had slipped away. The Frankfurt Assembly had of course no army though it did purchase a few old ships to found a navy. It therefore relied on the Prussian army and authorised it to fight the Danes to obtain Schleswig and to crush a Polish rebellion in Posen. In August 1848, however, the Prussians decided that foreign opinion was too hostile to their war in Schleswig and simply withdrew their army without any authority from Frankfurt. The radicals in Frankfurt were furious at this and on 26 September began a revolution. The Assembly had to call in Prussian troops to put down this rebellion. With the backing of his army Frederick William IV now felt strong enough to break with his own revolutionaries at home. In October the army marched back to Berlin and closed down the new Prussian parliament. Meanwhile the Hapsburg Empire was also climbing back to its feet. On 17 June the Bohemian Czechs had been crushed and brought back within the Empire. The Frankfurt Assembly, who wanted Bohemia to come within their Grossdeutsch Empire, gave this their full backing. On 31 October the Hapsburg army retook Vienna and on 2 December a new Emperor, Francis Joseph, took over with a tough new chief minister, Prince Felix Schwarzenburg. The Austrians would now have nothing to do with the Frankfurt Assembly's Grossdeutsch scheme because it would mean splitting up the Empire which they had every hope of keeping intact especially now that the wars in Italy and Hungary were beginning to go in their favour (p.19). It was in desperation therefore that on 3 April 1849 the Frankfurt Assembly offered the crown of a scaled down Kleindeutsch empire to King Frederick William IV of Prussia. To anyone who knew the King there could be little doubt what his response to this invitation would be. On 23 December 1848 he had added a postscript to a letter written to one of his ministers: 'Here is a little word of confession about the crown which the Frankfurt Assembly has for sale; every German nobleman is a hundred times too good to accept such a diadem moulded out of the dirt and dregs of revolution, disloyalty and treason...' (Bohme, 8, pp.65–6). When the King's official rejection of their crown reached the Frankfurt Assembly on 21 April 1848 most of the deputies returned sadly home having failed in their mission.

However the attempt to achieve German unity was not yet at an end. Chased out of Frankfurt the more determined radical members of the Assembly retreated to Stuttgart in Württemburg calling for further revolutions all over Germany. In Dresden their call was answered on 3 May 1849, when the citizens erected over 100 barricades, and in Baden, where a Republic was proclaimed. By early June, however, the Prussian army had crushed all the revolutions and dispersed the remainder of the Assembly. Out of a population of $1\frac{1}{2}$ million in Baden it has been estimated that 80,000 chose to emigrate after their defeat. (Kohn, 31, p.137) There was still even now, one last chance for a united Germany. Although he had rejected the Frankfurt Assembly's scheme Frederick William IV was in favour of any plan which could create a Kleindeutsch Germany safely under Prussian control. With this end in view the Erfurt plan was drawn up on 26 May 1849. In this scheme Prussia would retain control of the army and foreign policy in a federation of the German states. A parliament was called and met on 20 March 1850 at Erfurt, but four of the bigger states, Württemburg, Bavaria, Saxony and Hanover, refused to join. By the end of August 1849 the Austrian Empire had finally defeated the Italians and the Hungarians. Prince Schwarzenburg was determined not to accept the Prussian scheme. In the third week of May 1850 he organised a meeting of the smaller German states at Frankfurt and it was decided to restore the Diet of the German Confederation. So which was to triumph – the new Prussian union agreed at Erfurt or the old Diet? Matters came to a head in September when both sides tried to interfere in the state of Electoral Hesse. The Prussian King gave way; Tsar Nicholas I, who had already used the Russian army against the rebelling Hungarians, was backing the Austrians. At Olmutz in Moravia on 29 November 1850 the Prussians agreed to give up the Erfurt union and rejoin the Frankfurt Diet. So all the schemes had come to nothing and the settlement of 1815 had been restored. One man, who had managed to get himself elected to the Erfurt assembly and whose angry squeaky voice had been heard arguing against it, was delighted. Otto von Bismarck believed that even the Erfurt scheme gave away too much Prussian power. His performance at Erfurt drew the King's attention to him once again. He had a better scheme, or so he claimed later in his memoirs. According to Bismarck the period 1814–50 had been the time when nothing happened.

Study 25

This section on the period 1847–50 has not attempted to deal with the events in chronological order. Yet it is sometimes very useful to think of them in this way. Read back through pages 113–117 and study 5 on page 26 in the Italy section, and make a timechart set out as below

Month and year	Prussia	Austrian Empire	Rest of Germany – e.g. Frankfurt

CHAPTER 8

The Unification of Germany

1851-71

Prussia struggles to survive as a great power, 1851–62

The inner council of the German Confederation at Frankfurt was about to begin another of its sessions. The Austrian President sat smoking a long thin Havana cigar while the other delegates stood deferentially waiting for him to formally open the meeting and enable them to take their seats. Suddenly the tallest man in the room wearing his official diplomatic uniform, a gold embroidered jacket and black trousers with gold stripes, sat down next to the surprised President, pulled out a cigar from his gold case and asked him for a light. The man who had dared to break the traditional custom that only the Austrian envoy smoked at meetings, was the newly appointed Prussian envoy, Otto von Bismarck. Whether the story is true or not it illustrates very well the trend in the ten years which followed the Prussian humiliation at Olmutz. Like a boxer struck down by a vicious right hook in the first round Prussia had to show that she could continue the fight or acknowledge that she had failed to retain her position as one of the great powers in Europe. As all good boxers know, the best response to a first round knock down is to pretend that it was of no consequence and to bluff the opposition into thinking that the boxer is still full of energy and light on his feet. In his eight years at Frankfurt, constantly defying and annoying the Austrian delegate-President, this was basically what Bismarck did. The Austrian Chief Minister meanwhile went for the knock out. Prussia's one remaining source of power in Germany was the **Zollverein** (p.113). Schwarzenburg planned to destroy it and replace it with a vast new union including the whole of the Austrian Empire and with a much higher tariff to protect Austria's less efficient industries; in this way Austria would relegate Prussia to a minor power in Germany. 'Let Prussia be humiliated and destroyed', he said. But the Austrian attack failed completely; Prussia fought back and all that Austria gained from the initiative was a vague promise of entry to the Zollverein at some time in the future.

In the next rounds of the contest, as is frequently the case with boxers who have appeared to do well at the start, Austria began to make serious mistakes. Prince Schwarzenburg's death in 1852 had deprived it of the firm leadership it needed to deal with the Crimean war (see also p.64). Here the Austrians made the fatal error of breaking with their ally Russia. Nicholas I, the Tsar of Russia, had helped Austria in 1849 by using his army against the Hungarians and putting pressure on Prussia to give up her Erfurt scheme (p.117). But the Austrians repaid him in the Crimean war by threatening to join Britain and France unless he gave in. Prussia and the other German states wisely played no part in the war. By now Bismarck was arguing that the time had come for Prussia to take the offensive but his views were not trusted. In 1857 Frederick William IV finally plunged into complete insanity and his brother first took over as regent and then, in January 1861, as King William I. William hoped that it would be possible to co-operate peacefully with Austria and bring the 'fight' to an end. In 1859 Bismarck was removed from Frankfurt and became Prussian ambassador to Russia, where as Bismarck put it, he would be in 'cold storage'. Meanwhile the Austrians went on making mistakes. In 1859 they were lured into war with Sardinia and France (see also p.31). Again Prussia refused to assist Austria in the war though she did, much to Bismarck's helpless rage, mobilise six of her army corps on the Rhine. This helped to make Napoleon III withdraw from the war against Austria before he had completed the job of driving her out of north Italy.

Bismarck's position was now rather like that of someone in the front row of the audience at a boxing match. He felt convinced that Austria had now spent herself. The economic recession after the Crimean war had hit her hard; the cost of the war in Italy had been considerable. Now was the time, Bismarck argued, for Prussia to take the initiative and gain concessions in north Germany. But Bismarck was only in the audience. The Prussian boxer and his seconds did not have to listen to him; they were still hoping for a draw and were reluctant to take the initiative. In March 1862 Bismarck was recalled from Russia and in May he was appointed as ambassador in Paris. He was now 47 and despaired of ever attaining a position where he could make his views count. Between 25 July and 15 September he took an extended holiday. At Biarritz, on the French Atlantic coast beneath the Pyrenees, he met Count Orlov and his wife Kathy. The Count had been wounded in the Crimean war and was partially crippled. Bismarck wrote to his wife: 'My old vigour has returned... hidden from prying eyes, shaded by two rocks on which heather blooms, I look at the sea, which is green and white in the spray and sunshine. Beside me is the most charming of women, of whom you will become very fond when you get to know her... she has a personality all her own amusing, intelligent and amiable, pretty and young.' When he should have been back in Paris at the beginning of September he was still making up a threesome with the Orlovs in Provence. Was he, like so many men in their forties, about to change direction and throw over his career for a woman? But back in Paris, on 18 September, he received a telegram from the Prussian Minister of War, Roon. It read: 'Hurry. Delay is dangerous.' The following day, gaunt and sunburnt from his holiday, he was on the midday train for Berlin. Three days later, after an interview with King William I at his imitation Gothic castle near Potsdam, he had been made Prussian Minister President. For the next 27 years he was to remain in that position of supreme power.

But what had brought about this transformation? The truth is that the King's appointment of Bismarck was the last desperate gamble of a despairing man. In 1859 Prince William and Roon had drawn up a series of army reforms. The professional Prussian standing army at that time numbered about 150,000. The reforms were intended to increase its size to 220,000 by adding another 39 infantry and ten cavalry regiments. To support the army in time of war 40,000 young Prussians were called up each year and trained by the regular army for two years followed by two years in the reserve. Roon and Prince William wanted to increase the annual number called up to 63,000 and extend their service to three years followed by four in the reserve. After their four years training under the old scheme the men had joined the Prussian Landwehr (militia) where they continued to do occasional training but under their own officers and totally separate from the regular army. Roon and Prince William were determined that the men would form reserve regiments under the control of regular army officers and organised under the regular army regiments. The Landwehr would cease to be a fighting unit.

In February 1860 the reform scheme was put before the Prussian Landtag. This was all that remained of the Prussian parliament which the revolutionaries had forced Frederick William IV to concede in 1848. In this system the voters were divided into three classes according to how much tax they paid. The system worked out in such a way that a vote in the richest class was worth 17 times a vote in class three. Incredibly, in spite of this, the usually compliant members of the *Landtag* refused to accept the reforms. They made the mistake, however, of still voting the Government a large sum of money. Prince William went ahead and spent the money on the reforms. Throughout 1861 and early 1862 the *Landtag* kept up a barrage of protest. They refused to accept the reforms. They began to threaten to cut off any further tax grants. King William I's ministers tried to persuade him to make concessions but he refused. Most of them, except Roon, resigned. On 17 September Roon thought he had at last solved the problem when the Landtag seemed ready to agree to all the reforms as long as the period of service with the regular army was kept down to two years. Angrily, King William I refused to make even this concession. His range of choices was now very small. He could call new elections but this had already been tried, with the result that his conservative supporters in the Landtag lost more and more seats. There were now only eleven conservatives left and his liberal enemies controlled 80% of the votes! He could call the army into Berlin and close down the Landtag... but this would surely mean civil war. He could abdicate in favour of his son, Frederick, who was known to be in favour of making concessions...

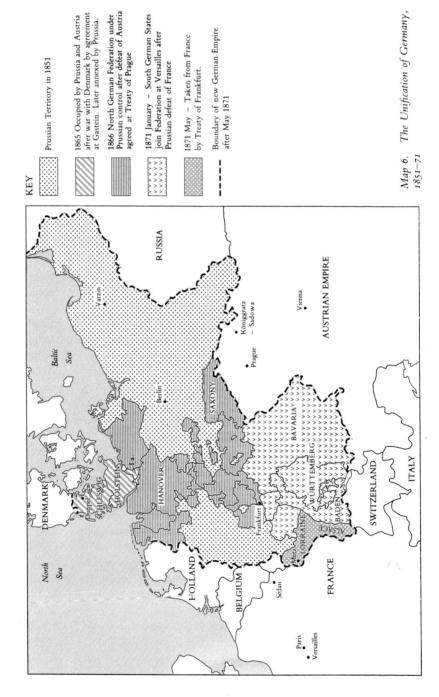

KEY

Prussian Territory in 1851

1865 Occupied by Prussia and Austria after war with Denmark by agreement at Gastein. Later annexed by Prussia.

1866 North German Federation under Prussian control after defeat of Austria agreed at Treaty of Prague

1871 January – South German States join Federation at Versailles after Prussian defeat of France

1871 May – Taken from France by Treaty of Frankfurt.

Boundary of new German Empire after May 1871

Map 6. The Unification of Germany, 1851–71

but this would be deserting his duty to God and the Hohenzollern dynasty. Bismarck in fact was his only hope and he clutched desperately at this last straw.

It makes sense to pause here for a moment and consider what all the fuss was about. What difference did the extra service under the close supervision of the regular army make? Max Duncker, Crown Prince Frederick's advisor, explained why in a conversation: 'People on all sides misunderstand the true character of the situation', he said, 'It is a struggle involving principles, it has become a class struggle, a struggle of the **bourgeoisie** against junkerdom.' (Palmer, 13, p.135) On their side the King and his conservative **Junker** supporters wanted the army to be directly under the King's control. In 1861 about 65% of the officers were nobles and they wanted to keep it this way. In the event of another revolution like 1848 it was vital that the army was loyal to the Crown. The three year service was absolutely necessary because, as the Prince had explained, 'discipline and blind obedience are things which can be obtained only by long practice and it is to these that a longer period of service is relevant so that in a moment of danger the Monarch can rely on his troops.' (Howard, 38, pp.70–1) However the bourgeois lawyers and officials in the Landtag saw things differently. They wanted to see Germany united into one country. To achieve that they believed that Prussia must be reformed so that her King and army were under parliamentary control. A three year service period would turn men into mindless robots under Junker domination. The Landwehr with its mainly middle class officers would be a popular army which would be more likely to fight for a unified Germany than the professional army with its junker officers who thought only of Prussia. What could Bismarck do to bring the conflict to an end? He tried once again to reach a compromise. Having failed in this he began to put into operation a very risky plan. He would simply ignore the Landtag and continue to collect the taxes in spite of their angry opposition. In the meanwhile he would put into operation his schemes for a Prussian take over in Germany. He gambled that if he could achieve this the Landtag would very quickly give up its opposition. Meanwhile he had to make sure that the King did not lose confidence in him. 'I foresee clearly how it is all going to end, they will cut off your head and a little later mine', the King told Bismarck in a famous railway carriage interview on 4 October 1862. 'How better to die', Bismarck is supposed to have replied, 'I struggling for the cause of my King and your Majesty for the right belonging to you by grace of God.'

Study 26

Map 6 on page 122 shows how Bismarck, having preserved Prussia's power, went on to achieve a united Germany under Prussian leadership. Use maps 5 and 6 and the information on pages 124–135 to fill in a simple chart like the one shown below:

Year	Names of areas gained	Battles	Treaties	Description of how Bismarck did it
1865	?	?	?	?
1866				
1871				

Prussia gains control of North Germany 1862–66

William I, Hohenzollern King of Prussia, lay sobbing on the sofa. Otto von Bismarck, also in tears, his legs trembling, dashed from the room wrenching off the door handle as he went. Back in his own apartments there was a loud crash as he flung a glass bowl against the wall. At the cost of a great expense of nervous energy Bismarck had just thwarted another Austrian attempt to retain her dominance in Germany. The Austrians had revived Schwarzenburg's idea of humiliating Prussia and seizing control of the Zollverein. They had decided to call a meeting of all the rulers of Germany at Frankfurt and sensing that the scheme they had in mind might arouse Bismarck's opposition they had delayed their invitation to William I of Prussia until the last moment. In the summer months it was the custom among the rich of Europe to do penance for their overindulgence of food and drink by 'taking the waters' at one or several of the fashionable spas. The Austrian Emperor delivered his invitation to King William while he was taking his annual cure at Gastein in Austria on 3 August 1863. This was only thirteen days before the meeting at Frankfurt. King William felt it was discourteous to refuse and it had taken Bismarck a lot of hard reasoning, culminating in the scene just described, to make him change his mind. The other German princes were not prepared to agree to the Austrian scheme in Prussia's absence so the meeting was a failure. However the Austrians were still pursuing what from their point of view was a much more promising line with regard to the Zollverein. On 18 August 1862, before Bismarck had become Minister President, the Prussian government had made a trade treaty with France on behalf of the Zollverein. But the rules of the Zollverein required the unanimous assent of all the other members. This was a time consuming task and the south German states could see that if they accepted the treaty, which involved lowering their tarriffs, there would be no chance that the Austrians could ever join them in the Zollverein. Meanwhile Bismarck had the crisis with the Landtag on his hands, and in January and February of 1863 he had been involved with the Polish crisis. He had signed the Alvensleben agreement with Russia on 9 February which committed him to help the Russians to put down a Polish rebellion. This had got him into serious trouble with Britain and France as well as with the liberals in Germany. It seemed an excellent moment for the Austrians to break up the Zollverein and replace it with a trade area of their own. With Austrian encouragement the southern German states had refused to agree to the French treaty. But here too Bismarck was not to be overawed. By threatening to break up the Zollverein completely he forced the southern states to give up their opposition. By October 1864 the Zollverein was safe and Austria was still outside. By then Bismarck had already come off the ropes and gone over to the offensive against the Austrian Empire.

Two events in Denmark triggered off the series of explosions which were to culminate in the Prussian conquest of north Germany. In March 1863 King Frederick VII of Denmark had issued a new **constitution** which tried to unite the two provinces of Schleswig and Holstein more closely to the rest of the Kingdom. This seemed to break the Treaty of London signed in 1852 in which all the great powers had promised to protect Denmark as long as she allowed the two provinces to retain their privileges. Since about 30% of Schleswig and Holstein's population was German King Frederick's constitution raised an outcry in the German states. On 15 November King Frederick VII died and his successor, Christian IX, immediately prepared to enforce the new constitution. The local assembly of Holstein, which was a member of the German **Confederation**, refused to accept Christian IX as King and demanded that, instead, Frederick of Augustenburg be made Duke of Schleswig and Holstein. This might be the chance that Bismarck was awaiting to silence his liberal critics in the Landtag by seeming to use Prussian power to support German nationalists. The Schleswig-Holstein problem, though, is complex. So pause here and consider the situation.

Study 27

The following are possible courses of action which Bismarck could take:
1. Call an international conference of the countries who had signed the original Treaty of London in 1852 (Austria, France, Great Britain, Russia and Sweden) before taking further action.
2. Send the Prussian army into Schleswig-Holstein to support the claim of the Duke of Augustenburg. In this case the provinces would become another state in the German Confederation.
3. Take the matter before the Diet of the Confederation at Frankfurt and offer to put the Prussian army at their disposal.
4. Persuade the Austrians to join Prussia and send in an army to force Denmark to obey the Treaty of London.
5. Send in the Prussian army to annex Schleswig and Holstein.

Now consider each course carefully, remembering that the other great powers are involved in this question as well as Prussia and Denmark.

(a) Which course of action do you think the liberals in the Prussian *Landtag* would want Bismarck to follow?

(b) Which course do you think Bismarck might choose?

Bismarck's actions were in fact extremely complex and very controversial (You will find a more detailed examination of them on pp.155–6). Hopefully, you realised that he would reject the first course because it would probably get him nowhere and the fifth because it might end up with all the great powers against Prussia not to mention his own Prussian Landtag, who were still claiming that he was governing illegally. By far the best of the remaining three courses of action was number four because it would be supported by the great powers, a possibly hostile Austria would also be neutralised, and it would not bind him to setting up yet another German state. The majority of Germans, of course, wanted him to support the Duke of Augustenburg and there was pandemonium in December 1863 when Austria and Prussia announced that they were sending their armies against Denmark to protect the Treaty of London! The two armies had little difficulty in taking over Holstein and Schleswig and on 20 April 1864 the Danes were defeated in the battle of Duppel. By that time an international conference had assembled in London. The Danes, however, refused to go back to the Treaty of London so the Prussian and Austrian armies renewed the war on 26 June claiming that they would liberate the provinces and unite them under the Duke of Augustenburg. No other country came to the aid of the Danes, partly because they seemed to have put themselves in the wrong, partly because the French were too much involved in military operations in Mexico to want to frustrate Bismarck's plans. On 30 October 1864 the Danes were forced to give in, and handed the provinces over to Prussia and Austria.

You might think that now the whole thing would end with the Duke of Augustenburg setting up a new German state. Not at all – Bismarck now insisted, in February 1865, that his army and navy would be under Prussian control and that he would have to take his Duchies into the Zollverein. The Austrians resisted this and war between the two seemed imminent. On 20 August, however, the two countries 'papered over the cracks' as Bismarck called it, in the Convention of Gastein. Prussia would take over the administration of Schleswig and Austria would take control of Holstein until such time as a complete settlement could be reached. Hopefully, you will have noticed that Bismarck has now almost obtained the fifth possible objective; especially since the Austrians had granted Prussia such special rights in Holstein as a naval base, and had agreed to allow them to purchase the adjoining territory of Lauenburg. Whether Bismarck actually planned to complete the Prussian annexation by going to war with Austria is a very much debated question (see p.155) but from this point the two countries were soon on a collision course. In his usual methodical way Bismarck made sure that if war came Austria would have no allies and only enemies. At a seaside villa in Biarritz in October 1865 he met the French Emperor Napoleon III and made sure that he would not aid the Austrians. On the 8 April 1866 he made an alliance with the Italians. In return for Venetia they promised to attack

Austria's southern frontiers (p.43). Bismarck was also in touch with various Hungarian nationalists who he hoped would mount a rebellion inside the Austrian Empire. By 30 May 1866 the Austrians finally despaired of forcing Bismarck to reach a final agreement about the two provinces and brought the whole matter before the Diet at Frankfurt. The Prussian army retaliated by invading Holstein on 7 June. On 14 June the German Confederation agreed to mobilise against Prussia by a vote of nine to five. At midnight of the fifteenth the Prussian army began to move. Besides Austria they now had the states of Hanover, Saxony, Electoral Hesse, Bavaria, Württemberg and Baden ranged against them.

Study 28

The general feeling throughout Europe was that the Prussian army would be defeated. Friedrich Engels wrote in the *Manchester Guardian*, 20 June 1866; 'Prussia has had no great war for 50 years. Her army is on the whole a peace army with the pedantry and martinetism inherent in all peace armies.' Examine the table below and say whether you agree that the Prussian army looks likely to be beaten.

	Austrian Empire	Prussia
Numbers	270,000 in Germany 50,000 in Italy	355,000 and reserves
Allies	Other German States 175,000	Italy 400,000
Recruitment & Training	Three years training for all but graduates, skilled professions exempt and the rich able to hire substitutes. 30 days training per year after this. No reserve army or militia.	Three years training with no substitutions or exemptions of any kind. Four years in the reserve and then in the *Landwehr* (militia).
Equipment: a) Infantry	Lorenz gun — a rifled muzzle loader (see **rifle**). Accurate up to 400 yards; had to be loaded from standing position.	Needle gun — a rifled breech loader; Accurate up to 600 yards; could be loaded while lying down; rate of fire four times as rapid as the Lorenz gun.
b) Artillery	736 rifled cannon, muzzle load. 58 smooth bores, muzzle load. All bronze. Accurate from 4–5,000 yards.	492 rifled breech loaders including 160 made from cast steel. 306 smooth bores accurate up to 1500 yards.

table continued.

	Austrian Empire	Prussia
Mobilization	Non-German regiments were garrisoned in areas far away from where the reserves would come. One railway line to concentration point.	Regiments in same areas as reserves. Five railway lines to concentration point.
Administration	Chief of Staff had little power; no maps prepared.	Chief of General Staff issued commands via King. Each unit had a member of General Staff to advise. These men were the top twelve in each annual class of the military academy. Special sections gave advice on maps, railways, military intelligence.
Battle tactics for infantry	Shock tactics — rush forward with bayonet, packed together tightly on narrow front.	Advance in small groups, widely spread, aiming and firing.
Supreme Commanders	Ludwig Benedek. Hungarian (aged 62). Very popular with troops. Successful as a division commander in Italy in 1849 and 1859. Had never served in Germany.	King William I (aged 70) but advised by Helmuth Von Moltke, (aged 66), the Chief of Staff who had been advisor to the Turkish army. Took over command in Danish war, 1864.
Battle Experience	Army had won in Italy in 1849 (see p.19) Fought gallantly in Italy though defeated in 1859 (p.33). Performed well in Denmark in 1864.	No recent battle experience. Army performed badly in Denmark in 1864.

Perhaps you may rate the Prussian army rather higher than Engels did? Now read on and find out how it actually performed.

Austrian hopes for useful support from her allies had been dashed when, by the end of June, the Prussian army had defeated and overrun Hanover, Hesse and Saxony. The Bavarians had opted to keep their army separate from the Austrians. On the other hand the Italians had been defeated (p.43) and the Saxon army had escaped and linked up with Benedek's troops. The main Prussian army had taken only fourteen days to mobilize and by early July was marching in three sections into Bohemia. The Austrian army had taken seven weeks to mobilize and Benedek had decided to place his army on the hills between Sadowa and Königgratz. His plan was to defeat and crush the Prussian first army before the second and the Elbe armies could come to its aid. Moltke's plan was to keep the main Austrian army occupied while the second Prussian army and the Elbe army encircled it. With up to 46,000 men involved in the fighting, the battle of Königgratz-Sadowa was to be the biggest and most decisive battle Europe had as yet seen.

Although it was misty and raining W. H. Russell, the special correspondent for *The Times* newspaper was able to watch the main developments in the battle from a high tower in Königgratz. On the morning of 3 July 1866 he saw the Austrian army with their bands playing take up their positions in 'squares and parallelograms of snowy white, dark green, azure and blue on the cornfields like checker work of a patchwork quilt.' (Craig, 5, p.102) Through the driving rain the grey green masses of the Prussian first army threw themselves against the Austrians as the fighting began at around 7.30 a.m. As the artillery opened fire Russell observed that 'the whole range of hills, valleys and slopes for nine miles and more was as if the earth had been turned into snow wreaths agitated in a wintry gale.' (Craig, 5, p.107) Until 1 p.m. the Austrians were doing well and withstanding Prussian attacks. Although the army of the Elbe had come into action they were being checked by the Saxons. But at that point from up in his tower Russell was amazed to see Prussian troops far out on the right of the Austrians. This he said was 'inexplicable and very serious for although on the left and centre the Austrians might be victorious, this movement threatened, by forcing back their right, to cut them off from Königgratz.' (Craig, 5, p.133) At about this time Moltke too saw the signs that his second army had reached the scene of the fighting. 'The campaign is decided', he told the King, 'Vienna lies at your Majesty's feet.' (Craig, 5, p.133) From now on Benedek was desperately trying to hold the gap open long enough to get his army out of trouble. Around 4.45 p.m. the Prussians took the village of Chlom. By throwing in a brave cavalry charge and sacrificing his artillery which kept firing right up to the last minute, Benedek managed to pull 180,000 troops out of the trap before it closed at around 6 p.m.

Things were much less romantic when viewed from the thick of the fighting instead of from Russell's tower. The Austrian artillery was superbly handled and with its longer range inflicted terrible casualties on the Prussian first army as it tried to seek shelter in the woods and villages. A Prussian soldier remembered that: 'The bombshells crashed through the clay walls as if through cardboard; and finally raking fire set the village on fire. We withdrew to the left into the woods but it was not better there. Jagged hunks of wood and big tree splinters flew around our heads... We all felt we were in God's hands.' (Craig, 5, p.113) On the other hand, the superiority of Prussian infantry weapons and tactics was continually demonstrated when the Austrians tried to counter-attack. In one typical charge against Prussian needle guns 4,000 men set out but only 1,800 limping and badly wounded men returned. Although Benedek had saved 180,000 troops from the wreck they soon deteriorated into a disorganised rabble. About 60,000 tried to reach the safety of Königgratz but 'the waterworks, which protected the town, were opened and the soldiers who were crossing the causeways found themselves suddenly in a sea of water that grew deeper and deeper. Hundreds drowned. On the narrow ways everyone shoved together, gun carriages overturned and the fleeing soldiers of the Italian regiments fired off their weapons.' (Craig, 5, pp.172–3) As usual the arrangements for taking care of the wounded were entirely inadequate. The Prussians had only 2,000 hospital orderlies to cover the 45 square miles of the battlefield; bleeding and dying men lay for as many as three days and nights among the high corn and dense woods. Prussian deaths amounted to 1,929, Austrian and Saxon to 5,793. Having descended from his tower later that night Russell saw the remains of the Austrian army 'wounded on all sides, fragments of regiments marching, the roadsides lined with weary soldiers asleep, dressing their wounds or cooling their feet; on both sides of us wagons, guns, cavalry of all kinds... the debris of an army.' (Craig, 5, p.178)

Otto von Bismarck had spent the day with the King and Moltke feeling, as he put it later, as though he were playing poker with a stake of a million thalers he did not possess. When darkness fell no quarters had been arranged for him. After falling into a manure pit he spent a part of the night trying to sleep under the colonnade of the market place. He soon realised that this one battle had been enough to defeat the Austrians. His job was now to obtain a lasting peace treaty as quickly as possible. But just as it had taken him an enormous effort to persuade the King to go against the Austrians in the first place, now it would cost him even more nervous energy to persuade him to stop the fighting. The King and his army commanders wanted to march on into Vienna and to annex huge tracts of territory. In the treaty of Prague which was finally signed on 23 August 1866 Austria lost no German territory though she was obliged to surrender Venetia to Italy. However, she did lose all further influence in Germany. She had to agree to the Prussian annexation of Hanover, north Hesse, Nassau, Frankfurt, Schleswig and Holstein; to the incorporation of all the other German states north of the river Main into a Prussian dominated north **Federation**, to the termination of the Bund at Frankfurt and to the payment of a war indemnity. The southern states were to be formed into a separate South German Confederation but Bismarck made a treaty with them in which they agreed that if Germany were attacked their railways and armies would pass under Prussian control. To persuade the King of Prussia to refrain from demanding further concessions took Bismarck three days of arguing, sobbing, shouting, and threatening suicide and resignation, and of course a large quantity of broken crockery!

Prussia gains control of South Germany 1866–71

It was a very different *Landtag* which was opened on 5 August 1866. Gone were all the criticisms of Bismarck. Some idea of the way people's minds can be changed by a military victory can be seen in the letters of Rudolf von Ihering. On 1 May he wrote, 'Never has a war been incited so shamelessly... as the one Bismarck is currently trying to start against Austria. My innermost feelings are revolted...' By 9 August his innermost feelings had undergone a slight change! Now he 'bowed before the genius of Bismarck, who has achieved a masterpiece of political planning and actions such as are only rarely to be found in the pages of history.' (Simon, 7, pp.110–12) On 3 September 1866 the long struggle over the budget came to an end when the *Landtag* passed an Indemnity Bill which approved all the taxes which Bismarck's government had been illegally collecting since 1861. By 1 July 1867 a new constitution had been agreed for the North German Federation and Bismarck, with the reward money voted to him by the *Landtag*, had bought a new estate at Varzin which was bigger than all the original Bismarck lands put together.

There remained the problem of how the South German states were to be brought into the new North German Federation. There were two main obstacles. First, the southern states themselves were Catholic, hostile to Prussia and anxious to preserve their independence. Second, the French government had insisted that the frontiers of the new Prussian Confederation must end at the river Main. Napoleon III had no wish to see an even more powerful Prussian-led Germany just next door. One way of getting around the obstacles would be to gradually unite the south to the north by further military and economic agreements and persuade France to change her mind. The other alternative would be to trick France into attacking the North German Federation so that the South Germans would be obliged to honour the treaty they had signed in 1866. The problem of Luxemburg very soon offered an opportunity which might help either method. Luxemburg belonged to the King of the Netherlands but many of its inhabitants spoke a German dialect; it had been in the German Bund and there was a Prussian garrison in the Duchy. On 29 August 1866 the French ambassador had given Bismarck a written proposal that if France recognised a union between North and South Germany, Bismarck would allow the French to acquire Belgium and Luxemburg. Bismarck filed this piece of paper away carefully. On 19 March 1867 the King of Holland agreed to sell Luxemburg to the French. Immediately there was an outcry in Germany and talk of war. On 5 April the Dutch King, who had made his final acceptance conditional on Prussia's approval, changed his mind. In May at a conference in London it was finally agreed to make Luxemburg a neutral power and the Prussians consented to withdraw their garrison. Bismarck had high hopes that the French plans would persuade the South German states to join the North. He was disappointed. Very reluctantly they agreed to adopt the Prussian military system but mostly with serious reservations. Bavaria for example would not use the needle gun. Worse still, they only reluctantly agreed to his idea to strengthen the *Zollverein* by having an elected parliament to help run it. Bismarck's plan was that the Zoll parliament might grow into a real parliament for Germany. But when the elections were held in March 1868, 49 out of the 85 seats were won by men who wanted to keep their states independent. For the moment it looked as if the movement for Prussian domination of Germany had come to a halt.

Before the end of 1868 events in Spain set things in motion again. In September the Spanish Queen Isabella was deposed and the new Spanish government began to search for another ruler. In September 1869 they offered the throne to Leopold of Hohenzollern, the son of Prince Charles Anthony Hohenzollern. On the advice of his father, Leopold turned down the offer. However, in February 1870 Spain approached him again. This time the Prince and his son agreed and a telegram went off to Spain on 21 June accepting the throne. By 24 July the French government had heard the news. On 6 July the French Foreign Minister made an angry speech in the French parliament. He accused the Prussians of threatening France and hinted that France might use force if Leopold did not withdraw. The next day the French newspapers and the French public were howling with anger over this insult to their country.

Now we need to pause here for a moment to consider why the French were so annoyed. Leopold's branch of the Hohenzollern family was closely related to the Hohenzollern ruling King, William I of Prussia. The French reasoned that this was therefore part of a Prussian plot, engineered by Bismarck, to surround France with hostile powers. From their point of view events since 1866 looked very much like that. To the south-east was a new united Italy, who had allied with Prussia in the war against Austria; to the north-east was a much enlarged Prussia now in control of North Germany; their efforts to gain some sort of compensation by buying Luxemburg had been defeated; now they were being asked to tamely put up with a pro-Prussian royal family on their southern frontier. Gramont, the French foreign minister, decided that Prussia must be forced to admit that it had all been a carefully designed plot and be obliged to make Leopold withdraw. The French ambassador, Benedetti, rather like the Austrian Emperor almost seven years before (p.124), found the 74 year old King of Prussia taking the cure – this time at Ems. On 9 July William I admitted that he and Bismarck had discussed the matter and told the French ambassador that the family was reconsidering the candidature for the Spanish throne. On 12 July Prince Charles Anthony withdrew his son's offer to be King. So far it looked like a tremendous victory for the French. When Bismarck heard what had happened he considered resigning. The new North German Federation seemed to have been exposed in some double dealing and had then been forced to eat humble pie in a most humiliating fashion. But now Gramont made a terrible blunder. He pushed his luck too far by sending Benedetti back to the King on 13 July with the fresh demand that he should promise to *never* renew the Hohenzollern candidature again. This the King politely but firmly refused to do. Later that evening Bismarck was having dinner with Moltke and Roon when a telegram arrived from the King explaining what had happened. Bismarck edited the telegram to make it seem as though the king had humiliated Benedetti and then sent it to the newspapers for publication. The boot was now on the other foot; the French had been humiliated. On 19 July the French government declared war.

Study 29

Most experts thought that the French army would be too good for the Prussians. Since the war with Austria the Prussians had made the following changes –
a) The army of the North German Federation now numbered 983,064 with, of course, the *Landwehr* in reserve.
b) All the South German States honoured their agreement of 1866. This put the total strength up to 1,183,339. Their decision was helped by Bismarck's publication of the French plans of 1866 (p.131).
c) The artillery had converted completely to steel rifled breech loaders.
Now consider the table below and compare the two armies. Do you agree with the experts? If not where do you think they have gone wrong? You will need to look back to the table in study 7 (p.127) for information on the Prussian forces.

Numbers	Probably about 500,000 when mobilised.
Allies	None as neither the Italians nor Austrians would join them.
Recruitment & Training	Since January 1868 everyone had to do five months training but in each year group a minority who were unlucky in a ballot had to do five years followed by four on the reserve. They could buy substitutes. A reserve of *Gardes Mobiles* was formed for the rest who did fourteen days training per year but all on separate days.
Equipment a) Infantry b) Artillery	Chassepot: a rifled breech loader. Range 1,600 yards. Bore narrower than Needle Gun. Mitrailleuse – 25 barrels: 150 rounds per minute: range 2,000 yards. Rifled muzzle loaders as used in 1859 war.
Mobilization	Reservists had to proceed first to regimental depots which were not usually in areas where they lived. Then to concentration areas. Railways were under civilian management for mobilization.

table continued.

Administration	Maps of Germany had been prepared but not of France.
Supreme Command	Napoleon III, who was very ill, was in command but the Army Commanders, the War Cabinet and even the Empress could issue orders.
Battle experience	Crimean War. Italy 1859. Algeria. The army had won all three wars.

By 2 September France seemed to have been completely defeated. Her first army was shut up in the fortress of Metz and gradually being starved into submission. Her second army, over 100,000 complete with the Emperor himself, had been forced to surrender at Sedan. The German army had mobilised efficiently, the French army's mobilisation had been a disaster. The railway lines were clogged by supply trucks which could not be unloaded. Of those soldiers who had managed to reach their concentration points one in ten were with the wrong units. One group of reserves left Lille for their regimental depot on 18 July but their regiment was captured at Sedan before they even joined them! Even when the army finally went into action it was undermined by conflicting orders. The soldiers fought well and the new Chassepot rifles were effective. But the advantage of these and the Mitrailleuses were more than counteracted by the deadly efficiency of the Prussian artillery. A German soldier saw for himself the terrible effect of the steel Krupp breach loaders: 'In the large heaps of ruins the defenders lay all around... fearfully torn and mutilated by the German shells; limbs and bodies were blown from 30 to 50 paces apart, and the stones and sand were here and there covered with pools of blood... Some French were found burnt in their defensive positions and a large number of the wounded showed marks of the flames which had destroyed both uniforms and limbs.' (Howard, 32, p.171).

Just as Bismarck thought that the war had been won and peace was within his grasp, it was snatched away by revolution. On 4 September a republic was proclaimed in Paris and the Empress fled to England. The new government refused to make peace and the war went on. Very soon Paris was surrounded by 50 miles of Prussian siege lines. On 19 September, with the last telegraph lines cut, the French capital city seemed to be cut off from the outside world. Tenuous communication was, however, kept open by the use of balloons. Out of 65 flights from Paris, two were lost over the Atlantic and five were captured. The remainder succeeded in transporting 164 passengers, 5 dogs, 11 tons of dispatches, $2\frac{1}{2}$ million letters and numerous baskets of pigeons, into the provinces. The pigeons carried messages back to Paris on microfilm contained in tubes fitted to their tails. In this way the army in Paris tried to keep in touch with the new armies being formed in the provinces. Here the war became bitter and brutal. Guerilla units were formed to harass the Prussian army.

Foreign volunteers like Garibaldi joined the French in the fight. 'Murder and burning is now the order of the day on both sides', wrote a German officer in November (Howard, 32, p.379)

While the war dragged on Bismarck was fighting three campaigns of his own. He was persuading the southern German States to give up their independence and enter a Federation with the North. He was working hard to make King William I forget he was a Prussian and allow himself to be styled German Emperor. He was fighting Moltke and the army chiefs to get more control of the conduct of the war so that a peace treaty could be made at the earliest opportunity. The events of 18 January 1871 proved that his first two campaigns had succeeded. The 80 yards of the Hall of Mirrors at the Palace of Versailles were packed with German princes, aristocrats and high ranking generals to hear the proclamation of the new German Empire. Meanwhile Paris was being starved and bombarded into submission. The last rats, pets and animals from the Paris zoo were being eaten. Henry Labouchère, a reporter from the English Daily News, commented: 'I had a slice of spaniel the other day; it was by no means bad, something like lamb but I felt like a cannibal... experts tell me that poodle is by far the best...' On 2 January Bismarck finally got his way and the bombardment of Paris which he had been urging the army to undertake was begun. While Bismarck and the army leaders drank wine and argued at Versailles the Prussian guns were pumping up to 400 shells into Paris each day. Edmund de Goncourt's diary mentioned: 'streets full of handcarts trundling a few sticks of furniture... cafe proprietors replacing the mirrors shattered by the blast of exploding shells,... a first floor balcony hanging menacingly over the street.' Every so often there was an attempt at a break out but always with dreadful and horrifying casualties. An aide de camp found 'a little infantry man, barely 22, who had had both legs smashed at the ankle joint by the bursting of a shell. One of his feet had been completely torn off and the other was still hanging by the sinews and a strip of flesh.' With food rations exhausted, the news that the armies in the provinces had been beaten, and the defeat of the last attempted break out, the city surrendered on 26 January 1871. On 1 March the Prussian army were allowed a triumphal march through the defeated capital city and on 10 May the Treaty of Frankfurt finally brought the war to an end, France was to hand over the provinces of Alsace and Lorraine, and maintain a Prussian army of occupation until a war indemnity of five billion francs had been paid. The last of the three wars which had achieved German unity had been fought and won. The cost in German lives had been 28,208 dead and 88,488 wounded.

Study 30

The Baroness Spitzemburg was the wife of Charles Spitzemburg, the Württemberg envoy to Berlin. Throughout the main events of German unification she kept a diary. Read the extracts shown below and then answer the questions. This will help you to make sure that you have mastered the main events.

a) 8 July 1866: 'Until today it has been impossible for me to recall the days that have just gone by partly for lack of time but chiefly because I have been in too sad a mood to write down what I would like to forget...'

b) 19 August 1866: 'My dear husband looks splendid and is very pleased with the peace which is being concluded in Berlin...'

c) 13 July 1870: 'After supper a telegram arrived from my husband. It ran, "The Prince has renounced the candidature"... we women rejoice over a hateful evil averted...'

d) 14 July 1870: 'We had scarcely risen from table when a new telegram announced that: "After the renunciation of the Prince, Benedetti made further demands and was repulsed. Warlike events are in front of us, Charles."... we sat until 9 o'clock quite stiff from fear, anger and astonishment.'

e) 3 September 1870: 'The following telegram came very early. "2 September, 1.30 pm... the whole army has been taken prisoner." What a turn of events! Any German would be proud to have lived through this day! God be praised.'

f) 3 March 1871: 'What a peace treaty for us Germans! More magnificent and glorious than ever. United into one Reich, the greatest, the most powerful, the most feared in Europe... we are fortunate in that we not only saw the star of Germany's greatness rise but are still young enough to warm ourselves under its rays.' (Bohme, 8, pp.230–40).

Questions
1) In extract (a) what would the Baroness want to 'forget' and why?
2) In extract (b) what 'peace' is her husband pleased with and why?
3) In extract (c) explain what 'candidature' is referred to and why the Baroness is 'rejoicing'.
4) What were the 'further demands' referred to in (d)? Why are 'warlike events' in front of them? Why are they frightened, angry and astonished?
5) What event is referred to in extract (e)?
6) What peace treaty is referred to in (f) and why is the Baroness' point of view transformed between 1866 and 1871? Explain what this change is, when it first becomes obvious and why you think she changed her mind.

Study 31

Pictures 10–13 show Bismarck at different stages of his life. Study them carefully. First arrange them in chronological order and then complete a chart like the one below:

No. of picture	Year	Bismarck's age	Important events in Germany or in Bismarck's career at that time
	1834		
	1848		
	1870		
	1895		

Photographs opposite:
Bismarck at various stages of his life. 10 (Hulton Picture Library), 11 (Mansell Collection), 12 (Hulton Picture Library), 13 (Hulton Picture Library).

10.

11.

12.

13.

CHAPTER 9

German Nationalism

1815 – 71

In chapters 7 and 8, we have seen Germans demonstrating, risking prison sentences and exile, fighting on the barricades and dying on the battlefield, to make their 39 separate states into one German Empire. This chapter is intended to help you investigate two problems relating to this movement for unification. What caused it? How powerful was it? Before examining any of the evidence it is worth considering some of the theories which have been suggested by historians.

One explanation for the rise of German **nationalism** goes like this; during the Napoleonic Wars the 360 German states were invaded and conquered by the French. Humiliated by seeing their land overrun and their culture, language and institutions threatened by the invaders, the German people developed an aggressive nationalism. Their small states were ill equipped to compete with the superior resources of modern centralised and efficient countries like Britain and France. Leading German writers and philosophers put forward the view that to survive in the modern world the German states must unite into one Empire. This alone could deter invasion and the collapse of the German language and culture. These ideas were spread to most Germans through the education system, books, newspapers and mass meetings. German historians and philologists helped to encourage a pride in German culture by writing about great events in the past and collecting folk tales and music. The result was the emergence of a German nationalist movement.

2. An alternative explanation for the rise of German nationalism has been derived from the work of Karl Marx (1818–83). Marx was himself a German who was driven into exile in the 1840s. The modern theory of **communism** is based on his writings. History, Marx argued, is not made by ideas; rather, ideas like nationalism are themselves shaped by economic factors. Human behaviour and thought are the product of economic conditions, Marx believed. It is perhaps helpful to think of Marx's theory in terms of an iceberg. On the visible part of the iceberg are all the great theories and religions, mankind's visible thoughts. But, as everyone knows and as the Titanic discovered to its cost, the most important part of an iceberg is the nine-tenths of its mass which lies beneath the surface of the

water. Here lie all the economic motivations, like poverty and unemployment, which are the real factors controlling human actions and which themselves, superficially invisible, create the grand and noble theories. Applying Marx's idea to the rise of German nationalism the following explanation can be constructed: between 1815 and 1870 German society was under immense pressure caused by the impact of an industrial revolution on a very traditional conservative society. This conflict produced four frustrated and disorientated groups. There were industrialists and merchants whose businesses were unable to cope with overseas competition from Britain because of the obstacles imposed by numerous tariff barriers, different systems of currency, commercial law and weights and measures. There were migrants from the countryside into the towns whose family and village traditions had been uprooted. There were craftsmen and domestic workers whose traditional way of life and standard of living had been undermined by competition from the new factory produced goods. There were ever increasing numbers of the sons of **Junker** families and the professional classes trying to obtain the security and respectability of posts in the state bureaucracies. Now when the fabric of society is under stresses of this type a new religion or philisophy is desperately needed to replace the old beliefs which can no longer satisfy. People need a new belief to replace the old loyalties to family and local community; belief in a German nation or state which could remove all the painful pressures and set things to rights could be a perfect replacement.

3. Some German historians have seen the nationalist movement in Germany as enormously powerful; so powerful in fact that, even without Bismarck, unification would have eventually resulted.

4. Other historians, however, regarded the nationalist movement as pathetically weak. O. Pflanze (21) has argued that 'as an autonomous movement German nationalism was patently lacking in vitality before 1870. For six decades German nationalists had been confronted with the challenging task of uniting a badly divided people but only once in 1848 did the ideal of national unity generate sufficient popular support for the attempt. The achievements of 1864 and 1866 were attained by the Prussian state over the bitter opposition of the national movement.' (Pflanze, 21, pp.12–3) The nationalist movement, it has been suggested, was confined to a small group of mainly middle class Germans from the Protestant northern states rather than from the south. It rarely spread to the lower urban or rural classes which were essentially conservative. Only in exceptional circumstances, as for example in 1848, when serious unemployment and famine forced them into blind action, did the lower classes participate in the movement.

Study 32

As you have probably guessed, if you have read chapters 3 to 5 on Italian nationalism, you are about to be asked to use some evidence to decide for youself which of the theories are nearest to the truth. However, before doing this it is helpful to consider what sort of evidence would be needed. To support the first you would obviously need to find plenty of examples of nationalist writers and philosophers. Up to a point this evidence has already been provided on pp.109–11, chapter 7. But to show merely that there were plenty of nationalist writers between 1793 and 1815 is not enough to prove the validity of the first theory. The same reasoning would also apply to the second alternative theory. The work of List, explained in chapter 7, page 110, would certainly provide evidence for the idea that nationalism was an economically motivated theory espoused by disgruntled manufacturers and merchants. However, it does not go far enough to prove the whole idea. Finally, to decide whether the nationalist movement was powerful, as suggested in three, or weak as argued in four, you will need to consider what sort of evidence would prove the matter one way or another. Before going on to study the sources set out below, make charts like this one for each theory:

Theory 1

Types of evidence which would be needed to prove the theory	Examples found	Reference
Actual examples of the work of German nationalist writers.	Lectures of F. Schlegel The Grimm brothers' fairy tales	Ch.7, p.111, Ch.7, p.111.

Evidence on Nationalism

A. Literacy and Education

1. Ratio of children in school to adult population in following in the 1820s: Germany, 1 to 8; Holland, 1 to 12; England, 1 to 16; France, 1 to 30; Russia, 1 to 700. (Hamerow, 26, p.279). For further literacy comparisons see chapter 3, p.56, evidence 19.

2. Annual per head publication of newspapers in 1862: Austria, 0.98; Prussia, 3.73; Saxony, 3.15; Württemberg, 4.49; Baden, 3.66; Hanover, 2.94; France, 5.65; England, 20.82; Switzerland, 9.85. (Hamerow, 26, p.290)

3. Prices of Newspapers in 1860s in Prussia. Yearly subscriptions: *Volks Zeitung*, 9 marks; *Neue Preussiche Zeitung*, 30 marks; *Social-Demokrat*, 7 marks. (Hamerow, 26, p.292)
   At this time 70% of the working population earned less than 300 marks a year.
   'Even a generous approximation of the ratio of readers to subscribers suggests that out of a population of 19 million there could have been little more than about $1\frac{1}{2}$ million with an understanding of public affairs derived from the press. This would represent about 20% of the adult population.' (Hamerow, 26, p.292)

B. Participation in Politics and Pressure Groups

4. *Participation of voters in elections to Prussian Electoral College 1849–63.* (Hamerow, 26, p.302)

Classes of voters	Average tax paid	No. of eligible voters for each member of electoral college chosen.	Average partici-pation of eligible voters
First class	168 marks	7.4	53.2%
Second class	54 marks	19.9	40.6%
Third class	less than 9 marks	128.0	23.5%

Note: elections to the Prussian lower house were indirect (see **indirect voting**) and voters were divided into three categories according to their wealth.

5. *Occupations of members elected to Prussian lower house 1848–66* (Hamerow, 26, p.306)

Occupation	*1849*	*1855*	*1862*	*1866*
Agriculturalist	17.4%	22.3%	23.6%	23.9%
Civil service	16.0%	33.7%	12.9%	20.5%
Judicial officers	20.9%	16.0%	26.7%	15.6%
Merchants & industrialists	6.9%	4.3%	7.2%	8.1%
Clerks, handcraft workers, labourers	0	0	0.9%	0

6. *Occupations of members of Frankfurt Parliament 1848–9* (Hamerow, 27, p.124)

Occupation	No.	Occupation	No.
Jurists	200	Nobles	90
University professors	49	Principals & teachers	40
Writers & journalists	35	Merchants & industrialists	30
Clergy	26	Physicians	12
Handicraft workers	4	Peasants	1

7. Participation of voters in elections to Frankfurt Parliament 1848: The percentage of those eligible to vote who actually voted in: Annaburg (in Prussia), 25%; Leipzig (in Saxony), 40%. The average for all German states was about 50%. (Hamerow, 27, p.123)

8. *Membership and size of the Nationalverein* ★ 1859–66 (Hamerow, 26, p.322)

Year	Number of members	Newspaper sales
1860	5,000	5,000
1861	15,000	
1862	25,000	6,000
1863	23,000	
1864	21,000	
1865	11,000	
1866	5,000	

★ The Nationalverein was founded in 1859 to promote German unification. The yearly subscription was 4 marks.

9. *Distribution of membership of Nationalverein, September 1860* ★ (Hamerow 26, pp.323–4)

State	No. of members	% of pop.	State	No. of members	% of pop.
Baden	433	0.05	Bavaria	193	0.005
Bremen	191	0.59	Frankfurt am		
Hanover	194	0.06	Main	98	0.37
Hamburg	163	0.24	Hesse Darmstadt	32	0.16
Saxony	124	0.02	Nassau	109	0.10
Württemberg	45		Prussia	3,073	0.04

★ Note: you should see map 5, page 108, with this distribution table.

10. Occupational distribution of members of Nationalverein from a sample of 588 members who attended local meetings or who subscribed to funds (Hamerow, 26, p.325):

Lawyers	133	Physicians	32
Merchants	75	Landed Proprietors and Rentiers	25
Professors and Teachers	56	Editors and Journalists	24
Judicial Officers	54	Booksellers	20
Industrialists	37	Apothecaries	20
Municipal Officials	36	Master Craftsmen and Handicraft Workers	19

11. Speech by J. C. Bluntschli, Professor of Law at Heidelburg during a banquet celebrating a convention of German jurists: 'All these phenomena which we have for several years been finding once again in Germany in the most diverse branches of life, all these organisations of singers, gymnasts★, sharpshooters★★ economists★★★, jurists etc have a political significance. They are symptoms of a political life which exists and grows in the nation. I would like to compare all these organisations to brooks which flow towards a great river which continually grow bigger until the

river embraces them and carries them away★★★★. That is how the electric current of unification flows through the hearts and the mind of the German nation, a current which sweeps all of us along and which also takes with it him who does not want to go.' (Hamerow, 26, p.339)

★ Between 1859–64 the number of gym societies grew from 100 to 2,000 (Hamerow, 26, p.376)

★★ In 1862 the total membership of the sharpshooting societies stood at 11,000. (Hamerow, 26, p.357)

★★★ The congress of German economists at Stuttgart in 1859 attracted over 300. (Hamerow, 26, p.340)

★★★★ 'The total number of members in the various political and quasi-political associations was small, no more than a few hundred thousand. But they experienced a powerful influence over public affairs on the basis of property, status and education. They constituted the decisive classes of society. The others paid taxes, bore arms, obeyed, fought and died.' (Hamerow, 26, p.358)

C Participation in riots

12. Occupations of the 230 killed in the March Days 1848, Berlin (see chapter 7, p.114):
    74 of the dead were handicraftsmen, 13 were merchants, 2 were students (Hamerow, 27, p.102). 40% of the dead were journeymen (Kitchen, 24, p.326). Two thirds of the dead were born in Berlin; at that time the percentage of the Berlin population who were actually born in the capital was less than 50% (Tilly, 29, p.216).

13. Involvement in the 1848–9 revolutions:
    (a) There were an estimated 600,000 man days of violence, which if evenly distributed would have involved more than one German adult out of every 50. Newspaper reports reveal 2,200 deaths.★
    (b) In 1851 the Prussian police had a list of 279 wanted revolutionaries. These represented nearly 100 different occupations; nearly one third were from the upper-middle class – army officers, merchants, lawyers, estate owners. (Tilly, 29, pp.221–2)
    ★ Most of the figures used in Tilly are based on an index of collective violence which was constructed from newspaper reports on incidents involving more than 20 persons.

14. *Urbanization and disorders* (Tilly, 29, p.215)

(a)

Years	% of disorders registered in cities	Year	% of population in cities
1816–47	55	1840	15
1850–1913	75	1880	40

(b)

Indicator	1816–47*	1850–81**	1882–1913**
Number of disorders	175	201	194
% growth of urban population	99	200	149

    ★   Prussia, Bavaria, Saxony
   ★★ Prussia, Bavaria, Saxony, Kassel, Wiesbaden, Schleswig-Holstein

15. *Violent Events and Food Prices* (Graph from Tilly, 29, p.214)

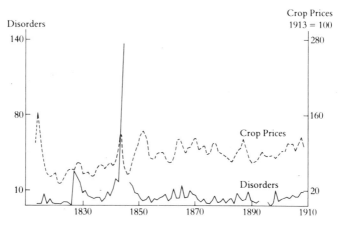

About one fifth of the disorders in 1830 and more than two-thirds of those in 1846–7 were related to food prices.

16. *Duration and size of disorders* (Tilly, 29, p.212)

Period	Number of disorders	Average duration (days)	Average size	Man days per year
1816–47	323	1.5	3,200	48,450
1848–49	197	1.2	3,000	354,600
1850–81	236	1.1	1,120	9,086

17. *Violence and Migration* (Tilly, 29, pp.211 and 216)

Areas with more than 20 disorders 1816–48	Were they gaining or losing population by migration?
Nassau	Losing
Electoral Hesse	Losing
Breslau/Silesia	Losing
Berlin	Gaining

D. Occupations and Social Pressures

18. Posts in the government bureaucracies and judiciaries of German states:

    (a) Length of time before a qualified person obtained a job in the bureaucracy: 1830s – 6.6 years, 1850s – 10.4 years. (*Past and Present.* no. 41, December 1968, p.118)

    (b) Only 2% of university graduates managed to obtain well paid posts. (Sagarra, 24, p.266)

    (c) Many job hunters had to accept unpaid posts while they waited to get in to the bureaucracy or legal profession. In 1840, 2,500 unpaid lawyers were employed in the judiciary. (Sagarra, 24, pp.266–7)

    (d) The career of the Oldenburg District Governor before the 1848 revolutions:

    14–19: Grammar School ⎫
    19–22: University ⎬ Parental support required
    23–27: Unpaid and Junior posts ⎭

    30: Paid post   Still insufficient to marry on (Sagarra, 24, pp.266–7)

19. Illegitimacy rates (per 100 births):

    (a) 1845–50
    Saxony – 14.8   Prussia – 7.5   France – 7.4
    England – 6.7   Bavaria – 20.5 (Hamerow, 27, p.233)

    (b) In Bavaria.
    1700s – 3   1800s – 20   1850s – 24 (Sagarra, 24, p.377)

20. *Emigration Overseas* (Cipolla, 30, p.123 and statistical appendix) Population in millions, emigrants in hundreds.

	1821–1850		1851–1870	
	Pop.	*Emig.*	*Pop.*	*Emig.*
Germany	25.0–34.0	645	40.8	1,450
Austria-Hungary	30.7		35.8	71
France	30.5–35.8		36.1	63
Britain	14.1–20.8		26.1	2,885
Italy	19.7–24.4		26.8	32

21. Employment in the craft industries

    (a) The percentage of the Prussian population in the artisan class:
    1843 – 12.8,   1849 – 16.5,   1852 – 16,   1861 – 14.9. (Hamerow, 26, p.80)

    (b) Numbers of Prussian journeymen and apprentices for every 100 Masters:
    1849 – 76,   1852 – 81,   1855 – 83,   1858 – 93,   1861 – 104. (Hamerow, 26, p.78)

(c) Memorial from Erlangen Guild Organisation to Bavarian parliament, 1827–8:

'The presiding officers... propose by this petition to present a picture of the overcrowding of those engaged in industry in this city, for out of 9,000 inhabitants there are 1,200 practising a craft... because of this overcrowded condition we have an increase in destitution and complete impoverishment...'(Hamerow, 27, pp.30–1)

E. Contemporary Comment

22. Bismarck's Memoirs (written 1890):
'In order that German patriotism should be active and effective, it needs as a rule to hang on the peg of dependence on a dynasty... It is as a Prussian, a Hanoverian, a Württemberger, a Bavarian or a Hessian rather than as a German that the German is disposed to give proof of patriotism, and in the lower orders and the parliamentary groups it will be long before it is otherwise.' (Hamerow, 27, p.19)

23. August Ludwig, 1869:
'The civic struggle for freedom in Germany has down to the most recent years been waged exclusively by the middle classes... the mass of the people stood aloof from this struggle, devoting to it even the mere interest of a spectator only in certain moments, and particularly in a few cases which affected them directly.' (Hamerow, 26, p.269)

24. G. Rumelin. Letter about the election campaign to bring Württemberg into the North German Federation after the war with Austria in 1866:
'We have two great main schools of thought... the one agitates for direct entry into the North German Federation... To it belong the great majority of all educated people, the liberals and supporters of the Nationalverein, the protestant clergy... On the opposite side are three different parties: (1) the dynasty with the Court, (2) the Democrats whose goal is a South German and Swiss Confederation with cantons... (3) the Catholics...' (Hamerow, 26, p.383)

25. The Views of Ernst Arndt (1769–1860):
'Let us hate the French strongly, and let us hate our own French who dishonour and ravage our energy and our innocence.' (pamphlet 1818)
'What is the fatherland of the German? Name me the great country! Where the German tongue sounds and sings lieder in God's praise, that's what it ought to be... That is the fatherland of the German where anger roots out foreign nonsense, where every Frenchman is called enemy, where every German is called friend...' (poem 'The German Fatherland'). (Kedourie, 40, pp.601, 69)

26. The Views of Richard Wagner⋆ (1813–83):
'When we have liberated the German folk we shall sail across the seas,

plant here and there a young Germany... bring up the noblest of children, children like unto Gods... We shall do things Germanly and grandly... the rays of German freedom and gentleness shall light and warm the French and cossacks, the bushmen and the Chinese, (Speech to a patriotic club, Saxony, 1848). 'One thing is now clear to me... with Germany's well being stands or falls my art ideal; without Germany's greatness my art was only a dream: if this dream is to become reality, then, as a matter of course Germany must also achieve its predestined greatness.' (Letter) (Kohn, 31, pp.196–7, 210)

* Wagner was a German composer who, as a republican (see **republic**), took part in the 1848 revolutions. His dream, which he finally fulfilled, was to turn the German folk legend of the Nibelungen into a series of operas.

27. Heinrich Heine* (1797–1856), Letter from exile in Paris, August 1848: 'The news which I received from my country increases my anxiety... our enemies have got the upper hand in Germany. The so called national parties, the fanatics of Germanism, are strutting about in their overbearing conceit, as ridiculous as they are coarse. Their boastful rantings are incredible. They dream that their turn at playing the leading role in world history has arrived and that they will gather all the lost German tribes from East to West to the fold of German nationalism.' (Kohn, 31, p.113)

* A German poet. Born a Jew, he converted to protestantism but his sympathy with the ideals of the French revulution led to his exile in Paris from 1831.

28. Leopold von Gerlach: 'Why do I detest **patriotism**, the dearly beloved fatherland and things of that sort? Partly because of their hypocrisy and emptiness, but there is also something wrong with them. Loyalty to the king and love for our fellow men, which can just as well be extended to Russians, Englishmen, Frenchmen, are quite enough.' (Hamerow, 26, p.191)

29. Friedrich Engels* (1820–95) 'The longing for a unitary fatherland had a very material background... it was the demand of the practical merchant and industrialist, arising out of direct business need, for the clearing away of all the historically transmitted rubbish of the petty states which stood in the way of the free development of trade and man. It was the desire for the removal of all the superfluous friction which the German businessman had to overcome at home if he wanted to enter the world market... German unity had become an economic necessity.' (1895) (Hamerow, 26, pp.381–2)

* Engels was born in Germany but like his friend Marx spent most of his life in England. He worked with Marx on some of his most famous books.

Study 33

Don't worry if you have found this rather a confusing package of evidence. It was deliberately designed to include every type of evidence from memoirs to quite difficult graphs and statistics. If you have read the previous section on Italy (see ch. 6) you should be now be developing some skill in deciding which can be trusted and which must be treated with care. Below are some statements intended to help you sort out which of the theories on German nationalism you support. Each statement is followed by the numbers of the evidence from the above list which relate to it. Write down the theories you prefer. You will need your notes to write the essay at the end of chapter 11, p.174!

A. Causes of German nationalism

1. German nationalism developed as a reaction to French power and aggression (25, 26, 27).
2. Germany between 1815 and 1870 was a country undergoing severe economic and social stress and was therefore ripe for the growth of nationalism (14, 15, 16, 17, 18, 19, 20, 21, 29).
3. Although there was stress in nineteenth-century Germany, there is little evidence to suggest that the people who supported nationalism were the same groups as those who suffered most from these tensions (10, 14, 15, 16, 17, 18, 19, 20, 21, 29).
4. The standard of German education and other cultural media was high enough to make the transmission of the new idea of nationalism relatively simple (1, 2, 3, 4).

B. Extent of German nationalism

5. German nationalism was a powerful and widespread movement which embraced all sections of the population and all regions (4, 7, 8, 9, 10, 11, 12, 13, 22, 23, 24, 28).
6. German nationalism was a weak and divided movement which declined after 1848, failed to spread to any class other than a small group of middle class merchants and industrialists, and never penetrated south Germany (4, 5, 6, 7, 8, 9, 10, 11, 12, 13, 22, 23, 24, 28).

Now carefully record your reasons for agreeing/disagreeing with each of the statements, referring to the numbers of the pieces of evidence which you regard as important. The figures in brackets are intended to help you by referring to the pieces of evidence which relate to each statement.

CHAPTER 10

Bismarck and German Unification
1815 – 71

The Problem

Between 1815 and 1863, German unification seemed to make no progress at all. Yet it was finally accomplished in the space of only six years between 1864 and 1870. To most German historians and many others, the explanation was quite simple and straightforward. Unification was made possible by the arrival of Otto von Bismarck as the King's chief minister. In 1879, Dr Moritz Busch wrote: 'In a hundred years Prince Bismarck will take his place in the thoughts of our people, by the side of Luther: the liberator of our political life from the pressure of the foreigner by the side of the liberator of our consciences from the tyranny of Rome.' Symbolic statues representing Bismarck as Germany's armourer forging German unity became fashionable. Rudolf von Ihering was not the only German who looked upon Bismarck as a sort of long awaited Messiah. On 19 August 1866 he wrote, 'Oh my friend what enviable luck to be living in this time... for years I have envied the Italians that they succeeded in what seemed for us to lie only in the distant future. I have wished for a German Cavour and Garibaldi as Germany's political messiah. And overnight he has appeared in the person of the much abused Bismarck...' (Hewison 3, p.112). Well into the twentieth century, this view was still being expressed by German historians. P. Kluke wrote: 'The final act of the foundation of the reich was the personal achievement and performance of one great statesman...' (Bohme, p.36). However, as in the very similar case of Cavour (p.62) contemporary historians are not nearly so ready to accept this belief in the power of one individual to shape the course of history. In this chapter, you will be given a chance to look at both the legendary view of Bismarck and some of the arguments of its critics. As before you will be expected to make your own decisions and argue your case in an essay.

'The Wasted Years'

According to Bismarck, the reason why nothing was achieved in the long period between 1815 and 1863 was that no-one had realised that a vast change like the unification of Germany could only be accomplished by force. This is what Bismarck meant in his famous speech to the Landtag financial committee in 1863: 'Prussia must build-up and preserve her strength for the favourable moment which has already come and gone many times. Her borders under the Treaties of Vienna are not favourable for the healthy existence of the State. Germany is not looking to Prussia's liberalism, but to her power;... the great questions of the day cannot be settled by speeches and majority decisions – that was the great mistake of 1848 and 1849 — but by iron and blood.' (Simon, 16, p.196) The liberal university professors and lawyers who were elected to the Frankfurt Parliament in 1848 thought that a new Germany could be created by argument, voting and persuasion. Yet even after their failure the German liberals (see **liberalism**) still persisted with this dream – that if only they could reform Prussia and turn her into some sort of constitutional monarchy the rest of Germany would troop voluntarily into a united Germany. In 1862, when Bismarck was made Minister President they had still not learnt the lessons of 1848–9 and Bismarck had to fight their opposition as well as Austria's. Prussia's kings and ministers, in Bismarck's view, were no better than the liberals. They could not seem to understand that Prussia was a great and powerful state who could unite Germany by force. If only they had taken firm action in 1849–50 instead of copying the liberals with the feeble Erfurt plan. If only Prussia's rulers had had the strength and determination to throw off their foolish feelings of loyalty and respect for Austria and take full advantage of the Crimean war or the war in northern Italy (p.120) they could have unified Germany before 1862. According to Bismarck therefore Prussia had wasted her opportunities before 1863. Bismarck, against the misguided opposition of Prussia's King and liberals, had a hard struggle to put her on the right path.

But is this picture of the great minister struggling single handed to unify his nation against almost impossible odds really acceptable? In a book written in 1958, W.E. Mosse argued: 'If Bismarck played his hand with great skill, it was a good hand in the first place.' (Mosse, 41, p.372) The best card in his hand was that in 1862 the diplomatic situation in Europe was exceptionally favourable for German unification. The major obstacles to German unification were the Holy Alliance between Austria and Russia and the hostility of France. Yet by 1862 these had both been removed. Austria had failed to help Russia in the Crimean war and Russia had made an alliance against Austria during the war in northern Italy (p.64). The two countries now hated and distrusted each other and the Holy Alliance was in ruins. France was ruled by Napoleon III who dreamed of overthrowing the 1815 settlement and replacing it by re-organising Europe along the lines of nationalism. By 1862 he had already begun this process and a new Kingdom of Italy stood on Austria's southern borders. Friendless, her trade stagnating, her different racial minorities causing more and more trouble, defeated in war, Austria was no longer the formidable barrier to change in Germany that she had been in 1848–9. The much abused professors of the Frankfurt Parliament and the supposedly feeble King Frederick William IV of Prussia did not have this strong diplomatic card in 1848–51. At that time the Austro-Russian friendship was still intact and Austria's power was still formidable. Bismarck, it could be argued, had inherited a very favourable diplomatic situation.

Nor was this all; Bismarck held some other very useful cards. One of his strongest was that by 1860 Prussia's economic strength was formidable. The rapid growth of its population, the expansion of the **Zollverein** (p.113), the railway network and new joint stock companies and banking facilities had brought about an industrial revolution. In 1850–60 the length of railway line in Prussia increased by 46% and the weight of goods carried by the railways went up 6 times. The cost of transporting a ton of coal in Prussia's Ruhr industrial area fell from 40 pfennigs in 1820 to two pfennigs in 1850. Between 1815 and 50, 37 joint stock companies had been founded in Prussia; by 1859, 107 more were in existence. The output of coal in Prussia's Ruhr coalfields increased from 1,961,000 tons in 1850 to 8,526,000 tons in 1865. In 1846, Berlin's 33 machine-building shops employed 2,821 workers; by 1861 there were 67 firms with 6,313 workers (Millward and Saul, 28, pp.380–410).

All this rapid economic growth had three important consequences for Bismarck's position in 1862. First Prussia had already gone a long way towards gaining economic control over Germany. By 1860 the Prussian bank note, the Prussian coinage and the Prussian commercial legal code dominated the Zollverein. After 1859 the Austrian currency had virtually ceased to circulate even in Bavaria (Millward and Saul, 28, p.385). Second, Prussia could rely on an excellent iron and steel industry for her weapons and plentiful railways for mobilising her army. Third, Bismarck had the money to fight his wars. Previous Prussian governments had sensibly made sure that they had a share in the increasing economic prosperity. The 1842 Prussian Railway Law ensured that in return for providing one seventh of the capital for building each private railway line the government could collect a useful amount of interest. With this income supplemented by the increasing import and export dues from the Zollverein, the sales of timber from the Crown lands for such things as pit props and railway sleepers, the large royalties paid for mining rights and the money from the state monopoly on the production and sale of tobacco, the Prussian government had a very healthy annual tax surplus and had built up an enviable state treasury. Bismarck was able to write on 24 March 1865, 'Our financial balance for 1864 shows that we need only two million from the state treasury for the Danish war. Everything else is covered by the surplusses for 1863–4. (Stern, 15, p.63) Unlike poor King Charles I of England, Bismarck was therefore able to fight his first war without having to ask the angry Landtag for extra taxes. With the aid of his clever Jewish banker and financial advisor, Bleichroder, he also succeeded in fighting the war with Austria without the need for extra taxes. When the Cologne-Minden railroad had been built the Prussian government had been given the right to take over the railway at some future date. Bleichroder arranged for this right to be sold back to the private owners of the railway for 13 million thalers. In his retirement Bismarck paid tribute to his banker. 'Bleichroder put at my disposal the necessary money for war. That was an undertaking which, under the circumstances of those days, when I was almost as close to the gallows as to the throne, compels gratitude.' (Stern, 15, p.48). When Bismarck came to power he therefore had an enormously useful advantage denied to his predecessors – he had the blood, iron, coal and gold needed to unify Germany.

Another strong card which Bismarck held in 1862 was the Prussian army (see page 127 for details). Generations of Prussian leaders had regarded the army as the main item for government expenditure. In 1855 for example, out of a total spending of 335 million marks, 91 million went on the army and navy. This should be compared with 7 million on public education and 5 million on penal institutions (Hamerow, 26, p.276). Generally, the money had been put to good use. By the time Bismarck came to power the Needle gun (p.127) had already been accepted as the main infantry weapon. Bismarck himself admitted his debt to the army when he remarked after his retirement, 'Cavour and Crispi were greater men than I. I had the Prussian state and army behind me; these men had nothing.' Nor was Bismarck as isolated and friendless as he liked to make out. Most Prussians, including the king himself, resented what they called, 'the defeat or humiliation of Olmutz', and were not opposed to Bismarck's anti-Austrian policy. Indeed, before Bismarck came on the scene they had beaten off several Austrian attempts to break up the Zollverein (p.119). Also the Prussian liberals, although they were putting up a fight against Bismarck in the Landtag, were already psychologically prepared to trade in their liberal views in exchange for German unification. Generations of German students had been taught Hegel's philosophy that the state is 'the divine idea as it exists on earth.' As long ago as 1836 Menzel had written 'The hero and statesman who subjects everything to his tyrannical will and tramples upon justice can be excused if historical situations demand his terrorism' (Kohn, 31, p.98). Ludwig von Rochau had argued, 'Neither a principle, nor an idea nor a treaty will unite the splintered German forces, but only a superior force which swallows up the rest.' (Pflanze, 21, p.48). The businessmen of the Nationalverein (p.142), desperate to remove the remaining obstacles to their commercial and industrial prosperity, were arguing that Prussia must take the lead in unification. It would only need a clear lead from Prussia, some small success, before they abandoned their liberal opposition and welcomed Bismarck's policy.

There is a strong case, therefore, for arguing that Bismarck was very fortunate. When he came to power in 1862 the economic, diplomatic, military and intellectual foundations for German unity had already been laid.

So far from being 'wasted' the years before 1862 had played an important part in the final achievement of German unification.

Bismarck the Master Planner

The other part of the legend about the reasons for the success of German unification is the idea that it was all due to Bismarck's master plan. Bismarck, the argument runs, had a very clear and precise aim and a carefully formulated stage by stage plan by which the aim was to be realised. His aim was to use Prussia's strength to unify Germany. His master plan was supposed to have worked something like this. First, to obtain Russian neutrality or friendship for Prussia. This it is claimed, he did with the Alvensleben Convention of 1863 (p.124). Second, to find a way of tricking Austria into declaring war on Prussia so that King William I and his supporters were forced to fight. It is alleged that this was his reason for intervening in the Schleswig-Holstein affair in 1864 (p.126). Third, to ensure French neutrality in the coming war with Austria. This was supposed to have been achieved in the Biarritz meeting (p.126). Fourth, to make sure that after Austria had been defeated she was treated leniently. This was because another war, this time with France, would be needed to bring in the south German states. An angry Austria might have allied with France against Prussia. That was why, the argument runs, Bismarck worked so hard to make the King and the army give up their plans for marching into Vienna (p.130). Fifth, to manipulate France into declaring war on Prussia so that the south German states would come to Prussia's aid and a united Germany would be attained. The Hohenzollern candidature and the Ems telegram were, according to the legend, the clever means by which Bismarck achieved this (p.133). So between 1863 and 1870 everyone was manipulated by Bismarck, the clever puppet master, according to the scenario he had planned. Bismarck the master planner succeeded in unifying Germany where all others had failed.

However, critics of this view do not even agree that Bismarck's aim was to unify Germany. 'Bismarck had nothing to do with the nationalism of the nineteenth and twentieth centuries and its blind fanaticism,' argued the German historian Ritter (Pflanze, 21, p.4). Bismarck's aim was to preserve and extend the power of Prussia. He was a Prussian and not a German nationalist. Unless something was done quickly the unification of Germany would swallow up Prussia and terminate her separate identity. It was Bismarck's task therefore to take over the leadership of the German unification movement and manage it in such a way that Prussia emerged intact and more powerful than before. It was important therefore that the new Germany should be **kleindeutsch** and not **grossdeutsch**. The inclusion of the Austrian Germans would overwhelm the Prussians. But why did Bismarck think it was so important to preserve Prussia? Because he believed that the Prussian form of government and society was an excellent one. A King governing through a loyal bureaucracy and army recruited from his **Junker** landowning families; local rural society dominated by stern but kind local landowners; this was a workable system worth retaining. It made Bismarck's task all the more challenging that the industrial revolution was threatening the Junker aristocracy which he wished to preserve. In 1816, the percentage of Prussians employed in agriculture, fisheries and forestry was 78; by 1867 it was down to 48. Between 1824 and 1834 in Prussia east of the Elbe, 230 Junker estates were declared bankrupt. Some Junkers escaped from the agricultural depression by working hard to modernise their farms. Others transferred their attentions to obtaining posts in the government bureaucracy and army. In 1820 the nobility held 24% of the regular administrative posts; by 1852 they had increased their share to 32%. The sons of landowning families were to be found studying hard at university to gain the necessary qualifications. Between 1820 and 1870 the landowners' share of those studying law as a preparation for the civil service rose from seven to fifteen per cent (*Past and Present*, no. 41, December 1968, pp.113–4). In 1861, 65% of Prussia's officers, 86% of her Generals and Colonels and more than 70% of the holders of the leading diplomatic posts were aristocratic (Hamerow, 26, p.60). It was not Bismarck's aim to unify 'Germany' but to preserve and enlarge this sort of society. 'I am a Junker and I want the advantages of being one' he said in a speech in 1849.

Nor do all historians believe that Bismarck had a well worked out master plan. This is a legend spread by Bismarck's memoirs and embellished by German nationalist historians. Bismarck's own comments elsewhere on his methods in fact suggest an entirely different approach: 'There is no exact science of politics... the professors and their imitators in the newspapers constantly decry the fact that I have not revealed a set of principles by which I direct my policies... politics is neither arithmetic nor mathematics...' (Pflanze, 21, p.88) 'In chess one should never base a move on the positive assumption that the other player in turn will make a certain move. For it may be that this won't happen and then the game is lost... one must always have two irons in the fire.' (Pflanze, 21, p.90). In fact, Bismarck had no master plan but was, like Cavour, brilliant at making use of whatever opportunities came his way. He often made bad mistakes but he was clever enough to remedy them. A re-examination of the alleged five stage master plan outlined on p.153 will demonstrate this.

1. *Obtaining the friendship of Russia and France — Alvensleben, 1863.* (p.124)

Did Bismarck's handling of the Polish rebellion really pave the way for uniting Germany under Prussia? There must be serious doubts about this. First of all it seems that his motive for intervening had nothing to do with German unification. What Bismarck feared was that the revolt might spread to Prussia's Polish subjects in Posen, and that the Russian government might be too tolerant to the Poles. Bismarck had an almost irrational hatred and fear of the Poles. They were Catholic and the German liberals often supported them. Two years before, in a letter to his sister, he had declared his intention to 'Harry the Poles so that they despair of their lives. I have every sympathy for their plight, but if we are to exist we can do nothing other than exterminate them.' (Pflanze, 21, p.186). His excessive haste in fact almost ruined the excellent diplomatic position which he had inherited when he came to power. There was almost a French, English and Austrian alliance against Prussia because of the strong liberal sympathy for the Poles in all three countries. His action even threatened the good relations between Prussia and Russia because the Russians resented his interference, and because the publicity attracted by the affair led the other three great powers to gang up against Russia. Luckily he had the good sense to lie low after making the initial mistake, and in the end the friendship with Russia emerged intact: 'Our dear Bismarck is a terrible blunderer,' remarked Tsar Alexander II (Palmer, 13, p.83): Austrian relations with Russia had become even worse, because the Austrians had dared to oppose Russia's Polish policy. But if this was the first step on the road to Prussian control of Germany it was surely a step sideways rather than forward. (Taylor, 4, p.51; Palmer, 13, p.82: Medlicott, 19, p.35; Mitchell, 2, p.19; Taylor, 20, p.10; Moses, 1, p.42; Pflanze, 21, p.185; Crankshaw, 14, p.148).

2. *Using the Schleswig-Holstein affair to trick Austria into declaring war, 1864–6* (p.126)

Even before studying the evidence, the idea that when Bismarck persuaded the Austrians to join Prussia in the war against Denmark he was already looking ahead to 1866 and a way of tricking Austria into declaring war on Prussia, seems far fetched. If this was his aim why bother to 'paper over the cracks' at Gastein (p.126)? Why not have the war right away? Because, say the supporters of the legend, Bismarck needed to make sure of France and required really clear evidence of Austrian aggression to convince King William I that he must fight a fellow German Monarch. This may be true but another view seems much more likely. Bismarck probably had two policies, two 'irons in the fire.' At least up until the Gastein agreement he hoped that he could persuade Austria to give up north Germany without a fight. In fact he would have preferred this solution. On 6 August 1864, he wrote to the Prussian ambassador in Austria: 'A true German and conservative policy is only possible when Austria and Prussia are united and take the lead. From this high stand point, an intimate alliance of the two powers has been our aim from the outset... if Prussia and Austria are not united politically Germany does not exist...' (Bohme, 8, p.128). From the start of the Schleswig-Holstein crisis Bismarck's aim was to annex the two duchies to Prussia. The joint action with Austria was a means to this end. Without it the other powers would be more likely to intervene, as in 1848–9, or German nationalist opinion would succeed in promoting a union of the Duchies under Augustenburg. Gradually his aim widened to acquiring Prussian predominance in north Germany but while he was prepared to fight Austria to achieve this if he had to, he always hoped that Austria could be persuaded to give way without a war. This explains why he was prepared to 'paper over the cracks' at Gastein and why, as late as May 1866, he allowed an intermediary to explore possible compromises. There was no master plan, only a clever exploitation of every lucky incident which arose on the way. Bismarck could not be sure that the Danes would refuse to compromise over the Duchies, that the Austrians would begin troop movements in March 1866 and break their agreement with Prussia by taking the problem of the Duchies to the Diet on 30 May 1866. He merely exploited such incidents when they came. (Pflanze, 21, p.233; Moses, 1, p.44; Taylor, 20, p.114; Mitchell, 2, p.22; Medlicott, 19, p.38; Palmer, 13, p.90; Taylor, 4, p.54; Crankshaw, 14, p.163, and chaps X–XII.)

3. Making sure of French neutrality at Biarritz on 4 October 1865 (p.126)

According to the legend Bismarck tricked Napoleon III at the famous meeting in Biarritz. In return for some vague promises about possible territorial compensation along the Rhine or in Belgium or Luxemburg, Napoleon III promised not to help Austria in any future war with Prussia. This view seems very unlikely. For a start, we shall never know what happened at the meeting because no official records were kept. Bismarck had not yet decided whether he would need to go to war with Austria. The main point of discussion seems to have been Venetia. Napoleon III wanted to acquire it for Italy and was trying to make sure that Bismarck had not promised to help Austria to defend it. If Bismarck had hoped to tie Napoleon III down to a definite agreement then he failed. He told an official at his Foreign Ministry on 23 October that 'Napoleon will dance a cotillion with us, without being clear in his mind when it will begin or what figures it will include' (Palmer, 13, p.108). This may be true but since Napolean III was not tied down by any definite agreement Bismarck could not be sure at what point he might end the dance. When, and if, Bismarck went to war with Austria, Napoleon III was an unknown factor waiting in the wings. No wonder Bismarck felt like a gambler as he watched the Prussian army go into battle. If the war turned out to be a long one Napoleon III might interfere and take any of the gains that had been made. (Taylor, 4, p.62; Medlicott, 19, p.50; Rohl, 12, p.106; Mitchell, 2, p.25; Crankshaw, 14, pp.199–200; Pflanze, 21, p.259).

4. *Making sure that Austria was treated leniently in the Treaty of Prague, 23 August 1866.* (p.130)

The Bismarck plan was to complete unification by fighting a war with France, so the legend goes. He was therefore determined to make sure that Austria did not become a revengeful enemy. But was he really that far sighted? The documentary evidence suggests that right up to at least 1869 Bismarck was hoping to unite the south German states to Prussia by peaceful means. His real reason for terminating the war quickly and therefore offering the Austrians reasonable terms was a much more immediate one. Napoleon III, the unknown factor waiting in the wings, had suddenly emerged into the open. On 4 July he had written to King William I proposing an armistice. If Bismarck had refused, the consequences could have been serious: the mobilisation of a French army on the Rhine; time for the Austrians to transfer some of their victorious troops from the Italian front; the weakening of the Prussian army from the cholera which had been reported to be spreading. In any case, Napoleon III's terms were generous; he agreed to the setting up of the Prussian dominated north **Federation** and all he seemed to want in return was a promise that the south German states should be allowed to form their own federation independent of Prussia. Considering that Bismarck had been anticipating making much greater sacrifices this was reasonable. On 30 April for example, Bismarck had suggested that the Prussian cabinet should sell the state owned mines in the Saar to private investors. He had clearly anticipated that he might have to buy off France with the Saar. By the time the French changed their minds and began to make further demands, Bismarck had made his peace with Austria and could reject them. As usual Bismarck's diplomacy had not been fastened in the straightjacket of a single master plan but had been opportunist and flexible. (Craig, 22, p.3; Pflanze, 21, pp.295, 309; Palmer 13, p.122; Taylor 20, p.118; Moses 1, p.50; Mitchell, 2, p.29; Medlicott, 19, p.56; Taylor, 4, p.66; Crankshaw, 14, pp.215–23).

Study 34

I hope you have noticed that the discussion you have just been reading is far from satisfactory. This is because many of the arguments, both of the legend version and its opposite, have not been supported by adequate evidence.

1. Copy out the chart overleaf, work through the arguments again, decide whether the evidence presented, if any, is adequate and if not, suggest additional evidence.

One of the columns has been filled in to give you a clearer idea of how to proceed but you need not necessarily agree with it! Although the passage on the Prussian economy does include useful evidence on Prussia's railways and financial position this is surely inadequate to prove the argument. Perhaps the economy of other countries had also been improving? If so Bismarck's position in 1863 would be no stronger than Prussia in 1848. Before accepting the argument, therefore, some facts and figures on other countries are needed.

Argument: Unification succeeded because:	No evidence presented	Inadequate evidence presented	Convincing evidence presented	The sort of additional evidence needed
Bismarck inherited:				
a. a favourable diplomatic position				
b. a strong Prussian economy		X		Statistics on other economies
c. a powerful Prussian army				
d. ministers & politicians ready to back him				
Bismarck had a clear aim to:				
e. unify Germany				
f. preserve & increase Prussia's power				
g. Bismarck had a well worked out master plan				
h. Bismarck was a clever opportunist				

2. Read the additional evidence set out below. Make notes on it in the form of a chart like this:

Evidence and source	Which arguments does it support and why?
1. Prussian population	This may support (b) and (c) because it shows that Prussia's population was growing faster and that Prussia's age structure was young. This would mean a stronger economy and plenty of men in the younger age groups to fight.

3. Follow up some of the further reading references. You should find quite a lot of disagreement between the different books.

4. Make a brief report on your position so far. Which explanations for the German unification do you prefer? Which do you reject? Then, look at the next chapter which deals with the Hohenzollern Candidature (p.163) in much more detail.

Further Evidence

1. Prussian Population Figures:
   (a) 1815–64: Prussian population increased by 87%; Bavaria by 30%; Württemberg by 24%.
   (b) 1850–69: 46% of Prussia's inhabitants were aged under 20; 41% between 21–50 years; 13% over 50 years old. (Hamerow, 26, pp.45–6)

2. Economic Growth Statistics

Country	Population (millions)			Coal (million metric tons)		
	1820–1	1850–1	1860–1	1820–1	1850–1	1860–4
Austria-Hungary	25	30.7	32	0.1	1.4	4.1
France	30.5	35.8	37.4	1.1	5.3	10.1
Germany	25.0	34.0	36.2	1.2	9.2	20.8

Country	Pig Iron (thousand metric tons)			Rail Open (kms)	
	1820–4	1850–4	1860–4	1850	1860
Austria-Hungary	73	221	309	1,579	4,543
France	150	561	1065	2,915	9,167
Germany	75	245	613	5,856	11,089

(*Source:* Cipolla, 30, pp.747, 770, 773, 782)

3. Bismarck's Speech in the Landtag Debate on Erfurt Union, September 1849: 'What preserved Germany from the revolution of 1848 was that which constitutes the real Prussia. It was what remains of that much stigmatised Prussian stock which outlasted the revolution: that is the Prussian army, the Prussian treasury, the fruits of an intelligent Prussian administration of many years standing, and that vigorous spirit of co-operation between King and people which exists in Prussia. It was the loyalty of the Prussian people to their hereditary dynasty. It was the old Prussian virtues of honour, fidelity, obedience, and bravery which permeate the army... The army are satisfied with the name Prussia and proud of the name Prussia... Prussian we are and Prussian we wish to remain.' (Pflanze, 21, p.74)

4. Report from the Württemberg Central Office for Industry and Trade on whether to remain in the Zollverein or join a new Union with Austria; 17 December 1851:
   'Württemberg's trade routes go in the main towards the North Sea... a breach of the tariff links with Prussia, who rules the Rhine for a long stretch on both banks would cause the most damaging disturbance of

trade... during the 18 years that the Zollverein has existed contacts in trade have become so many and the interests of the business men have so interlocked with each other that the tearing apart of these countries would be accompanied by the most damaging effect upon industry and trade and connected with enormous losses of capital... our considerable paper manufacturers have a large sale in North Germany and could not continue without it on their present scale...' (Bohme 8, pp.85–6)

5. Bismarck's report to Manteuffel, Prussian foreign minister, from Frankfurt; 26 April 1856:
'I only wish to express my conviction that we shall be obliged sooner or later to fight Austria for our existence and that it does not lie in our power to evade the fight because the course of events in German history can have no other outcome. If this is correct, which of course remains more a matter of faith than knowledge, then it is not possible for Prussia to take self denial to the point where she puts her own existence at stake in order to protect the integrity of Austria...' (Bohme 8, p.89)

6. Bismarck's statement in a conversation with Disraeli held over dinner at the Russian Embassy, London; June 1862:
'I shall soon be compelled to undertake the conduct of the Prussian government... As soon as the army shall have been brought into such a condition as to inspire respect, I shall seize the first best pretext to declare war against Austria, dissolve the German Diet, subdue the minor states and give national unity to Germany under Prussian leadership.' (Bismarck refers to the incident in a letter to his wife, 30 June 1862: (Palmer, 13, p.70, n.26) Disraeli also mentioned it but A.J.P. Taylor argues that the story may have been manufactured later (Taylor 4, p.39, n.1). It is recorded by the Russian ambassador, Vitzthum von Eckstaedt in his memoirs published in London in 1887 (Medlicott and Coveney, 10, p.30; Palmer, 13, p.176; Crankshaw, 14, p.122)

7. Thun, Austrian ambassador to Prussia reports to Rechberg, Austrian Chief Minister; 5 January 1863:
'Herr von Bismarck said, "I am quite inaccessible to this emotional policy of sentiment; I have no sense of German nationality; for me a war against the King of Bavaria or the King of Hanover is just as serious as one against France" (He might just as well have said the Emperor of Austria)' (Bohme, 8, p.116)

8. Instructions from Bismarck to the Prussian Ambassador in St. Petersburg; 24 December 1863:
'The question is whether we are a great power or a state of the German

confederation, and whether, as would correspond to the former, we are to be ruled by a monarch or, as would be permitted by the latter, by professors, local magistrates, and small town gossips. The pursuit of the phantom of popularity has cost us our position in Germany and Europe and we shall not win it back by allowing ourselves to drift, but only by standing firmly on our feet and by being a great power first and a state of the confederation afterwards... For the moment I regard it as the right policy to have Austria on our side; whether the moment for separation arrives and on whose part we shall see... (Simon, 7, p.102)

9. Letter from Bleichroder* to Baron James**, 7 September 1864:
'The great intimacy with Austria has reached its term and a great chill will follow. Schleswig's future is still deeply veiled. My good source*** still thinks that we must reach an understanding with the French and keep Schleswig for Prussia... Russia would not object and Austria and England would remain silent however unhappy they might be. For the time being this ideal is frustrated by the will of the monarch who... is inclined to the Duke of Augustenburg.' (Stern, 15, p.51)
(this letter was found with others in the attic of the bank of Paris).

*   Bismarck's Jewish banker and financial adviser; often used by Bismarck to spread political information.
**   Head of the French banking family of Rothschild in Paris.
*** Bismarck.

10. Extracts from the Constitution of the North German Federation, 1867:
5.   The legislation of the Federation is performed by the Federal Council (Bundesrat) and the Diet (Reichstag).
6.   The Federal Council consists of the representatives of the members of the Federation, amongst whom the votes are divided according to the rules for the full assembly of the late Germanic Federation, so that Prussia, with the late votes of Hanover, Hesse-Cassel, Holstein, Nassau and Frankfurt,* has 17 votes, Saxony four... Mecklenburg-Schwerin two, ... Brunswick two, (all other states one each), total 43...
11. The Presidency of the Federation appertains to the Crown of Prussia which... has the right of representing the federation internationally, of declaring war and concluding peace, of entering into alliances and other treaties with foreign states...
20. The Diet (Reichstag) emanates from general and direct elections with secret voting...
63. All the land forces of the Federation form one single army, which in war and peace is under the command of his Majesty the King of Prussia, as Federal Commander-in-Chief...

78. Alterations of the Constitutions take place by way of legislation, but a majority of two thirds of the votes represented in the Federal Council is necessary thereto.' (Kertesz, 42, p.150)

* Annexed by Prussia after 1866 war.

CHAPTER 11

Bismarck and the Franco-Prussian War

1866–71

Accident or Design?

The Problem

The Franco-Prussian War and the Hohenzollern candidature which led up to it (p.132) played a vital part in the final unification of Germany. According to one version, Bismarck intended all along to go to war with France in order to force the south German states into the German Empire. Just as he was supposed to have planned the Austro-Prussian intervention in Schleswig-Holstein knowing it would lead to war with Austria in the end, so he was supposed to have planned the Hohenzollern candidature feeling sure that somehow it would provoke war with France. On the other hand Bismarck himself always denied that he ever had anything to do with the Hohenzollern candidature. The purpose of this chapter is to allow you to look into the evidence in more detail and reach a verdict of your own. For the sake of simplicity it would be possible to reduce the numerous theories about Bismarck's policies between 1867 and 1870 to the following four:

1. Bismarck's aim was to unite the south German states to the rest of the German **Federation**. His master plan was to provoke an incident which would force the French to declare war on Prussia and thus drive the south German states into the Empire. He deliberately and cynically encouraged the Hohenzollern candidature because he was sure it would give him the war he needed.

2. Bismarck wanted to bring the south Germans into the Federation but he aimed to do it peacefully by agreement with the south German states themselves and with France. He saw the Hohenzollern candidature as a chance to force the French to do a deal with him. However his plans went wrong and the result was a war which he had not originally intended.

3. As always Bismarck had more than one plan for realising his aim to unite the rest of Germany. He had one plan of peaceful persuasion and another for war with France. It was the reckless behaviour of the French which finally made sure that the war plan was the one that went into operation.

4. Bismarck had no immediate plans for bringing the south German states into the Federation. They were Catholic and hostile to the Protestant north. He never planned the Hohenzollern candidature. It was the warlike behaviour of the French and German national hysteria which forced him to manipulate the Ems telegram and carry out the unification long before he intended it.

Study 35

What recent historians have said

It makes sense to begin our investigation by looking at the verdicts of historians. Read each of the quotations below and write down which of our original four theories they appear to be supporting.

A. 'Certainly there is not a scrap of evidence that Bismarck worked deliberately for a war with France, still less that he timed it for the summer of 1870' (Taylor, 4, p.90).

B. 'The explanation that the conflict was planned by Bismarck as the necessary climax to a long matured scheme for the unification of Germany is one which does not today command general assent.' (Howard, 32, p.40)

C. 'Bismarck's goal was not an alliance, but a crisis with France. He deliberately set sail on a collision course with the intent of provoking either a war or a French internal collapse. The partisans of his innocence ask us to believe a most improbable case: that the shrewdest diplomatic mind of recent history permitted Germany to be drawn into a war which he was eager to avoid... In the end war came because Bismarck believed it necessary and opportune and because the French cabinet had neither the wisdom nor the firmness of will to avoid it.' (Pflanze, 21, pp.449, 457).

D. 'Some historians have recently... endeavoured to prove either that the whole affair was an example of *brinkmanship* which went wrong, or even that Bismarck's aims were peaceful and defensive, and that no-one was more surprised than he at the result... what we seem to have in this case is an example of Bismarck's skilful pursuit of alternative courses. There were two possibilities; either that France would acquiesce in the Hohenzollern election, in which case Prussia would be no worse off... or France would not, in which case there might be a war, for which he was ready. What we must reject is that he was innocently unaware of this second possibility.' (Medlicott, 19, p.81).

E. '... This is not to say that Bismarck planned the Hohenzollern candidature in order to trap France into a war which would result in the accession of the south German states to the Confederation... To impute to Bismarck the prior planning of every detail of developments as they occurred is to make of him a kind of superman, to whom nothing could happen that he had not intended.' (Simon, 16, p.206).

F. It now seems fairly certain, on the basis of newly discovered documents and a reinterpretation of old ones, that Bismarck planned a war from the very beginning.' (Kent, 18, p.71).

G. 'The Hohenzollern candidature, far from being designed to provoke a war with France which could complete the unification of Germany, was intended rather to make German unification possible without a war... He had neither planned the war nor even foreseen it. But he claimed it as his own once it became inevitable.' (Bohme, 8, p.92).

Study 36

You have probably found that the extracts from the historians were too short for you to be absolutely certain which of the four theories they were closest to. My count, which you may disagree with, is that only one (F) seems to go for theory one. The majority go for theory two (four of them). Two more or less seem to be arguing for theory three but nobody seems definitely committed to theory four. It is now time to have a look at some of the documents. Before doing so it is very important that you:

1. Re-read chapter 8. You cannot follow the documents unless you have a clear picture of the sequence which the events took and can relate the documents to them.
2. Read the general advice on documents and sources given in pages 75–6. As you read each document below register your views on it in a table like this:

Document and date	Type of source and reliability, see pp. 75–6	Which theory does it support?

A September 1868 to February 1870

Hohenzollerns uninterested in offer of Spanish Throne:

1. 26 February 1869, Bismarck to Werthern, Prussian envoy to Munich, Bavaria:
   'I also think it probable that German unity will be forwarded by violent means. It is quite another matter however, to bring about such a violent catastrophe and to bear responsibility for the choice of time for it. Such arbitrary interventions in the development of history... have always had as their consequence only the striking down of unripe fruit. It is self evident in my opinion that German unity at this moment is not a ripe fruit... We can put our clock forward but time does not go any faster because we have. The capacity to wait while circumstances develop is one of the prerequisites of a practical policy.' (Bohme, 8, p.202–3)

2. 25 May 1869, Theodore Von Bernhardi arrived in Madrid on a special mission for Prussia. In 1899 the British historian Lord Acton wrote: 'What Theodore Bernhardi did in Spain has been committed to oblivion... The Austrian First Secretary said that he betrayed his secret one day at dinner. Somebody spoke indiscreetly on the subject (of the Hohenzollern candidature) and Bernhardi aimed a kick at him under the table which caught the shin of the Austrian instead. Fifty thousand pounds of Prussian bonds were sent to Spain at midsummer 1870... they came over here (to London) to be negotiated, and I know the banker through whose hands they passed.' (Steefel, 23, p.15) In 1903 the German Government suppressed the publication of pages in Bernhardi's memoirs which showed he had been in contact with Berlin during his mission (Bonnin, 9, p.19). There are 38 days unaccounted for in his memoirs between 18 March and 8 May 1869 (Steefel, 23, p.15).

3. 11 May 1869, Bismarck to Solms, Prussian Ambassador in Paris: 'Herr Benedetti★ visited me on the eighth... the only thing that seemed to pre-occupy him was the question whether Prussia would give a King of any sort to the Spaniards. I turned this question aside with a joke and told him that of course we had taken soundings recently in the princely house of Hohenzollern to see whether the hereditary Prince had any wish to accept the Crown but that both he himself and his father said they were for declining it and that his majesty the King, when he later learnt of it, said that he understood that very well.' (Bohme, 8, p.215)
   ★ French Ambassador to Prussia.

4. 20 November 1869, Bismarck to King William I: 'In regard to the South German situation I think the line for Prussian policy is set by two diverse aims... the one distant, the other immediate... The distant and by far the greater aim is the national unification of Germany. We can wait for this in security because the lapse of time and the natural development of the nation which makes further progress every year will have their effect. We cannot accelerate it unless out of the way events in Europe, such as some upheaval in France or a war of other great powers among themselves offer us an unsought opportunity to do so... Every recognisable effort of Prussia to determine the decision of the South German Princes will endanger our immediate aim. I consider this to be... to keep Bavaria and Württemberg in such political direction that neither will co-operate with Paris or Vienna... nor find a pretext to break all alliances which we have concluded...' (Bohme, 8, p.203).

5. 24 February 1870. Bismarck in conversation with Moritz Busch★: 'The question of German unity is making good progress, but it requires

time... one year perhaps or five, or indeed possibly even ten years. I cannot make it go any faster...' (Pflanze, 21, p.435)

* Moritz Busch was Bismarck's press attaché. He had his dialogues published in 1898 as *Bismarck: Some Secret Pages of his History.*

B February 1870 to July 2 1870

The candidature is secretly accepted:

6. 25 February 1870, Charles Anthony of Hohenzollern to King William I: 'Had I to follow only my family feeling and the dictates of my conscience I should be able most positively to declare to your majesty in the name of my son and in my own that we absolutely declined the candidature... I have considered it, however, my duty to appeal to your majesty's judgement since the present case and the decision associated with it are of a high significance... over the context of the affair as a whole I have today given some exact particulars to Count Bismarck which he will doubtless put before your majesty.' (Bohme, 8, p.215)

7. 28 February 1870, Bismarck in conversation with Busch: 'The French Arcadians (war party) are watching the course of events in Germany and waiting their opportunity. Napoleon is now well disposed to us but very changeable. We could now fight France and beat her too, but that war would give rise to five or six others; and while we can gain our ends by peaceful means, it would be foolish, if not criminal, to take such a course. Events in France may take a warlike or revolutionary turn, which would render the present brittle metal there more malleable.' (Pflanze, 21, pp.436-7).

8. 9 March 1870, Bismarck to King William I of Prussia: 'I am of the opinion that it would serve Prussian and German state interests and bring indirect advantages if the acceptance of the candidature takes place... For Germany it is desirable to have on the other side of France, a country on whose sympathies* we can rely and with whose feelings France is obliged to reckon.' With a friendly Spain 'the armed forces that France could put in the field against Germany may be estimated at not less than two fewer army corps.** We have in the long run to look for the preservation of peace, not to the goodwill of France, but to the impression created by our position of strength.*** The prosperity of Spain and German trade with her would receive a powerful impetus under Hohenzollern rule. In the event of a rejection, the Spaniards would probably turn to Bavaria... Spain would have a ruling house which looked for support to France and Rome...' (Simon, 7, p.140; Bonnin, 9, p.68-73; Steefel, 23, pp.57-61)

The King's marginal comments:

*   How long would these sympathies last?

**   What potentate in Spain would be in a position to guarantee such a policy?

*** Agreed

(This document was not fully published until the secret files of the German foreign office were captured after World War Two.)

9. 20 March 1870, Charles Anthony of Hohenzollern to Prince Charles of Rumania, 1894–1950:
   'The question of the candidature is a great pre-occupation here. Bismarck desires acceptance on dynastic and political grounds, but the King desires it only if Leopold answers the call willingly. On the fifteenth (March) there was a very... important council here presided over by the King at which the Crown Prince, we two, Bismarck, Roon, Moltke, Schleinitz, Thile and Delbruck were present. The unanimous conclusion of the deliberators was for acceptance as the fulfilment of patriotic Prussian duty.' (Bohme, 8, p.215; Bonnin, 9, pp.291–4; Steefel, 23, pp.61–5)

10. Prussian Reports on policy of new French Foreign Minister, Gramont, appointed 15 May 1870:
    On the margins of the three reports Bismarck wrote, "War!" (Pflanze, 21, p.448).

11. 28 May 1870, Bismarck to Prince Charles Anthony of Hohenzollern:
    'If his serene highness the Hereditary Prince or one of your highness' younger sons were inclined to render service to both Germany and Spain I think that a still unanswered telegram addressed to me by Marshall Prim* after the latest refusal would offer a possibility for me to re-open the question.' (Simon, 7, p.145; Bonnin, 9, p.158)
    * Marshall Prim was Prime Minister of the Spanish provisional government.

12. 5 June 1870, Prince Charles Anthony to Leopold:
    'I have to inform you that yesterday I talked for half an hour... with the King and Bismarck... the King accommodates himself to the political constraint of Bismarck. The latter triumphs... Had we again refused we should have had to pay for it; for the question of the Spanish throne is a prime factor in Bismarck's political calculations... perhaps some European event or other will yet come between to prevent it – if so all the better.' (Bohme, 8, p.220)

13. 19 June 1870, report from Thile* to Bismarck on meeting with King William I:
    When the King heard that the candidature was being further discussed he

said it was 'very extraordinary that this sort of thing was going on without his authorisation.' He wanted to be informed 'of everything that Prim's agent brings either by word of mouth or in writing before any action is taken...' ** (Pflanze, 21, p.444; Bonnin, 9, pp.190-191; Steefel 23, pp.96-7)

★ Thile was Bismarck's principal aide in the Foreign Office.

** Bismarck wrote these comments in the margin:
  'That beats everything! So his majesty wants the affair treated with official royal interference? The whole affair is only possible if it remains the limited concern of the Hohenzollern princes, it must not turn into a Prussian concern, the King must be able to say without lying: I know nothing about it.'

14. 19 June 1870, Diary of Max von Versen★:
Versen and Bucher met Prince Karl Anton and his son who agreed to accept the candidature. 'Then there came various scruples on Karl Anton's part. What would France say about it? Would it not give rise to complications? I said, 'Bismarck says that is just what he is looking for.'

★ Versen was sent as an emissary to Spain in April 1870 whilst Bucher was handling the Hohenzollern candidature with the Spanish government. In June Versen had been sent by Bismarck to negotiate with Leopold of Hohenzollern. In 1897 the German government banned the publication of a chapter in a biography of Versen dealing with the Spanish affair. (Bonnin, 9, p.278; Steefel, 23, p.246)

15. Bismarck's instructions to Bucher★ June 1870:
When Leopold's election becomes known 'it is possible that we may see a passing fermentation in France, and, without doubt, it is necessary to avoid anything that might provoke or increase it.' Bismarck wanted to avoid all appearance of being involved in the candidature. 'Thus we shall have an unassailable position before the European public. If there is an outburst in France we shall simply ask: 'What do you want? Do you wish to dictate the decisions of the Spanish nation and of a German private citizen... Undoubtedly they will cry 'intrigue', they will be furious against me, but without finding any point of attack.'** (Pflanze, 21, pp.446–7, n.43; Bonnin, 9, pp.41–4)

★ Bucher was Bismarck's envoy in Spain.

** The document was alleged to have been found in the Spanish Archives by Piralea, a Spanish historian, in 1876 but no-one since then has ever been able to locate it. Some historians think that the document was not actually Bismarck's but Bucher's notes. It was not found in the German Foreign Office's secret files after World War Two, nor has it been found in the Spanish Archives.

C 2 July to 19 July

The secret of the candidature leaks out and leads to war:

16. 21 June–2 July, the story of how the secret leaked out:
    'Sheer chance ultimately prevented Leopold from becoming King of Spain. On 21 June, the elated Spanish agent telegraphed through the Prussian foreign service to the President of the Spanish Parliament, the news that he would arrive in Madrid "about the 26th" bearing Leopold's acceptance and terms. A clerk in the Madrid embassy inexplicably decoded it as "about the 9th". The consequence was disastrous. On 23 June the President prorogued the Parliament. Madrid was sweltering, the deputies idle and impatient. He sent them home until November. But the secret could not be kept until then. By 2 July it had reached Paris. The fat was in the fire. (Pflanze, 21, p.445)

17. 5 July 1870, King William I to Queen Augusta:
    'The Spanish bombshell has suddenly exploded but in quite a different way from how we were told it would... In Berlin the French chargé d'affaires has already spoken to Thile, who naturally said that the matter had been kept entirely from the Prussian government.' (Bohme, 8, p.220)

18. 5 July 1870, Bismarck to Abeken★:
    'I communicate for use in speaking to the King some views on the handling of the Spanish question. In my opinion Herr von Werther★★ should have repulsed any discussion of the matter as one foreign to himself and to his government. He must make his journey to Ems pass for courteous readiness to inform himself about the matter and to procure as speedily as possible all available enlightenment for a friendly French government... France is more afraid in my opinion, of a serious breach than we are. If we let the belief gain ground that we are the more afraid, French arrogance will very soon leave us no other choice but war...' (Bohme, 8, p.221)
    ★ Abeken was the Prussian foreign ministry official with King William I at Ems.
    ★★ Werther was the Prussian ambassador to France. He didn't know about the Hohenzollern candidature so when questioned about it by the French he promised to go to Ems to ask King William.

19. 6 July 1870, Gramont's speech to the French Chamber:
    'We do not believe that respect for the rights of a neighbouring people obliges us to suffer a foreign power, by putting one of its Princes on the throne of Spain, to alter the present balance of power in Europe to our disadvantage and to endanger the interest and honour of France. This eventuality we firmly hope will not be realised. To prevent it we count both on the wisdom of the German people and the friendship of the

Spanish people. If things fall out otherwise, strong in your support and in that of the nation, we shall know how to do our duty without hesitation and without weakness...' (Bohme, 8, p.221)

20. 7 July 1870, Gramont to Benedetti:
'We are pressed for time because we must strike first. In the event of an unsatisfactory reply, and for the campaign to begin in a fortnight, the troops must begin to move on Saturday... if you obtain from the King the withdrawal of his consent to the Prince of Hohenzollern's candidacy, that will be an immense success and a great service. The King will have assured the peace of Europe. If not, it means war...' (Bohme 8, p.221)

21. 9 July 1870, Bleichroder★ to Bismarck:
'On my part I do not believe in the extreme seriousness of the political situation★★ and have therefore not done any selling on your excellency's account. Should I be mistaken, however, and should your excellency think that many more unpleasant incidents are to be expected I respect-fully beg you to warn me by a single syllable.' (Stern, 15, p,128)
★ Bleichroder (p.161) was Bismarck's banker and managed Bismarck's extensive portfolio of stocks and shares. His letters to Bismarck were found above the stables on the Bismarck estate at Friedrichsruh.
★★ Bismarck put in an exclamation mark here.

22. Joanna Bismarck to Bleichroder, 10 July 1870:
'My husband, who is very busy coding and uncoding, asks me to answer your letter of today in this way: he does not indeed believe in war because despite all the frivolity of some people he thinks it improbable that anyone would suddenly attack us because Spain did not vote the way one wanted it to. But he thought there could still come moments when the belief in war would be stronger than now, and since he needs more money anyhow, it might be a good idea to sell the railroad shares. But you should be a better judge of the stock market than my husband; perhaps the market is not so jittery as some of the diplomats are. But it is just as impossible to predict the political decisions of irritated people of either sex as it is to predict the weather.' (Stern,15, p.128)

23. 10 July 1870, King William I to Prince Charles Anthony:
'Preparations for war on a large scale are in progress in France... the situation is , therefore, more than serious. Just as I could not bid your son accept the crown, so I cannot bid him withdraw his acceptance. Should he, however, so decide my 'adherence' will again not be wanting...' (Bohme,8, p.221)

24. 12 July 1870, Gramont receives reports from 80 French prefects:
According to the historian Lynn Case, writing in 1954, 63 of these reports argued that the French people were ready to go to war to get the Prussian

Prince out of Spain. The report from Charente Department said: 'I summarise public opinion in these words; no one wants a Prussian Prince in Spain; they hail war patriotically; they prefer peace with a moral victory; they would not forgive the government if it showed weakness or even timidity.' (Steefel,23, pp.229, 248)

25. 12 July 1870, Bismarck's first dinner with Moltke and Roon, told in Bismarck's *Reflections and Reminiscences*★:
'During dinner at which Moltke and Roon were present, the announcement came from the embassy in Paris that the Prince of Hohenzollern had renounced his candidature in order to prevent the war with which France threatened us. My first idea was to retire from the service because I perceived in this extorted submission a humiliation of Germany for which I did not desire to be responsible... I was very depressed for I saw no means of repairing the corroding injury I dreaded to our national position from a timorous policy unless by picking quarrels clumsily and seeking them artificially. I saw by that time that war was a necessity which we could no longer avoid with honour...'

★ Bismarck's *Reflections and Reminiscences* were written with the help of Lothar Bucher (see doc. 15) after his resignation as Chancellor in 1890, and published in 1898. In another section of them he wrote: 'I was convinced that the gulf which had been created in the course of history between the South and North of the fatherland by a variety of dynastic and racial sentiments and modes of life, could not be more effectively bridged than by a common national war against the neighbouring nation, our aggressor for centuries.' (Bohme,8, p.361) Bucher's letters to Busch, which were published in 1899 (p.167) show some of the problems he encountered. The ex-chancellor tried to deny a diplomatic initiative over the Hohenzollern candidature which Bucher himself had tried to carry out, 'he tells a story one way today and quite differently tomorrow,' 'he will never admit that he played any part in things which went wrong,' 'his thoughts are with the present which he desires to influence.' (Palmer,13, pp.260-1)

26. 3.50 pm, July 13 1870, telegram from Abeken in Ems to Bismarck in Berlin:
'His Majesty writes to me, "Count Benedetti spoke to me on the promenade in order to demand from me, finally, in a very importunate manner, that I should authorise him to telegraph at once that I bound myself for all future time never again to give my consent, if the Hohenzollerns should renew their candidature. I refused at last somewhat sternly, as it is neither right nor possible to undertake engagements of this kind 'for ever'"... His Majesty, having told Count Benedetti that he was

awaiting news from the Prince, has decided with reference to the above demand... not to receive Count Benedetti again but only to let him be informed through an aide-de-camp... His Majesty leaves it to your excellency whether Benedetti's fresh demand and its rejection should not be at once communicated both to our ambassador and to the press.' (Simon,7, p.233)

27. 13 July 1870. Bismarck's second dinner with Moltke and Roon, as told in his *Reflections and Reminiscences*:

'Having decided to resign... I invited Roon and Moltke to dine with me alone on the thirteenth... During our conversation I was informed that a telegram from Ems was being deciphered... I read it out to my guests whose dejection was so great that they turned away from food and drink... in the presence of my two guests I reduced the telegram by striking out words to the following form:"After the news of the renunciation of the hereditary Prince of Hohenzollern had been officially communicated to the Imperial government of France by the Royal Government of Spain, the French ambassador at Ems further demanded of his Majesty the King that he would authorise him to telegraph to Paris that his Majesty the King bound himself for all future time never again to to give his assent if the Hohenzollern should renew their candidature. His Majesty the King thereupon decided not to receive the French ambassador again, and sent to tell him through his aide de camp on duty, that his Majesty had nothing further to communicate to the ambassador."... After I had read out the concentrated edition to my two guests, Moltke remarked: "Now it has a different ring; it sounded before like a parley; now it is like a flourish in answer to a challenge." I went on to explain: "if in execution of his Majesty's order I at once communicate this text... not only to the newspapers but also by telegraph to all our embassies it will be known in Paris before midnight... and it will have the effect of a red rag upon the Gallic bull..." Suddenly the two generals... had recovered their pleasure in eating and drinking and spoke in a more cheerful vein.' (Simon,7, p.233).

28. 16 July 1870, Bismarck's speech in Bundesrat:

'It is known... that the Spanish government had been negotiating for months with his Highness the hereditary Prince Leopold of Hohenzollern to accept the Spanish Throne, that these negotiations... were carried through in direct consultation with the Prince and his father, without the participation or invention of any other government... The foreign office of the North German Bund, and the government of His Majesty, the King of Prussia had had no knowledge of these proceedings...' (Medlicott and Coveney,10, doc. 9, p.72)

Study 37

1. If you would like to see what some of the main writers on German history have to say on the problems, here are the references:
   (Craig,22, p.14; Palmer,13, ch.9; Taylor,4, p.88; Medlicott,19, p.33; Rohl,12, ch.5; Moses,1, ch.5; Mitchell,2, ch.19; Crankshaw,14, ch.XXV)

2. Read through the table you made of the documents in study 36. Write down your views on the following problems
   (a) Which are the most reliable sources? Bismarck told Moritz Busch in February 1871 that 'Diplomatic reports are for the most part just paper smeared with ink... as for using them someday as material for history, nothing of any value will be found in them... the main point always lies in private letters and confidential communications, also oral ones and these never find their way into the records.' (Stern,15, p.306) Do you agree?
   (b) Do you think that Bismarck was planning war with France *before* the Hohenzollern candidature arose?
   (c) Did Bismarck deliberately manipulate the candidature?
   (d) Were his motives over the candidature warlike or peaceful?
   (e) Was Bismarck telling the truth in document 28?
   (f) Did his handling of the candidature proceed like smooth clockwork with no errors?
   (g) Is there any evidence that the French were just as guilty of causing the war as Bismarck?
   (h) Which of the original four theories on pages 163–4 at the beginning of this chapter came nearest the truth? Arrange them in your order of preference.

3. Bring together the material from chapters 9, 10, and 11 to write an essay entitled: *Account for the unification of Germany between 1864 and 1870.* Before writing make decisions on the following problems:
   (a) How important were the favourable factors, such as the diplomatic position, the strength and type of German nationalism, the Prussian economy and army, in leading to unification? Could unification have proceeded without Bismarck?
   (b) Did unification come about because Bismarck had a master plan for uniting Germany or...
   (c) Did Bismarck influence the course of unification by aiming at the expansion of Prussia, making no grand plans but manipulating each chance as it came along?
   (d) Are you going to use the 'Aunt Sally' technique for planning your essay (see p.73). This would mean first setting up your Aunt Sally – the Bismarck legend of why unification took place; second, demolishing it; third, replacing it with your own explanation. Or...
   (e) Will you choose a more orthodox essay plan? For example examine first the theories you think are not important (I would vote for 'Bismarck the master planner' as belonging to this category but don't let me influence you!) Then go on to review the more acceptable theories – perhaps the various ways in which Bismarck was helped before he had even become chief minister; his skilful opportunist style of diplomacy...
   (f) What will you put in your introductory paragraph? You could perhaps discuss the sources available for solving the problem and their various weaknesses. Or you could *very briefly* recount the main outlines of the story of unification.
   (g) How many paragraphs will you divide your essay into? What will the key sentences be? (See pages 58–9)

CHAPTER 12

German Unification

1871 - 1914:
Triumph or Disaster?

In 1945, as Russian soldiers drew even nearer to her home, a German lady shot herself. She was 80 years old, her home was Schönhausen, and she was Bismarck's niece (map 5, p.108). While Hitler's body was incinerated in Berlin, the Bismarck's family home was burnt to the ground by the Russians, and the German national state, which Bismarck had helped to create, ceased to exist. Since the end of the Second World War, West and East Germany have become separate nations. Berlin is divided by the notorious wall across which Berliners venture at their peril. The Bismarck family home now lies in East Germany and Varzin, the estate which was bestowed on him by a grateful King of Prussia, is in Poland. East Germany is a communist state lying behind the 'Iron Curtain' and under the political and economic protection of Russia. West Germany is under the political protection of NATO and has surrendered some of her economic independence to the European Economic Community, (the Common Market). The German Empire which was proclaimed in the Hall of Mirrors at Versailles did not even last a century.

These are the facts of twentieth century history. But how and why did the German Empire disappear so rapidly from the European map? If anyone had laid a bet back in 1870 surely they would have backed the German Empire as having a much better chance of survival than Italy? Germany was altogether in a different league from the point of view of population, military strength and economic resources. Moreover Germany had the advantage that Bismarck enjoyed another 20 years of power to guide the new state on its way, whereas Cavour died prematurely. Bismarck survived as Chancellor of the German Empire until a new Emperor, William II, grandson of William I, forced him to resign in 1890. Twenty four years later, Germany and Europe plunged into the First World War. Defeated and humiliated, Germany was split into two parts by the hated Polish corridor (see map 7, p.197). The Prussian Hohenzollern Royal family was replaced by the Weimar Republic. But the new regime was not to last. Adolf Hitler and the Nazi party came to power in the 1930s and proceeded to dismantle the Republic and replace it with their Fascist state (see **Fascism**). Hitler's desire not only to regain the territory lost after the First World War, but also to extend German control over other areas of Europe, paved the way for World War Two from which the German state failed to emerge intact. The obvious explanation for Germany's failure to survive is that her leaders after Bismarck must have committed fatal errors; that her disastrous collapse was all the fault of Hitler and the Nazis. However, some historians have begun to suggest that perhaps this is too simple an explanation; that perhaps there was a serious flaw or weakness in Bismarck's creation. Writing in 1945, the German historian Meinecke observed,: 'The staggering course of the first, and still more the second, world war no longer permits the question to be ignored whether the seeds of later evil were not already present in the Bismarckian Reich.' (Pflanze, 21, p.3)

It is the purpose of this chapter to encourage you to consider this problem. The method used will be to present you with two deliberately exaggerated points of view. The first will argue that Bismarck's Germany was indeed flawed and played an important part in bringing about Germany's ultimate ruin. The second will take the view that there was nothing fundamentally wrong with Bismarck's Germany. As usual you will be asked to reach your own verdict after comparing the two versions.

Bismarck's Germany was a disaster

Between 1871 and 1890, when he was dismissed, Bismarck had nearly 20 years to lay the foundations of a stable German Empire. There were three essential problems which he needed to solve. First he had to develop a method of government which would be capable of gradual development so that it involved the whole of the Empire in decision making. What was needed was a form of government which would unite the different states and involve all classes of German society. Bavarians and Hanoverians must be made to feel that they were as important as Prussians, middle class business men and workers must feel that they were as much part of Germany as **Junkers**. Any form of government which attempted to locate power in the hands of one man, one state, or one class would in the end lead to disaster. Second, he needed to develop a society in which all classes and groups had an equal chance of making progress and had freedom to hold their views and state their opinions. The Empire contained Catholics as well as Protestants, Poles, Danes, French and Jews as well as Germans. All needed to be reassured that they were acceptable members of the New Empire, and that they could criticise and make suggestions freely. Third, Bismarck must be able to show the rest of Europe that the new German Empire was stable, contented and ready to live at peace with its neighbours. Failure to achieve this would have the inevitable result of growing tensions and ultimately war. It was Germany's tragedy and ultimately the world's that Bismarck completely failed to achieve any of these three objectives. As H. Kohn remarks (Snyder 34, p.241): 'It was Germany's misfortune that she had a Bismarck and not a Gladstone, and not even a Cavour.'

Although the constitution which Bismarck handed down to Germany had the outward appearance of a modern **democracy** it was in fact a cunningly designed vehicle for preserving the power of the Prussian King, his chancellor, Bismarck, the state of Prussia, the Junker class and the army. The new Empire, it is true, had a parliament, the Reichstag, which was elected regularly by all males over the age of 25. But as a contemporary observer of the German scene put it, 'It is a common error among newcomers... in Berlin to take for real the Parliamentary system as it exists here; ... one quickly realises that Germany is endowed with a fine... facade... faithfully representing a picture of a constitutional system; (there are) turmoils in the corridors, lively debates, defeats inflicted on the government but behind the scenes, at the back of the stage, intervening always at the decisive hour and having their way, appear the Emperor and the Chancellor...' (Kent, 18, p.98). In fact the Chancellor and his ministers were appointed by the Emperor and not by parliament; they were not even members of the Reichstag themselves, nor did they require a majority there. The Emperor was in full control of foreign affairs, the making of treaties, declaring war and was commander-in-chief of the armed forces. All these matters were outside the control of the Reichstag. As Karl Liebknecht, a socialist, put it, the Reichstag was 'a fig leaf covering the nakedness of Absolutism.' Laws also needed the approval of an upper house, the Bundesrat. This seemed to be a method of giving the other states a fair say in the running of the Empire's government. Each state sent representatives roughly in proportion to the size of its population. However, closer scrutiny reveals that any important measure, for example, one designed to alter the Empire's constitution, could be vetoed by the votes of fourteen out of the 56 Bundesrat members. Since Prussia had 17 votes, the Prussian King effectively controlled the chamber. Furthermore the President of the Bundesrat was always the Imperial Chancellor, who was usually the Prussian Prime Minister. Since, in addition, the Prussian King was by definition Emperor of Germany Prussian domination was assured.

Politics in Germany was therefore a career which led nowhere. Members of the Reichstag were not paid until 1906 and their quality suffered as a result. Nor were the civil servants in a much better state. Bismarck was so domineering that any individualism was discouraged. A royal edict of 1882 announced that the Emperor was responsible for all policy and that civil servants were bound by oath to support this. The secretaries of state were only twice called to a meeting to discuss policy and Bismarck even stopped them from corresponding with each other without his permission. He tried to regulate everything down to the last minor detail. By 1890 the Foreign Office contained 32 volumes of his instructions on such matters as the size of blotting paper, abbreviations and the use of non stain red covers (Holliday, 11, p.149). Holstein, who was a German civil servant during the Bismarck era, gives a clear view of what it was like to serve under Bismarck. He treated people, he said, 'just as tools; like knives and forks which are changed with each course.' (Stern, 15, p.231) 'It was a psychological necessity for Bismarck to make his power felt by tormenting, harrying, ill-treating people...' (Crankshaw, 14, p.384) In the end, of course, Bismarck fell a victim to his own system. Since all his power ultimately depended on the Emperor, the death of his old master William I signalled danger. The Crown Prince, Frederick, seemed to be the main problem as he had liberal views and was married to Vicky, the eldest daughter of Queen Victoria of England and was one of Bismarck's major critics. But he died of a painful throat cancer only months after succeeding to the throne. In the end though, the new heir to the throne, William I's grandson, Kaiser William II, proved to be no more amenable to Bismarck. Bismarck fell from power leaving to Germany a parliamentary system which was powerless in the face of his two other legacies to his country, an over-powerful junker aristocracy and an independent army.

Thanks to Bismarck's self-identification with the Junker class and their values, Germany in 1914 was still dominated by them. In 1908 it has been estimated that 83% of all the chief administrative officials of the provinces and 40% of all the Empire's ministers were nobles. (Sagarra, 24, p.186) In 1910, 75% of Prussia's officials were themselves sons of former officials, army officers or landowners. Between 1888 and 1891, 83% of the directors of police were drawn from the nobility. When the threat of imported food from the new world became apparent in the 1870s the Junker nobles, unlike the British landowners, had the power to obtain protection. In Prussia the constitution remained unreformed and based on the old estates system (p.121). This gave the Prussian junkers a firm power base. Between 1879 and 1887 the tariffs against foreign food imports went up five times. Meanwhile the junkers maintained a firm hold on the army. As late as 1913, and in spite of the great increase in the army's size, 30% of all officers, 80% of cavalry officers, 48% of infantry officers and 41% of field artillery officers were nobles. In the Prussian units of the army this phenomenon was even more marked. In 16 regiments the officer corps were exclusively noble (Sagarra, 24, p.186). What made matters worse was that this army was not controlled by the Reichstag but by the Emperor. After 1870 there was not even an Imperial Minister of War. In 1874 the Reichstag lost its battle to try to control the amount of money spent on the army on a yearly basis. Bismarck forced them to accept a seven year army budget. Since a new Reichstag was elected every three years this meant that their control was now very slight. As Bennigsen, one of Bismarck's liberal opponents remarked: 'The defence constitution and the army organisation are to a very large extent the backbone of the constitution of any state, and so, if these are not successfully absorbed into the constitution, it is not really possible to speak of that state as a constitutional one.' In 1913, on the eve of World War One, military expenditure represented 75% of the budget (Sagarra, 24, p.243). A newspaper in 1899 described the typical attitudes of an officer in the German army as 'devotion to the dynasty, absolute loyalty to the person of the monarch, high patriotism... and hostility towards anti-patriotic, anti-monarchic attitudes.' (Sagarra, 24, p.241). 'The army,' said Count Waldersee, Chief of the General Staff, 'is a corporation like a family whose most intimate concerns are not for the public eye.' It was typical of the way Bismarck's Germany had developed that William II's first act on becoming Kaiser was not to talk to his people but to address his army. He made regular arrangements to meet his service chiefs three times per week but had no routine for meeting his Chancellor (Sagarra, 24, pp.237–8)

Bismarck's Germany seemed to be a modern parliamentary state with a thriving economy but this was an illusion. Behind this facade things were run by an antiquated hereditary monarchy and its allies the junker aristocracy and the army. Unfortunately, the values of these institutions also began to infect the rest of German society. The most comical aspect of this was the incredible addiction to uniforms. Everyone wore them – even the Berlin cabdrivers boasted a uniform consisting of red braided jackets with black patent top hats. Bismarck himself, whose acquaintance with the army had been very slight, usually wore the uniform of the cuirassiers. William II took things to an absurd length; he insisted on appearing at a performance of Wagner's opera, the Flying Dutchman, wearing the full dress uniform of an admiral. This obsession was symbolic of a society which was dominated by junker military traditions. A junior lieutenant with noble birth could appear at the Hohenzollern court in Berlin while a middle class civil servant would have to have risen very high up the ranks of his profession before he would be welcome. Eminent scholars were expected to step off the pavement if an officer in uniform approached from the opposite direction. Since the middle classes were competing for jobs with this aristocracy they tended to imitate their values, or try to buy themselves into their ranks. Typical of this trend was William von Eynern, a Westphalian industrialist. Of his five children, one son bought an estate in Upper Silesia, three others lived off their investments, the fourth son made his way into the army as a cavalry officer and the daughter was safely married off to a gentleman with an estate (Sagarra, 24, p.297). In return for titles the middle classes accepted the system. The industrialists joined the junkers between 1879 and 1887 in their campaign for protective tariffs. Germany's political and social development had been retarded by the system of government which Bismarck had devised.

In Bismarck's Germany any group of individuals who opposed him was likely to be deprived of their equality of opportunity or basic human rights. At various times it was disastrous to be a Catholic, a Jew, a Socialist or even a liberal (see **liberalism**). When the German Catholics and their allies the Polish and French Catholics from Alsace and Lorraine combined to form the Catholic Centre Party, Bismarck saw it as a threat to the unity of the new German state. A series of laws were passed banning the Jesuits from Germany, forcing Catholics to accept civil marriage, preventing priests who had been educated abroad from teaching, and curtailing religious education in schools. Although Bismarck began to relax these laws in 1878, and made an agreement with the new Pope Leo XIII so that the Centre Party became one of his most loyal groups of supporters, Catholics were still far from being accepted as full citizens of the state. Given that a third of the population of Germany was Catholic it would seem reasonable to expect that they would be well represented in Germany's politics. In fact between 1888 and 1914 out of a total of 90 chancellors and ministers only eight were Catholics (Sagarra, 24, p.270). To be a Polish Catholic was even more disastrous. In 1885, 30,000 Poles were expelled from Germany's Eastern provinces. Bismarck also undertook a campaign against one of Germany's other biggest political parties, the Social Democrats. To him they were a communist party, hostile to the idea of nationalism and a threat to the German state. The anti-socialist law of 1878 made it illegal for them to hold meetings, collect funds or publish their literature. With the permission of the Bundesrat the state police could even forbid known socialists from residing in certain prohibited areas. Between 1878 and 1890 over 150 periodicals were suppressed and over 1,500 people arrested.

Only after Bismarck's fall from power were the anti-socialist laws repealed. By then, another unpleasant phenomenon had appeared: anti-semitism. Germany's leading musician, Wagner, had always been anti-semitic. In a letter to his patron Ludwig II of Bavaria in 1881 he said, 'I hold the Jewish race to be the born enemy of humanity and all that is noble.' But the disease now entered politics. The court chaplain, Adolf Stoecker, campaigned to end the legal equality of Jews. In a debate in parliament he declared: 'Recently a corpse was found in a district not far from here. The corpse was examined and at hand was a Jewish district physician, a Jewish surgeon, a Jewish judge, a Jewish barrister, only the corpse was German.' (Stern 15, p.517). Although Bismarck did not give way to this campaign he did little to discourage it. He himself referred to Lasker, one of the German liberal leaders, as that stupid Jew-boy, and to a Jewish minister as a 'Semitic shit in the pants.' He was not above using anti-semitism as a vote catcher as, for example, in the 1884 elections. His treatment of the Jewish liberal leader Lasker was typical of his authoritarian style in politics which insisted on branding any criticism of his government as treachery to the German state. While on a tour of the USA Lasker died and the American House of Representatives sent an offer of sympathy. Bismarck refused to allow it to be read in the Reichstag and no government representatives appeared at the funeral. Not suprisingly Jews, Socialists and Liberals were as far as possible kept out of the German civil service. Between 1885 and 1914 not a single Jewish officer appeared in the Prussian army (Stern, 15, p.488). Promotion for civil servants with liberal or socialist views was denied.

Under Bismarck the tradition was firmly established that the individual was subservient to the state. With this end in view Bismarck did not hesitate to use every means at his disposal to undermine the freedom of the press. The Wolff press agency, one of the main rivals to Reuters, was given a government monopoly but only if it accepted censorship, precedence for the government's political dispatches, and control by the government of its head and agents. Bismarck had at his disposal the Welfenfond, popularly known as the 'Reptile Fund'. This large sum of money had been confiscated from the Hanoverian crown when Hanover was annexed by Prussia. Bismarck did not have to account for this to the German parliament and in fact only one set of accounts has survived. Bismarck referred to one group of Hanoverian pressmen as 'reptiles' and this gave the fund its popular nickname. The money was used, among other purposes, to help Bismarck's system of planting stories in the newspapers. Bismarck was entirely unscrupulous in his use of the press. When King Frederick lay dying of throat cancer Bismarck did not hesitate to whip up a press campaign against his English wife. The government powers of censorship were also used to the full. When a German professor attempted to publish King Frederick's diary, Bismarck declared it was a forgery and took criminal proceedings against the unfortunate man. Bismarck's successors carried on this policy of censorship. The historian Sybel was forced to omit a large section of his book on German unification because, in the words of Caprivi, the new Chancellor, it 'questions the ideas hitherto publicised and officially confirmed about the causes of the 1870–1 war and might be expected to cast doubt at home and abroad on the trustworthiness of our political attitudes at that time.' (Bonnin, 9, introduction).

Of course Bismarck did not himself create the powerful image of the supremacy of the German state over the individual. The famous and popular Grimm fairy tales, supposedly based on German folk legends, are full of authoritarian symbolism (Snyder, 34, p.44). The story of the sole, for example, contains this very illuminating passage: 'The fishes had for a long time been discontented because no order prevailed in their kingdom. None of them turned aside for the others, but all swam to the left or to the right as they fancied, or darted between those who wanted to stay together or got in their way... "How delightful it would be," said they, "if we had a king who enforced law and justice among us." And they met together to choose for their ruler the one who would cleave through the water most quickly and give help to the weak ones.' The problem was that Bismarck's politics reinforced this basic tendency to **authoritarianism** and established it as part of the German state. Former liberals like the influential professor of history at Berlin University, Treitschke, continually preached the same doctrine to their students. 'The core of the state,' said Treitschke, 'is power! The state is not there for the citizen. It is an end in itself. Since the state is power, it can obviously draw into its sphere of influence all human activities.' 'It does not matter what you think as long as you obey.'

Perhaps Bismarck's most serious failure was that the Germany he built up between 1871 and his fall was hated and feared by the other European states. The unification of Germany had been carried through by the fighting of three wars and the forceful annexation of Alsace and Lorraine from France. Although Bismarck realised that the annexation was likely to pose impossible problems he did nothing to prevent it and probably even approved of it. He told Odo Russell, the British emissary to Versailles, that 'the more completely France was vanquished the better in the end for Germany and the more lasting the peace.' (Stern, 15, p.146). Bismarck did nothing to prevent the senseless celebrations which followed the defeat of France and which helped to poison the relations between the two countries. The Berlin victory parade of June 1871, with its laurel wreaths, triumphal arches, its 81 captured French flags and eagles and generals in their military uniform and medals, cost Germany more than the 150,000 thalers which were needed to pay for the spectacle. Together with the annual Sedan fairs which commemorated the Prussion victory they helped to make the French desire for revenge a strong one. Crown Prince Frederick confessed his fears in the diary which Bismarck tried to suppress. On 31 December 1870 he recorded: 'Bismarck has made us great and powerful but he has robbed us of our friends, of international sympathy and of our own clear conscience. I still stand by the view that Germany without blood and iron but using her just influence could have made "moral conquests" and become united, free and powerful. She would then have gained a superiority quite different from that gained solely by force of arms, because German culture, German science, and the German nature could not but win us esteem, love and honour. This bold and violent Junker wanted it otherwise,' (Hertz, 17, p.327) The victories of the German army brought about a senseless veneration for war which Bismarck did little to combat. Felix Dahn, professor of law and history, wrote the following poem which was typical of the period:

> 'And the hammer flew out of Thor's hand,
> flew over the whole earth,
> fell down in the farthest south,
> so that everything became his.
> Since then it has been the joyful right of the Germans
> with their hammer to acquire land:
> We belong to the race of the hammer God.
> and we wish to inherit his world wide Reich.   (Kohn, 31, p.162)

Treitschke believed that 'the grandeur of war is in the utter annihilation of puny men in the great conception of the state.' Periods of peace, he believed, were 'exhausted, spiritless, degnerate periods.' 'War is both justifiable and moral and the ideal of perpetual peace is not only impossible but immoral as well.' Writing in 1899 Carl Franke praised the Grimm fairy tales because 'they have enabled us in understand that we, the German people, bear the power and conditions in ourselves to take up and carry on the civilizations of old times, that we are a folk with a high historical mission.' Far from trying to combat this extreme nationalism Bismarck at times even stirred it up. In 1875, for example, he wanted to obtain a Reichstag which was less critical of his policies so he deliberately planted news of a war scare with France in the papers. It seems likely that the German colonial Empire which Bismarck built up between 1885 and 1890 was not created because be believed in colonialism. In 1871 he had told Moritz Busch (p.167), 'I do not want colonies at all. Their only use is to provide sinecures... for us Germans, colonies would be exactly like the silks and sables of the Polish nobleman who had no shirt to wear under them.' (Mitchell, 2, p.111) He stirred up all the emotions of colonialism because he needed to create hostile relations with Britain. A hostile Britain might embarass the Crown Prince and his English wife, should he become King, and could perhaps help Bismarck to ally with France against a common adversary. In the event Frederick died before he could effectively become King and the rift with France, caused by Bismarck's own annexation of Alsace and Lorraine, proved impossible to repair in this way. So Germany now had a colonial Empire which after Bismarck's fall was to be used as an excuse for building a powerful navy. This navy would further inflame the suspicions and fears of Germany which paved the way for World War. I.

When Bismarck fell from power his legacy to Germany and Europe was a dangerously unstable authoritarian state which he had taught to base its actions on military power, the undermining of individual freedom and empty assertions of German nationalism. In 1954, in his book, *The Social and Political Conflict in Prussia*, E.N. Anderson wrote: 'Did Bismarck settle the constitutional conflict? The answer can only be that he did not, that he glossed over it by nationalism and success in international relations. He solved none of the crucial internal social and political problems; he only postponed a settlement. The evidence for this conclusion is found in the fact that within three generations the Bismarckian Reich was destroyed, the Junker conservatives were ruined, and the Hohenzollerns had lost their throne.' (Hollyday, 11, p.125) In addition the Bismarckian Reich had paved the way for Hitler's Reich. His domination of affairs had removed the essential element of democratic conflict from German political life. With no experience of democracy the German people were unable to make the Weimer Republic of 1919–34 work and fell easy victims to Hitler's Nazi dictatorship. Hitler's anti-semitic and nationalistic policies fitted easily into the atmosphere which had been encouraged by the Bismarckian regime. Indeed in 1936, the two Nazi writers, Von der Goltz and Theodor Stiefenhofer, hailed Bismarck as part of the line which led up to Hitler. 'We see the *volkisch* line which stretches from Arminius through Henry I, Luther, the great Prussian Kings, Stein and Bismarck to Adolf Hitler, and we nurse the steadfast belief that it will continue to stretch into a brilliant future so long as the German people remain at all times, in fortune and misfortune, in good days and bad, a nation pledged to pull together, whatever fate has in store for it.' (Rohl, 12, p.3)

Bismarck's Germany defended

It is interesting to speculate on why the view of Bismarck's Germany as being a sort of prototype for Germany militarism, World War One, Hitler, and World War Two, has been so popular. There can be little doubt that the propaganda influence of two World Wars, in which British and American governments were obliged to use all the resources at their disposal to prove that the German nation was fatally flawed, may have a lot to do with it. Faced with the problem of explaining why their countries have had to fight the same national enemy twice within 50 years it is tempting for historians to look for answers such as the German character and the flaws in Bismarck's unification. Even an historian like Namier, writing a book review in 1947 of Taylor's *The Course of German History* (20), was capable of trying to fix a national stereotype on the Germans. 'Why do individual Germans in non-German surroundings become useful decent citizens but in groups develop tendencies which make them a menace to their fellow men?' he asked. 'We call the German inhuman: for sometimes he behaves like a beast and sometimes like a robot.' (Callao, 35, p.62) Yet it is now over thirty years since World War Two, the German nation has remained divided, and still the legend persists. The reason lies within the complicated twists and turns of the 'Cold War.' NATO needed West Germany as an ally against a possible invasion of west Europe by the Russion dominated Warsaw pact forces. Before this could be achieved west Europeans had to be reassured that Germans had admitted guilt for their past sins. West German historians began to do this. Ludwig Dehio contributed an article to a collection called *German History, Some New Views,* in 1954, in which he wrote, 'The majority of Germans see today in Hitler a terrible destroyer of their country. But we must learn to understand fully that the destruction started with Bismarck's work.' (Mitchell, 2, p.130) In contrast East Germany, a communist state behind the Iron curtain, was held to be perpetuating all the worst features of the Prussian state which Bismarck had imposed on the rest of Germany. The distortions imposed on history by the smoke screens of war time propaganda and the pressure of cold war politics have therefore denied Bismarck's Germany a fair trial. It has not helped that the Nazi propaganda machine sought to justify their policies by claiming that they had a good historical ancestry from Bismarck. To get anywhere near the real truth the historian must try to blow away the smoke and look at the problem objectively.

The methods used by those historians who have tried to link Bismarck's

Germany with the disasters of Hitler's Reich must be seriously open to question. They start by isolating the well known evils of Hitler's regime: authoritarianism, anti-semitism, the glorification of war, the subjection of the individual to the needs of the state. The letters and writings of Bismarck and other influential writers from that period in Germany are then ransacked to find evidence that they too sometimes gave support for such policies. Such methods are not properly historical. They fail to reveal that Bismarck and his contemporaries may also have given voice to totally contradictory views and that the selected extracts may have only been isolated fragments. They neglect the possibility that many Germans may have held other opinions and have sometimes succeeded in winning their case. Worst of all they fail to explore the possibility that the glorification of war, authoritarian thinking and anti-semitism may not have been confined to Germany in the Bismarckian period. William Shirer's famous book *The Rise and Fall of the Third Reich* (1960) was heavily criticised by Klaus Epstein in a book review in 1961 on the same grounds. 'Shirer documents his one-sided theme by presenting parallel passages from Hitler, Hegel and Nietzsche. It is superfluous to comment on this crude throwback to wartime pamphleteering.' (Rohl, 12, p.16).

A common British criticism of Bismarck is that he failed to establish Germany as a democracy. But how many other democracies were in operation between 1870 and 1914? When Bismarck gave the Germans universal manhood suffrage for all those over 25 he was in fact ahead of most other countries in Europe. The Russians could only vote in local elections; British agricultural labourers did not get the vote until 1884 and domestic servants not until 1918. In the USA the negroes of the south were deprived of their vote by their local states. Women were almost universally voteless. Of course the elected German Reichstag had few powers compared to the French Chamber or the British House of Commons but consider how many centuries of gradual change had been necessary before the House of Commons became sovereign in Britain. It is an unfortunate British prejudice that all new nations are expected to give birth to a ready made replica of democratic government. The history of new nations like Greece, Italy and the emergent African states suggests that this is not possible and probably not desirable. Even if Bismarck had wanted to give Germany a full democracy the opposition from the junkers and the army would have made it almost impossible for him to succeed. To have persuaded the King and the army to accept universal male suffrage and a Reichstag which could block government legislation was a considerable feat which Bismarck is given very little credit for. The Reichstag was given enough power to make the future development of democracy possible in Germany. The way in which Bismarck was always struggling to find majorities which would carry through his policies shows that its powers were not as slight as has often been made out.

When viewed in isolation the treatment of minority and opposition groups in Bismarck's Germany looks bad. But it must be remembered that most European countries were at that time trying to reconcile Catholicism with the powers of the state. In France there was a long struggle by the Third Republic to wrest control of education from the Roman Catholic Church, which culminated in 1905 when the Roman Catholic Church in France was disestablished. In Belgium in the 1870s there was a 'war of the schools.' Even in Britain Catholics had only just been admitted to the Universities of Oxford and Cambridge by the passing of the University Test Act in 1871. In Northern Ireland, of course, the restrictions on Catholics persisted until after the Second World War and are still causing trouble. The struggle with the Catholics in Bismarck's Germany was part of a European problem and not evidence of religious intolerance or lack of respect for minorities. The idea that life under the Bismarckian Reich could be compared to the lack of basic liberties in Hitler's Germany has very little to recommend it. Laws passed in 1874 guaranteed the German press against interference from the government and German **pressure groups** were just as strong and just as capable of looking after themselves as those in other European countries. When in 1904, for example, the Prussian Government attempted to nationalise the Hibernia Coal Mining Company it was easily defeated by industrialists. Despite the anti-socialist laws the German Social Democrat Party was able to gain more and more seats and soon became the largest parliamentary socialist party in Europe. It mounted massive peaceful demonstrations like the one in Berlin in 1910 in which 150,000 Berliners went on an 'electoral stroll' to demonstrate against the Prussian three class electoral laws. True the German government was often ruthless in dealing with its political opponents but can it be truthfully claimed that British governments were any less so in dealing with the suffragettes and the problems in Ireland?

Perhaps one of the biggest injustices done to Bismarck has been the attempt to saddle him with some of the guilt for Hitler's final solution to what he saw as the Jewish problem. Bismarck was far from being alone in letting slip statements showing anti-Jewish sentiments. Such attitudes were common everywhere at that time. The American Eleanor Roosevelt wrote of Felix Frankfurter in 1904 that he was 'an interesting little man but very Jew.' (Stern, 15, p.497) Do we therefore argue that the USA was paving the way for racialist policies? In fact Bismarck showed considerably less anti-semitism than was common at the time. Bismarck's banker, doctor and legal advisor were all Jews. In July 1892 Bismarck gave his views on the subject in a conversation with Heinrich von Poschinger. 'Bismarck considered that a combination of the Jewish and German elements was useful. There was something in the Jews that Germany did not possess... He considered the Jews to be useful members of the state of today and thought it unwise to molest them. The rich Jew especially was generally a regular tax payer and a good subject.' (Hollyday, 11, p.81) The pogroms against the Jews in Russia and the celebrated Dreyfus case in France show that other countries had much more violent anti-Jewish feelings than Bismarck's Germany. Even such a well known anti-semite as the German composer Richard Wagner did not hesitate to hand over the interpretation of his music to Jewish conductors and artists. Proof that this did not affect his personal relations with Jews was provided when Joseph Rubinstein, the Jewish pianist, committed suicide on his grave. If German society had been as anti-semitic as some have suggested the industrial depression of 1873–83 should have brought forward more dangerous movements than Stoecker's easily defeated group. In 1881 it has been estimated that Jewish people constituted 4.8% of Berlin's population, 8.6% of the city's writers and journalists, 25.0% of those working in the money market, 46% of the city's wholesalers, retailers and shippers. In the mid-1880s nearly 10% of all students enrolled in Prussia's universities were Jewish, that is seven times their proportion of Prussia's population (Stern, 15, p.499). It is a testament to the soundness of Bismarck's Germany that the depression failed to trigger the well known 'scapegoat' mechanism when a people blame a minority like the Jews or negroes for their misfortunes and actually persuade the government to take violent action against them. Bismarck's Reich was not at all like Hitler's.

Bismarck's Germany has often been described as a society dominated by the Junkers with militaristic values which glorified war and insisted on the subjection of the individual to the state. It was only, it is claimed, a short step from this type of society to Hitler's Nazi regime. When Germany is viewed in isolation this point of view seems plausible but when other countries are put under the microscope German society seems only part of a general European trend. For example, the German philosophers who argued that the nation state was more important than the individuals who comprised it were only saying the same, admittedly more crudely and forthrightly, as T.H. Green, Bosanquet and Bradley in Britain, Croce in Italy, and Bergson in France. In any case there is a lot to be said for the arguments of the 'Idealist' school of philosophers. Without the organisation, rules and discipline of the state it is surely true that there would be no real individual freedom. Most individuals are by nature aggressive and anti-social and the state must teach them to live together in harmony and to moderate their actions so that they do not limit the freedoms of others. Even the British liberals discovered that there could be no real freedom for individuals unless the state interfered to protect the weakest – that is how the Welfare State came to be formed. The idea that the Germans by nature are liable to accept discipline has often been put forward and evidence to support it has been derived from the authoritarian tone of alleged samples of German popular culture like the Grimm fairy tales. The argument loses something of its weight however when one enquires exactly where the Grimm brothers obtained their material for the stories. One recent analysis (Snyder, 34, p.44) suggests that a large proportion of their tales came from Frau Viehmenn, a descendant from a French Huguenot family which had emigrated to Germany bringing with them stories current in seventeenth century France!

The argument that Bismarck and the Junker class founded a Germany based on the glorification of war is also demonstrably untrue. Bismarck and the Prussian Junkers were satisfied with the Germany of 1871. They did not contemplate expanding its boundaries to include the Germans in the Austrian Empire or anywhere else, as Hitler did. It is true that Bismarck was prepared to use war but only if it was absolutely necessary and if it could be limited in aim. In 1867 he put his point of view to Count Eduard von Bethusy-Huc, a member of the German free conservative party: 'If foreign ministers had always followed their sovereigns to the front, history would have fewer wars to tell of. I have seen on a battlefield and what is far worse in the hospitals the flower of our youth carried off by wounds and disease; from this window I look down on the Wilhelmstrasse and see many a cripple who looks up and thinks that if that man there had not made that wicked war I should be at home, healthy and strong. With such memories and such sights I should not have a moment's peace if I had to reproach myself for making war irresponsibly, or out of ambition, or the vain seeking of fame.' (Crankshaw, 14, p.215) As A.J.P. Taylor has remarked, 'Bismarck's planned wars killed thousands; the just wars of the twentieth century have killed millions.' (Taylor, 4, p.79) The much maligned Junker class were in agreement with Bismarck over this. They wanted to retain an agricultural Prussia which imported cheap manufactured goods from Britain and supported a powerful army. A Germany expanded to include Austrian Germans would end their dominance so they were content with the smaller frontiers. Unfortunately the growth of the industrial middle classes made their ideal policy impossible and they had to compromise by accepting high tarriff barriers for German industry as well as agriculture. Most of the nationalist demands for colonies and a navy came from the middle class industrialists not the Junkers. It was from this group that the nationalistic poems and songs emanated.

Yet even these don't mean that Germany was particularly warlike or nationalistic. Every country in Europe between 1870 and 1914 was full of such sentiments. Children in Britain's public elementary schools were taught military drill. Charles Marley in his *Studies in Board Schools* (1897, p.292) described how, after the morning service at Clerkenwell Elementary School, 'the boy regiments file out, there is a trampling of many small feet upon the floor and six hundred small voices trill forth a gay air:

"With ribbons gaily streaming
I'm a soldier now Loisette
And of battle I am dreaming
And the honours I shall get
With a sabre by my side

And a helmet on my brow
And a proud steed to ride
I shall rush upon the foe
Yes, I flatter my Loisette
'Tis a life that well will suit
The gay life of a young recruit.'"

By 1914 over 200,000 youths in Britain were members of para-military type movements like the Boys' Brigade, the Church Lads, the Boys' Empire League, the Lads' Drill Association and the Boy Scouts. C. Fletcher and R. Kipling's history text book for schools (1912) told its readers, 'I don't think there can be any doubt that the only safe thing for all of us who love our country is to learn soldiering at once and be prepared to fight at any moment.' No doubt if Oswald Mosley and his Fascists had taken power in Britain between the wars as Hitler did in Germany, historians would be busy using this evidence to show that it was the fault of the British governments before the First World War. Aggressive warlike nationalism was not a German monopoly. The fact that it infected Britain, a country which was not open to invasion from three sides like Germany but safely protected by a moat of water, makes this point very clear.

The real cause of Germany's problems was not that the German people were wicked or that Bismarck had failed to set up a workable new national state but that there were too many pressures for her to cope with at once. Not only was Germany struggling to deal with the problems of national unity at a time when, as the last great nation to attain national unity, she was being regarded with hostility by the older European nations, but also she was facing all the complexities of one of the most rapid industrial revolutions the world has ever seen. Even in 1870 only about one third of the German population was urban; Germany was still predominantly a rural country. By 1914 the situation had reversed; two thirds of the German population lived in urban areas. The reason behind this rapid transformation was the growth of German trade and commerce. By 1914 Germany had risen to challenge Britain in factory production of textiles, coal mining and iron. At the same time as she was developing these basic industries she was also taking a lead over Britain in such newer industries as steel manufacture, electrical products and industrial dyes. The finance for this outstanding growth came almost entirely from within Germany and, incredibly, she was still able to find money to lend abroad. In 1914, 13% of the world's overseas investment was provided by Germany, compared to 43% from Britain, 20% from France and 8% from USA. All this was accompanied by a formidable growth in population: 160% between 1815 and 1914 compared to France's 40%. The pressures which the new state was subjected to as a result of this revolutionary growth were enormous. The growth of towns led to problems of health, housing and prostitution. Berlin's population grew from 172,000 to over two million between 1850 and 1910 and most of this came in the period after 1890. The numbers of prostitutes active in Germany were estimated to have increased from 100–200,000 in 1910 to 330,000 in 1914. (*Past and Present*, no. 70, February 1976, p.108). The growth of industry also led to problems of wages, working hours and conditions.

Incredibly the German state withstood most of the challenges remarkably well. Bismarck is often accused of failing to understand economic matters. Yet the discovery of his correspondence with his banker Bleichroder seems to reveal that he was much shrewder than most historians were at one time prepared to allow. Over the years there is no doubt that Bismarck received more money from the timber off his estates, carefully husbanded and sold for pit props and paper manufacture, than he obtained from his official salary (Stern, 15, p.296). It is hard to believe that the unification of Germany's currency, weights and measures, commercial law, postal, telegraph and communications services were reforms which Bismarck did not understand. Nor is it easy to maintain that the establishment of protection for German industry and the gaining of protected colonial markets were changes which Bismarck made merely as political games divorced from real calculations of Germany's economic needs. Perhaps his greatest achievement was his realisation that the social pressures created by Germany's rapid industrialisation must be dealt with by the State. The introduction of statutory sickness insurance in 1883, accident insurance in 1884 and old age insurance in 1889, made Bismarck the pioneer of the Welfare State. His ideas were copied by most other countries and not least in Britain. Although there was no system of unemployment insurance the idea of labour exchanges was soon added and by 1914 German workers probably had better protection against the hazards of industrialisation than those of any other country. In 1870 the life expectation of a male at birth was 36 years; in spite of the pressures in Germany it had risen to 45 years by 1913 (Cipolla, 30, p.122).

The disasters of Hitler's Germany should not therefore be blamed on Bismarck's Germany. He had nothing to do with the fanaticism of the twentieth century. The German state that he set up had a very good chance of success. But even the best creations cannot survive defeat in war, humiliation and repeated economic disaster as happened to Germany between 1914 and 1930. As D. Callao has argued, 'the lesson is not that the Germans are peculiarly wicked but rather that even a deeply rooted civilisation can rapidly descend into barbarism if put under sustained pressure.' (Snyder, 34, p.159). Ulrich von Hassell visited the Bismarck estates in July 1944 in the midst of the horrors of World War Two and recorded this very perceptive comment in his diary. 'During recent years I have studied Bismarck, and his stature as a statesman grows constantly in my estimation. It is regrettable what a false picture of him we ourselves have given the world – that of the power-politician with cuirassier boots – in our childish joy over the fact that at last someone had made Germany a name to reckon with again... In truth the highest diplomacy and great moderation were his real gifts...' (Rohl, 12, p.181)

Study 38

You have now read the two sides in the argument about Bismarck's Germany. Write a brief report giving your own views but first answer these questions in note form:

1. What are the main arguments of each side?
2. What are the main points of disagreement?
3. Which of the arguments on each side seem to you to lack evidence in their support? What sort of evidence, if available, could remedy these deficiences?
4. Arguments are often based on assumptions, for example, the author might assume that everyone would agree that murder is wrong. What assumptions are the two points of view based on? Do you necessarily agree with them? If not, why not?
5. It is often complained that some academic historians are guilty of playing clever games with words. They may set out, for example, to prove that there is no such thing as a desert; deserts are supposed to be dry and empty but you can prove that there are many living creatures in them, they do have rain, deep underground there is water, therefore deserts don't really exist! Do you feel that any parts of the two points of view are guilty of doing this? Which parts and why?
6. Can you find any further evidence for yourself? The relevant chapters of books 16, 20, 22, 24, 25, 30 might help. The second point of view really requires a comparative European history approach; the best book for this is D. Thomson *Europe Since Napoleon*, Longman, 1957, Part V.

Sources

For the Study of German Unification

Before consulting any bibliography it is essential to consider where the books in it have come from. How have they been written? What problems have had to be overcome? The construction of a book from the raw material can be illustrated by what is perhaps one of the most fascinating books to appear recently – F. Stern's *Gold and Iron* (15). This is a sort of 'double biography' which traces the relationship between Bismarck and his Jewish banker and financial advisor, Gerson Bleichroder. But what sources did the book use and where did they come from? Like many businessmen, Gerson Bleichroder kept files of his papers and personal correspondence. On his death, the business part of his archives was handed over to his banking firm and disappeared during the Second World War. But the private part consisting of thousands of letters written to Bleichroder between 1880 and 1893, turned up in New York and became the basis for Stern's book. However, these were obviously only letters written to Bleichroder (p.152). Stern was able to bridge the gap by using the letters which Bleichroder himself wrote to Bismarck (p.171). These had been unearthed above the stables on the Bismarck estate at Friedrichsrur. Finally, it was possible for Stern to study many other collections of letters which Bleichroder wrote. There was his correspondence with the Rothschilds of Paris which was discovered in an attic above one of their banks; there were over a thousand letters which he wrote to the British Prime Minister Disraeli which survived on the Disraeli estate at Hughenden.

As in Italy (p.100) Germany's state archives are very scattered. Each German state initially had its own library and centre for historical records so many documents are still held at this level. Worse than in Italy, Germany has now ceased to be one nation with the result that the archive situation has become even more complex. In 1919 a promising start had been made with the foundation of a central German Archive but after World War Two and the division of Germany between the Federal Republic (West) and the Democratic Republic (East) the archive has likewise been split between West German Koblenz and East German Potsdam. In the same way the Prussian state archives have become split between Merseburg (East Germany) and West Berlin (West Germany). Although permission to use the archives behind the iron curtain for documents before 1945 is usually given, it is unwise to assume that such access is guaranteed. The documents from the German Foreign Office were captured by the USA and Britain in the Second World War and are now in Bonn, West Germany (p.168). The British Government took the opportunity of having them photographed and as a result photostats may be consulted in the Foreign Office Library in London.

Bibliography

On German Unification

I.   A Brief and Basic List

1. A brief readable text, pamphlet dimensions: J. A. Moses, *Germany 1848–79*, Heinemann, 1972.
2. A recent account of Bismarck and his policies written for sixth forms: I.R. Mitchell, *Bismarck and the Development of Germany*, Holmes McDougall, 1980.
3. Documents: A. Hewison, *Bismarck and the Unification of Germany*, Arnold's Archive Series, 1970.
4. An argumentative biography: A. J. P. Taylor, *Bismarck, the Man and Statesman*, Mentor, 1965.
5. The story of a vital battle: G. Craig, *The Battle of Königgratz*, Weidenfeld and Nicholson, 1965.
6. A provocative short essay: L. S. B. Seaman, *From Vienna to Versailles*, Methuen, 1955, chapter 11.

II.   A More Detailed List

a. Documents and Sources

7. W. M. Simon, *Germany in the Age of Bismarck*, Allen and Unwin, 1968.
8. Ed. H. Bohme, *The Foundation of the German Empire*, Oxford University Press, 1971.
9. Ed. G. Bonnin, *Bismarck and the Hohenzollern Candidature for the Spanish Throne*, Chatto and Windus, London, 1957.
10. W. N. Medlicott and D. K. Coveney, *Bismarck and Europe*, Arnold, 1971.
11. Ed. F. B. Hollyday, *Bismarck*, Great Lives Observed Series, Prentice Hall, 1970.
12. Ed. J. C. G. Rohl, *From Bismarck to Hitler*, Longman, 1970.

b. Biographies

13. A. Palmer, *Bismarck*, Weidenfeld and Nicolson, 1976.
14. E. Crankshaw, *Bismarck*, Macmillan, 1981.
15. F. Stern, *Gold and Iron: Bismarck, Bleichroder, and the Building of the German Empire*, Knopf, 1977.

c. General Histories

16. W. M. Simon, *Germany: A Brief History*, Batsford, 1967.
17. F. Hertz, *The German Public Mind in the Nineteenth Century*, Allen & Unwin, 1975.
18. G. O. Kent, *Bismarck and His Times*, Southern Illinois Press, 1978.
19. W. Medlicott, *Bismarck and Modern Germany*, English University Press, 1965.
20. A. J. P. Taylor, *The Course of German History*, Methuen University Paperback, 1948.

21. O. Pflanze, *Bismarck and the Development of Germany: Unification 1815–71*, Holt, Rinehart and Winston, 1963.
22. G. Craig, *Germany 1866–1945*, Oxford University Press, 1978.
23. L. Steefel, *Bismarck, the Hohenzollern Candidature and the Origins of the Franco-German War of 1870*, Cambridge, Massachusetts, 1962.

d. Economic and Social History

24. E. Sagarra, *A Social History of Germany 1648–1914*, Methuen, 1977.
25. M. Kitchen, *The Political Economy of Germany 1815–1914*, Croom Helm, 1978.
26. T. S. Hamerow, *The Social Foundations of German Unification 1858–71*, Princeton University Press, 1969.
27. T. S. Hamerow, *Restoration, Revolution and Reaction. Economics and Politics in Germany 1815–71*, Princeton University Press, 1958.
28. A. S. Millward & S. Saul, *The Economic Development of Continental Europe*, Allen & Unwin, 1973.
29. C. L. & R. Tilly, *The Rebellious Century 1830–1930*, Harvard University Press, 1975.
30. Ed. C. Cipolla, *Fontana Economic History of Europe: The Emergence of Industrial Societies I and 2*, Fontana/Collins, 1973.
31. H. Kohn, *The Mind of Germany*, Macmillan, 1965.

e. Military History

32. M. Howard, *The Franco-Prussian War*, Hart Davis, 1961.
33. M. Kitchen, *A Military History of Germany*, Weidenfeld and Nicholson, 1975.

f. Essays and Articles

34. L. Snyder, *Roots of German Nationalism*, Indiana University Press, 1978.
35. D. Callao, *The German Problem Reconsidered*, Cambridge University Press, 1978.
36. Ed. T. Hamerow, *The Age of Bismarck*, Harper & Row, 1973.
37. B. Bond, 'The Austro-Prussian War, 1866', *History Today*, August 1966.

g. Other works referred to in text

38. M. Howard, *Studies in War and Peace*, Temple Smith, 1970.
39. J.R. Gillis, 'Aristocracy and Bureaucracy in nineteenth century Prussia', *Past and Present*, no. 41. December, 1968.
40. E. Kedourie, *Nationalism*, Hutchinson, 1960.
41. W.E. Mosse, *The European Powers and the German Question*, Cambridge University Press, 1958.
42. G. Kertesz, *Documents in the Political History of the European Continent*, Oxford University Press, 1968.
43. R.J. Evans, 'Prostitution, State and Society in Imperial Germany', *Past and Present*, no. 70, February 1976.
44. D. Thomson, *Europe since Napolean*, Longman, 1957.

III. Audio Visual Aids

a. Films

The Face of Germany, Open University, 1977, colour, 24 minutes (background to 1848). *Students and Revolution*, Open University, 1977, colour, 20 minutes (students in Heidelburg).

b. Slides/Filmstrips

The Franco-Prussian War 1870–1, Audio Visual Productions, 24 slides of filmstrip, (contemporary sketches).
The Franco-Prussian War, Slide Centre, 12 slides.
The Making of Modern Germany, Common Ground (Longman), black and white filmstrips.

c. Tape Recordings

The Making of the German Nation, 1815–1918, Educational Audio Visual (EAV), tape/cassette and two colour filmstrips.
Bismarck and Germany, a discussion between G. Barraclough and A. J. P. Taylor, Sussex Tapes, one hour (see also transcript printed in *Europe in the Nineteenth Century*, Sussex Books).
Bismarck and the German Problem, his aims and methods, M. Sturmer and Miss B. Williams, Audio Learning, 56 minutes.

d. Overhead Projector Transparencies

The Unification of Germany; 1812–67; 1871–1945, Audio Visual Productions, 5 OHP maps in each set.

Nationalism in the Modern World

The previous chapters have discussed why and how Italians and Germans succeeded in forming their countries into nations. They have also attempted to provoke consideration of what benefits their new countries brought them. But does it matter? Does studying what happened in Germany and Italy in the nineteenth century help us today in the twentieth century?

A main point to grasp is that the nationalist movements which began in Germany and Italy, went on to influence the whole modern world. Czechs, Slavs, Bulgars, Norwegians, Finns and many others, soon began to press their claims for nationhood. The Treaty of Versailles in 1919 yielded to their demands and the great European Empires of Turkey, Austria-Hungary and Tsarist Russia gave way to the small national 'succesor states'. Before the Second World War the idea of nationalism was already spreading to Africa and Asia. All over these continents after World War Two **decolonisation** took place and the Imperial flags of Britain, France, Italy, Spain and Portugal were hauled down. The world in which we live today is very much the product of the **nationalism** which had triumphed in Italy and Germany. To understand what happened then is therefore to gain an insight into the problems of the world today.

————— *Study 39* —————

Compare map 1 on page 2 and map 7 on page 197. Answer the following questions:
1. What new nation states took the place of the Ottoman Empire?
2. What successor states were created from the Austrian Empire?
3. What new nations emerged from the territory taken from Russia?
4. What other new countries, besides Germany and Italy appeared between 1815 and 1926? Your answers to these questions should serve to illustrate the argument that, in Europe at least, the period between 1815 and 1926 has seen the triumph of the idea of the nation state. To check on the further development of nationalism in Europe find a modern atlas and answer one last question:
5. What states have disappeared from Europe since 1926? Have any new ones appeared?

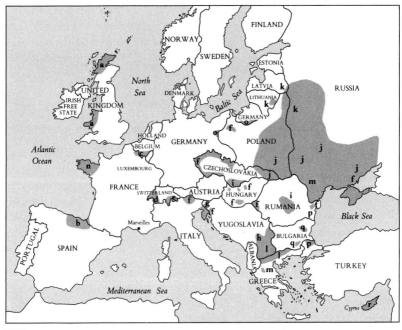

KEY

 Linguistic Minorities

a	Celtic	g	Slovene	m	Rumanian
b	Basque	h	Albanian	n	Breton
c	Walloon	i	Magyar (Hungarian)	o	Polish
d	French	j	Ruthene	p	Bulgarian
e	Italian	k	White Russian	q	Turkish
f	German	l	Macedonian	r	Greek

Map 7. Linguistic Minorities in Europe in 1926

Nationalist movements are still very much alive in all parts of the world. Map 7 above reveals that the distribution of languages, which are indicators of national groupings, wilfully refuses to be restrained within simple boundary lines drawn on maps. In Europe alone there are the Scottish and Welsh nationalist movements, the Basque ETA, and French speaking Walloons' attempt to obtain regional autonomy in Belgium. Outside Europe examples of nationalist movements are even more numerous. In the Middle East the Kurds have been attempting to establish their autonomy – an apparently hopeless task as they are split between Iran, Iraq, Turkey and USSR. Palestinian nationalists struggle to assert themselves against Jewish Zionists on the west bank of the river Jordan. In Canada French speaking Quebec has been trying for some form of autonomy. All these are examples of break away nationalists who are dissatisfied with the states in which they live and either wish to have more local autonomy or to become totally independent. But there are also national movements which are dedicated to extending their countries by including nationals who live across the borders under what they regard as alien rule. The most obvious examples of such movements are the IRA struggle to gain Northern Ireland for the Irish Free State, and the attempt by the Greek government to annex Cyprus. At the far end of the scale are the so called 'pan' nationalist movements, which dream of full Arab unity, or of an African nation.

The story of the unification of Germany and Italy could be taken to illustrate all three of the modern types of nationalism. Germans and Italians were attempting to break away from Austrian domination. The states of Piedmont-Sardinia and Prussia were trying to spread their territories to include the rest of their nationals living under alien rule. The many different German and Italian states were aiming at a sort of 'pan' German and Italian nationalism when they unified their territories. So if we wish to understand what is happening around us today, the lessons of Italy and Germany are relevant.

Study 40

One way of testing the continuity of history is to play the 'déjà vu' game. The term 'déjà vu' is used to describe a feeling which most of us experience at some time or other. We suddenly feel sure that something which is happening to us at the present has already happened before. Of course we are in fact suffering a distortion of the memory. But, to a historian, recent events often seem to have very close similarities to past ones. Consider each of the recent incidents listed below and say which events in the history of German and/or Italian nationalism they have a superficial similarity to. You have been given some page references to help trigger your 'déjà vu' historical memory! Usually on more careful consideration the incidents turn out to have fundamental differences – try to list these differences as well as the similarities.

1. On 27 August, 1979, the IRA blew up Earl Mountbatten and three others in his party, including a fourteen year old grandson (ch.2, p.28).
2. In 1982 Israel invaded its northern neighbour, Lebanon. The object of this attack was to hunt down the nationalist army of the Palestinian Liberation Organisation. They had taken refuge in the Lebanon and from there were carrying out guerilla raids on Israel and planning to recover what they regarded as their homeland, (ch.1, pp.10–11).
3. On 7 May 1981 the ETA carried out a terrorist attack in Madrid, Spain, leaving three dead, and seriously wounding the chief of the King's military household. The ETA is a secret organistion which was founded in the 1960s to promote greater autonomy for the Basques. (ch.1, pp.10–12)
4. Between 1 March and 3 October 1981, ten members of the Provisional IRA detained in 'H' block in the Maze prison, Northern Ireland, died

while on hunger strike in an attempt to gain political status as prisoners. The prisoners were hailed as martyrs and one, Bobby Sands was even elected to parliament (ch.1, p.14; ch.3, pp.52–3; ch. 7, p.112).

5. In April 1982, Argentina invaded the Falkland Islands which had been under British control since 1832. The Argentine government had always maintained that the islands belonged to Argentina and their seizure was accompanied by demonstration of popular enthusiasm (ch.2, pp.35–40 and p.43; ch.8, p.126).

6. In 1972 the British army had 22,000 soldiers in Northern Ireland. They were intended to prevent civil war between Protestant Ulster Unionists who wished to remain in the UK and Catholic Republicans who wanted to incorporate Northern Ireland into the Irish Free State. The soldiers still numbered 10,700 in 1981 (ch.1, p.15, and p.25; ch.2, p.43).

7. Nigeria obtained independence from Britain in 1960. The inhabitants spoke nearly 400 distinct languages. Between 1967 and 1970 the country was plunged into bitter civil war when the Ibos of Biafra tried to break away from the rest of Nigeria. They were defeated (ch.6, pp.91–2).

8. In 1980 the new nation of Zimbabwe was proclaimed after a seven year struggle between the white Rhodesian forces and terrorist groups from across the borders. In 1981 some 22,000 of the black guerrilla fighters were integrated into the new national army. This was only, however, after clashes between the rival two guerrilla groups, ZANLA and ZIPRA, led to 230 deaths (ch.6, pp.91–2; and pp.96–7).

9. On 1 February 1979 Ayatolla Ruholla Khomeini stepped out of a jumbo jet at Tehran Airport, Iran. After fifteen years in exile the conspiracies he had been planning had finally helped to drive out the Shah of Persia. There followed a religious nationalist revolution which led to anti-American demonstrations and the confinement of over 50 USA embassy hostages (ch.1, pp.11–12, p.14, p.20; ch.2, p.35).

The history of Italian and German unification should teach us to recognise these same basic patterns and rhythms which will keep re-appearing as long as nationalism is a key issue in the world. This is not to say that history exactly repeats itself. Each incident is unique and has notable variations from its earlier prototypes. But, despite the never ending variety of the patterns of nationalist behaviour, the ability to recognise them is an essential piece of equipment for a twentieth century citizen or politician. The necessary identification handbook can only be prepared by analysing the history of such earlier examples of nationalism in Germany and Italy.

Of course it would be even more useful if the history of national unification could provide more precise guide lines for politicians and nationalists. Would it be possible to build up a model which could tell us whether a particular national movement would have any chance of success? How should governments deal with nationalists? In the preface to the second edition of his book on nationalism, Elie Kedourie very properly commented, 'Some reviewers have remarked that I do not attempt to discuss whether nationalists should be conciliated or resisted... For an academic to offer his advice on this matter is... impertinent: academics are not diviners... ' (Kedourie, 5, preface). At the other extreme from Kedourie are writers like Lorenz, Ardrey and Desmond Morris who imply that the causes of nationalism can be pinned down to hereditary impulses which humanity acquired during its evolution as a species (Ardrey, 11, chs. 5-7; Morris, 10, chs. 5 and 8). Biologists have shown in researches into animal behaviour that there is an instinct to defend a territory. With lemurs, monkeys and apes this instinct was transferred from individuals to groups which combined to defend their chosen territories. The ape or monkey 'nation' preserves peace because if one group invades a neighbour's territory it will always withdraw quietly if confronted by the owners. Humans, unfortunately, are different. Besides having the impulse to defend their territory, to the death if necessary, they also have an aggressive urge to invade the territory of others.

While the attempt to link the causes of nationalism to hereditary instincts is an interesting one, it is not very helpful when applied to actual cases. If nationalism is caused by both aggressive hunting urges and a more defensive reflex to protect territory, why did nationalist movements not emerge in these countries before the nineteenth century? Why is it the idea of a nation state as a focus for territorial boundaries which has gained ascendency rather than the multinational empire, the tribe or some other grouping? The urge to defend or obtain territory may explain **patriotism**. But a multinational empire or a tribe may just as easily inspire patriotism as a nation. If we require guidance on such questions as, at what time is an outbreak of nationalism likely to occur and what are its chances of success, we need to turn to more orthodox methods of historical inquiry.

Events in nineteenth century Italy and Germany would suggest that for a nationalist movement to actually get off the ground the following conditions must be met:

1. There must be a clear national language and culture or at least a surviving memory of one.
2. The area needs to be subjected to a sharp shock, like a war or a revolution, which may shake the people out of their isolation.
3. The cultural group must be governed by another group which has either a different language or religion; the form of government must be strict enough to cause discontent but not so severe that all opposition is crushed.
4. The cultural group must be capable of producing writers, philosophers, poets, artists, composers, exiles and martyrs who can develop and transmit the idea of nationalism and turn it into a sort of religion with its own myths, flags, festivals and monuments.

5. There must be sufficient literacy, or other avenues for the communication of ideas, if nationalism is to spread.

6. The area needs to be subjected to the pressures of economic and social change. In a traditional society, unaffected by industrialisation and the growth of towns, life is structured; local customs upheld by the village and the family determine who you must marry, what job you will do, who you may leave your property to. Language is not important because everything is settled by custom and tradition. But when an industrial revolution arrives all this is changed. People become more mobile, they move into towns, the old family and village customs break down, whole regions become left behind and backward and look with envy at more prosperous areas. In this situation people need a new focus for their loyalty: the nation, the language, the culture may step into the gap. People become receptive to the idea of nationalism.

Even if all or most of these conditions are present the experiences of Germany and Italy would suggest that nationalism will still fail unless at least some of the following four further conditions can be fulfilled:

7. The international situation must favour changes. If all the great powers are opposed to alterations in an area there is little chance that the aspiring nation will succeed.

8. It will help if the ruling group against whom the nationalist rebellion is planned lose their will and their capacity to enforce it. They may for example be crippled by military defeat or a political or economic crisis.

9. Success will be more likely if the leaders of the national movement can make it really popular. The usual nucleus of intellectuals need to extend their movement to bring in merchants, businessmen, tradesmen, **peasants**, landowners, workers and students .

10. Final success may depend on whether a politician of sufficient skill emerges. Without such a person the revolutionary changes may not manage to by-pass the great powers or find acceptance among the movements' mixed group of supporters. Immense skills of diplomacy, tact and compromise are required to make a nationalist revolution acceptable. Indeed the original purity of the idea may have to be partially abandoned or corrupted if any success is to be achieved.

Study 41

Of course each movement for national independence will have its own particular balance of the ten conditions for success which have been outlined above. Carry out your own research on the differences between the German and Italian experiences. You might find it helpful to put your findings in a table as shown overleaf.

Condition number	Was it fulfilled strongly, weakly or not at all in		Reasons
	Italy	Germany	
e.g. 5	Weakly	Strongly	In Italy literacy was low compared to Germany and there was no readily acceptable national language. On the other hand other means of communicating simple ideas did exist — such as opera.

The history of the unification of Germany and Italy is important for another reason. Although nationalism has come to dominate the structure of the modern world it is at the moment being seriously challenged both from without and from within. Citizens, politicians and governments all need to make up their minds whether we should be trying to preserve nationalism or be presiding joyfully at its funeral. To make this decision will be impossible unless we have at our disposal a clear analysis of the first successful nationalist movements.

The case in favour of trying to retain national states in the twentieth century world could be put forward in the following arguments:

1. An individual who does not belong to a national state cannot be a complete personality. He or she will not be capable of displaying any of the higher qualities such as loyalty, self sacrifice, the capacity to put the honour of the nation above selfish interest.
2. A race of people cannot live happily in a multinational state. Their language, culture, art, music and poetry will become fossilised and their standard of living will decline. Sooner or later they will be deprived of their liberty and will have no share in their government. Only by forming their own nation state can they enjoy good government and realise their full potential in the modern world of industrialisation and rising living standards.
3. The boundaries of multinational empires depend on power, war and traditions. They are therefore unstable and always changing. Proper boundaries based on language and culture will be easier to draw and last longer.
4. Wars are generally caused by races of people being oppressed by multinational empires based around hereditary dynasties. When each race succeeds in escaping from such imperial domination the world will be at peace. There will be a healthy economic, sporting and cultural rivalry between a diversity of different nations, each with their own language and culture. World civilization will be free to progress at a much more rapid rate.

The case in favour of standing aside and abandoning nationalism to extinction could be put forward in these arguments:

5. An individual who belongs to a national state will be taking a backward step. For in order to reinforce his or her nationality the state will teach him or her to despise other nations. He or she will in fact lose sight of the most important civilising factor – the realisation that all people, whatever their race, colour or religion have an equal right to be treated as human beings.

6. There is no evidence that national states have done any better than multinational empires in bringing freedom, happiness and a higher standard of living to their people. Indeed in most cases, nationalism turns out to be the belief of a small minority of well-off people who indoctrinate the rest of the group with their myths and legends and deprive them of their rights of government.

7. The attempt to draw boundaries on the basis of language and culture has turned out to be a disastrous failure. The world's languages are too intermixed and complex for this to be practical. The only result of trying to apply this nationalist ideal has been to sacrifice the happiness of isolated minorities, who existed with reasonable contentment in the multinational Empires, but have been persecuted mercilessly or forced into exile by their new nationalist rulers.

8. Nationalism has caused wars not prevented them. The division of the world into national states has upset the balance of power, encouraged extremism and racial hatred and more and more quarrels over territory.

Study 42

We have now reached the point where you make up your own mind about nationalism. Of course it must be a very temporary and provisional decision. You have only had a chance to study the German and Italian varieties. New events may make you want to re-examine your views. To give yourself some final help try carrying through the following exercise:

1. Study the extracts below and decide which of the eight arguments each one is supporting. Remember that any one extract might be upholding more than one argument.

2. Which of the eight arguments in your view are most strongly supported by the history of nationalism in Germany and Italy?

Views of nationalism

(a) If we take the establishment of liberty for the realisation of moral duties to be the end of civil society, we must conclude that those states are substantially the most perfect which, like the British and Austrian Empires, include various distinct nationalities without oppressing them... A state which is incompetent to satisfy different races condemns itself; a state which labours to neutralise, to absorb, or to expel them, destroys its own vitality; a state which does not include them is destitute of the chief basis of self government. The theory of nationality therefore is a retrograde step in history....

(Lord Acton, *Essay on Nationality*, 1862. See Heater 2, p.16).

(b) 'Where the sentiment of nationality exists in any force there is a... case for uniting all the members of the nationality under the same government, and a government to themselves apart... Free institutions are next to impossible in a country made up of different nationalities. Among a people without fellow feeling, especially if they read and speak different languages, the united public opinion, necessary to the working of representative government, cannot exist...'

(J. S. Mill, *On Representative Government*, 1861. See Heater 2, page 5).

(c) 'How little worthy of respect is the man who roams about hither and thither without the anchor of a national ideal and a love of fatherland. How dull is the friendship which rests merely upon personal similarities of disposition and tendencies, and not upon the feeling of a great common unity for whose sake one can offer up one's life; how the greatest source of pride is lost by the woman that cannot feel that she also bore children for her fatherland and brought them up for it, that her house and all the petty things that fill up most of her time belong to a greater whole and take their place in the union of her people.'

(Schleiermacher (1768–1834), See Minogue, 6, p.73).

(d) 'A particular type of epic ballad's... accents ring so true, that the geographer, in search of Serbian boundaries, tries in vain to discover a surer guide to delimitation... Its tunes live within the hearts and upon the lips of every Serbian... To make Serbian territory coincide with the regional extension of this ballad implies the defining of the Serbian national area.'

(Leon Dominion, *The Frontiers of Language and Nationality in Europe, 1917*. See Minogue, 6, p.123).

(e) 'But the method (of using language to determine national frontiers) is not as plain and easy as it is represented... For, what is a language, and how is it to be distinguished from a dialect?...The method breaks down precisely in those mixed areas where the need for it seems to be greatest... A short while before the First World War, Epirus was the occasion of a quarrel between Greece and Albania, to decide which a linguistic enquiry was arranged. The partisans of Greece visited the villages in dispute and obtained answers in Greek; in the same villages the partisans of Albania obtained answers in Albanian; and occasionally it so happened that when questioned a village would answer in Albanian, 'I am Greek.'

(Minogue, 6, pp.123–4).

(f) 'The attempts to refashion so much of the world on national lines has not led to greater peace and stability. On the contrary it has created new conflicts, exacerbated tensions and brought catastrophe to numberless people innocent of all politics... the nation· states who inherited the position of the Empires were not an improvement. They did not minister to political freedom, they did not increase prosperity and their existence was not conducive to peace.'

(Minogue, 6, p.138; Heater, 2, p.16).

(g) 'There is room for both the Sleeping Beauty and the Frankenstein's monster view of nationalism. It brings millions of people out of traditional corners into the global commerce of the modern world, and it induces a psychological climate conducive to bitter, irrational struggles over contested bits of territory...'

(Minogue, 6, p.154).

(h) 'Nationalism, it seems to me, is a phenomenon of a certain stage in human history. It is neither good nor bad. It is like a coin on one side of which appear the venerable features of Garibaldi, on the other the obscene figure of the Commandant of Auschwitz...'

(H. Seton Watson, *Nationalism Old and New*, 1965. See Heater, 2, p.4).

Study 43

Consider the following questions and write a brief report on each.

1. Can a reasonable general explanation for the rise of nation states be assembled?
2. Has nationalism achieved anything of value. Should it be preserved?

Before writing your final reports you could

(a) use the booklist to carry out some more general research by reading one of the books listed 1–12, or:

(b) extend your knowledge beyond Italy and Germany through studying nationalism in another area by consulting books 13–21.

Bibliography

On Modern Nationalism

I. A Brief and Basic List

1. A good general discussion of nationalism aimed at sixth formers: M. Lamb, *Nationalism*, Heineman, 1974.
2. A useful selection of sources for the study of nationalism: Ed. D. Heater, *Nationalism*, General Studies Project Series, Longman for Schools Council, 1974.

II. A More Detailed List

a. Documents and Sources

3. H. Kohn, *Nationalism: Its Meaning and History*, Van Nostrand, 1955.

b. General Histories and Discussions

4. A. D. Smith, *Theories of Nationalism*, Duckworth, 1971.
5. E. Kedourie, *Nationalism*, Hutchinson 1960.
6. E. Minogue, *Nationalism*, Methuen, 1969.

c. Collections of Essays

7. L. Snyder, *Roots of German Nationalism*, Indiana University Press, 1978.
8. Ed. A. D. Smith, *Nationalist Movements*, Macmillan, 1976.
9. Ed. E. Kamenka, *Nationalism*, Arnold, 1976.

d. Biological Approaches

10. D. Morris, *The Naped Ape*, (ch.5: 'Fighting'), Cape, 1967.
11. R. Ardrey, *The Territorial Imperative*, Collins, 1967.

e. Case Studies in Particular Countries or Areas

12. Ed. A. C. Hepburn, *Conflict of Nationality in Modern Ireland*, Arnold, 1980.
13. S. Haim, *Arab Nationalism*, Berkeley, 1962.
14. R. Conquest, *Soviet Nationalities Policy in Theory and Practice*, Bodley Head, London, 1967.
15. Ed. J. Bracey, *Black Nationalism in America*, Bobbs-Merrill, New York, 1970.
16. A. Seal, *The Emergence of Indian Nationalism*, Cambridge University Press, 1968.
17. R. Storry, *The Double Patriots: A Study of Japanese Nationalism*, Chatto and Windus, London, 1957.
18. E. S. Munger, *Afrikaner and African Nationalism*, Oxford University Press, 1967.
19. D. Vital: *The Origins of Zionism*, Oxford University Press, 1975.
20. A. P. Whitaker and D. Jordan, *Nationalism in Contemporary Latin America*, Collier, New York, 1966.
21. E. Kedourie, *Nationalism in Asia and Africa*, Weidenfeld and Nicolson, 1970.

III   Audio Visual Aids

a. Tape Recordings

European Nationalism 1789–1870, Dr P. Savigear and Dr M. Biddiss, Audio Learning, 56 minutes.
European Nationalism 1870–1945, Dr M. Biddiss and Dr P. Morris, Audio Learning, 56 minutes.

b. Film Strip with Tape

Nineteenth Century Nationalism, EAV, cassette or tape with two filmstrips.
Twentieth Century Nationality (India and Vietnam), EAV, cassette or tape with two filmstrips.

Glossary

Words in this book which are in bold type can be looked up in the list which follows. Much fuller definitions can be found in encyclopedias, large dictionaries and in M. Cranston, *A Glossary of Political Terms*, Bodley Head, 1966. The page references indicate the chapters and pages in this book where the words have been used:

Anticlerical (ch. 6, p.92)
In favour of reducing the power of the church in politics and education.

Authoritarian (ch. 12, p.181)
A type of government in which law, order and discipline are regarded as more important than personal freedom.

Balance of Power (intro, p.3)
An international system in which peace is preserved by ensuring that no one state is too powerful or is tempted by the weakness of its neighbours to expand its territories.

Bourgeoisie (ch. 8, p.123)
A 'middle class' of people consisting of merchants, bankers, industrialists, who earn their income by making a profit.

Capitalism
An economic system in which industries, shops and farms are privately owned and run in order to make a profit.

Communism (ch. 9, p.138, ch. 12, p.180)
The belief, inspired by the writings of Karl Marx, that as long as workers were employed in trades and industries run by private owners for a profit, they would be overworked, underpaid and frequently unemployed. Inevitably they would rise against their masters, overthrow the government and introduce a fairer system in which all trade and industry would be publicly owned. Some communist parties, like the German Social Democrats before 1914, believed that since the revolution was bound to come, their main job was to wait patiently for the great day. There were, however, activists, who maintained that good communists should work to hurry the revolution on. Not until Lenin's success in Russia in 1917, was this element influential.

Confederation (intro, p.1; ch. 7, p.104; ch. 8, p.125)
A loose league of states in which each still retains the right to run its own foreign policy as well as its internal politics.

Constitution (ch. 1, p.17; ch. 2, p.27; ch. 6, p.92; ch. 7, p.114; ch. 8, p.125)
A set of laws and rules by which a government's powers are clearly regulated.

Cottage Industry (ch. 1, p.7)
A method of production where the machinery is sufficiently simple for the work to be carried out in the workers' own homes.

Decolonisation (conclusion, p.196)
The process whereby a governing country hands back control of an area to its local inhabitants.

Democracy (ch. 1, p.12; ch. 6, p.97; ch. 12, p.177)
A form of government in which decisions are made by an assembly elected by the people.

Fascism (ch. 6, p.88; ch. 12, p.175)
A form of government in which decisions are made by one leader and one dominant nationality in that state.

Federation (ch. 1, p.12; ch. 3, p.53; ch. 6, p.90; ch, 7, p.110; ch. 10, p.157; ch. 11, p.163)
A form of government in which decisions about foreign policy and other vital matters are taken by the central government but in which considerable powers of decision in other matters are left to the local states.

Feudalism (ch. 1, p.8)
An economic system in which permission to farm certain strips of land was only granted by the landowner on the understanding that he would be paid taxes in money, produce and labour service.

Grossdeutsch (ch. 7, p.110; ch. 10, p.153)
The belief that a new German state should include all German speaking people especially those within the Austro-Hungarian Empire.

Indirect Voting (ch. 7, p.112; ch. 9, p.141)
A system in which the voters elect local representatives, who often form an Electoral College, and who then elect further representatives to sit in the central assembly or parliament.

Junkers (ch. 7, p.106; ch. 8, p.123; ch. 9, p.139; ch. 10, p.154; ch. 12, p.176)
Aristocratic Prussian landowners who usually farmed a high proportion of their land themselves rather than rent it out to tenant farmers; these families provided most of Prussia's administrators and army officers.

Kleindeutsch (ch. 7, p.110; ch. 10, p.153)
The belief that a new German state should exclude Germans living in the Austro-Hungarian Empire.

Liberalism (ch. 2, p.27; ch. 6, p.97; ch. 7, p.116; ch. 10, p.150)
The belief that the main purpose of a government should be to ensure that people have as much personal and economic freedom as possible. Also that people of wealth and/or education should be represented in the government. Liberals are not necessarily nationalists and nationalists are not necessarily liberals.

Monarchist (ch. 1, p.15; ch. 2, p.40; ch. 4, p.62)
One who believes that a state should be governed by a hereditary King, Emperor or Duke.

Musket (ch. 2, p.21; ch. 5, p.79)
A weapon which was loaded by putting powder and ball down the muzzle and ramming them home with a rod. With disciplined training, four rounds per minute could be fired. Since the musket was smooth bored the ball did not fit snugly into the barrel and therefore accuracy beyond 50 yards was impossible. The improved percussion cap method of firing did at least make the weapon more reliable by reducing the appalling one in seven misfire rate of the flintlock to almost nil.

National Income (ch. 3, p.57)
A measurement of a country's total wealth. It can be calculated each year, providing the data are available, by adding up all incomes received, or all expenditure on goods and services, or the money value of all goods and services available to the country's economy. The standard of living of several countries may be compared by converting their national incomes into one standard currency and dividing these totals by their total populations (known as per capita income).

Nationalism (introduction, p.4; ch. 3, p.47; ch. 9, p.138; conclusion, p.196)
The belief that people with a distinctive language or culture should have the right to govern themselves, that the boundaries of states should be redrawn on this basis and that the world would become more peaceful and harmonious if this were achieved.

Patriotism (ch. 9, p.147; conclusion, p.200)
Devotion to one's country whether it is a nation, a republic, a multinational empire or a city state.

Peasant (ch. 1, p.7; ch. 7, p.106; conclusion, p.201)
A very vague term which can mean anyone from a small scale farmer who either owns or rents his small plot of land, to a labourer who owns no land but works on the land for others.

Plebiscite (ch. 2, p.34; ch. 8, p.90)
A special vote in which the people are asked to decide upon a single issue of importance. Also known as a referendum.

Police State (ch. 3, p.59)
A country whose citizens are rigidly controlled by their police forces. These often use extreme censorship, spies and informers.

Pressure Group (ch. 12, p.186)
An organisation which campaigns to promote a particular cause. It may use every possible legal kind of strategy from petitions to demonstrations in order to persuade the government to accept its arguments.

Radical (ch. 7, p.115)
One who demands very thorough reforms and is not prepared to accept delay or half measures.

Republic (introduction, p.3; ch. 1, p.7; ch. 4, p.61; ch. 9, p.147)
A state in which there is no King or other kind of hereditary ruler and in which the people of the country play a full part in the government.

Rifle (ch. 2, p.21, ch. 5, p.79, ch. 8, p.127)
A firearm with a barrel which is grooved so that the bullets fit tightly, rotate and reach the target much more directly than in the case of a musket. The early rifles had to be muzzle loaded and their rate of fire was slow. This was all altered by the development of breech loading in the 1840s which made seven shots per minute possible instead of the previous two.

Risorgimento (ch. 3, p.59; ch. 6, p.89)
An Italian word meaning resurrection and used to describe the movement for Italian Unification which began in the eighteenth century and reached its goal in the nineteenth century.

Romanticism (ch. 3, p.47)
A movement which was a reaction against the discipline and organisation and careful technique of the classical style. Romantic poets, musicians and artists believed in the wild and mysterious; in personal feeling and emotion.

Serfs (ch. 7, p.106)
Often confused with slaves. Serfs were allowed to farm land for themselves in return for paying rent and carrying out labour duties for their lords. Like slaves, however, they did have to put up with restrictions on their freedom – they could not leave their village, marry or inherit without their lord's consent.

Volksgeist (ch. 7, p.110; ch. 12, p.183)
The spirit of the nation which can be found in the language, folk music, ballads, customs and traditions of the ordinary people. Nationalists believe that these traditions must be preserved if the nation is to live.

Zollverein (ch. 7, p.113; ch. 8, p.119; ch. 10, p.151)
The economic union of the German states begun by Prussia in which common external tariffs were raised on foreign goods and which aimed at removing internal tariffs between its German member states.

Study 44

Test your understanding of some of the terms used in this book by trying the following exercises:

1. Use the cross references to find at least one person who fits each of the following: Federalist; Republican; Fascist; Liberal; Monarchist; Nationalist; Capitalist; Romantic; Bourgeois.

2. Write down one term which you think is opposite in meaning to each of the following: Capitalism; Clerical; The centralized state; Authoritarian; Monarchist; Radical.

3. Say whether each of the following was (a) a pressure group, (b) a federation, (c) a confederation, or (d) neither of these. Give your reasons:

   The *Zollverein* (ch. 7, p.113)

   The National Society (ch. 2, p.28)

   The German *Bund* of 1815 (ch. 7, p.105)

   'Young Italy' (ch. 1, p.11)

   The Kingdom of Italy 1861 (ch. 6, p.90)

   Nationalverein (ch. 9, p.142)

   The German Empire 1871 (ch. 12, p.177)

   The Frankfurt Assembly's Constitution for Germany 1849 (ch. 7, p.116)

Index